IMAGES
of America

HOLLYWOOD

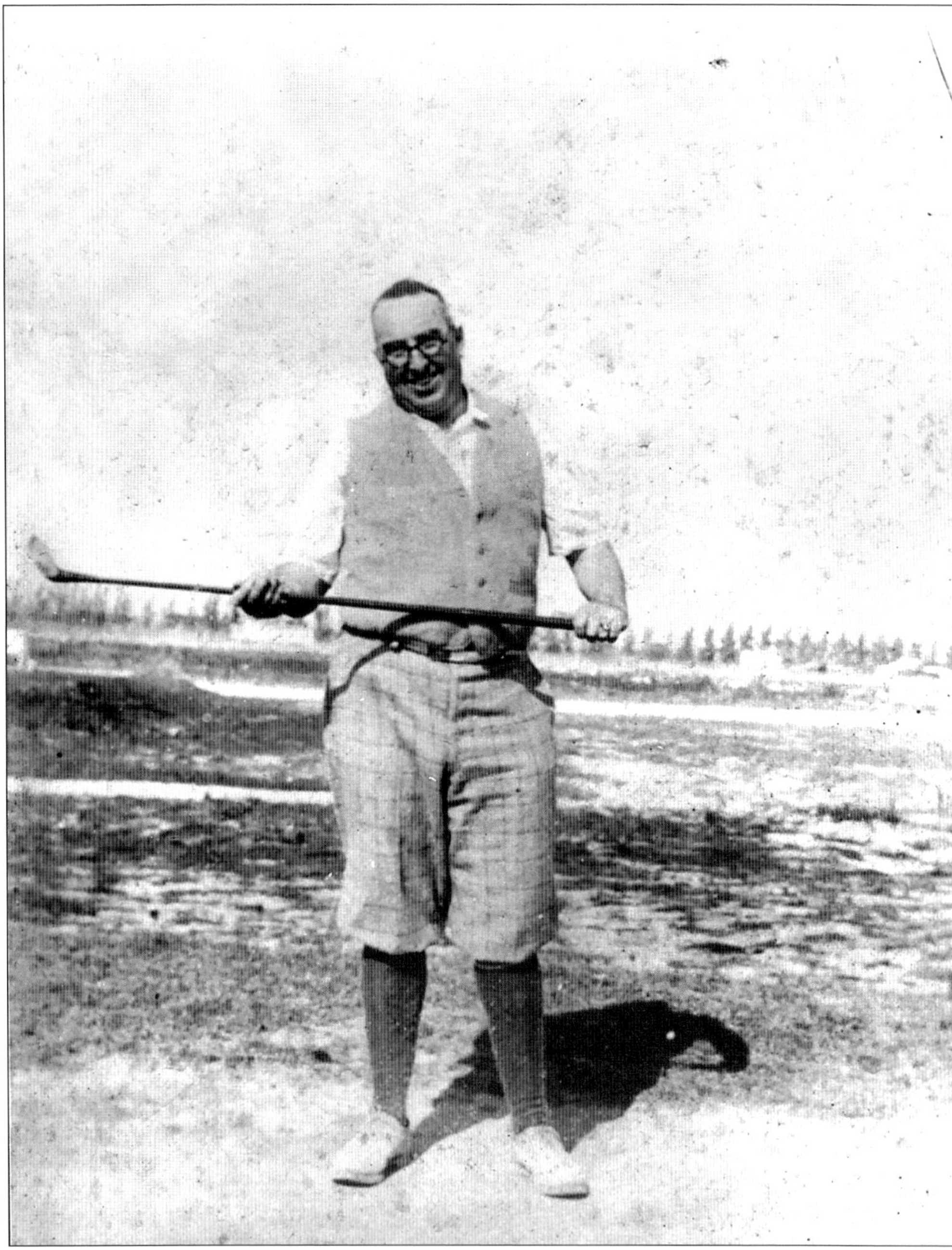

Joseph Wesley Young, founder of Hollywood, poses on the golf course in this undated photograph. Young, born in Gig Harbor, Washington, on August 4, 1882, died in his Hollywood home on February 26, 1934. (Whitson Collection.)

IMAGES
of America

HOLLYWOOD

C. Richard Roberts

ARCADIA
PUBLISHING

ISBN 978-0-7385-1482-6

Published by Arcadia Publishing,
Charleston, South Carolina

Printed in the United States of America

Library of Congress Catalog Card Number: 2002112075

For all general information contact Arcadia Publishing at:
Telephone 843-853-2070
Fax 843-853-0044
E-mail sales@arcadiapublishing.com
For customer service and orders:
Toll-Free 1-888-313-2665

Visit us on the Internet at www.arcadiapublishing.com

Longtime Hollywood residents know that Cathleen Anderson is a legend in her own time. She is a Broward County native and a fourth-generation Floridian who began her uninterrupted service on the Hollywood City Commission in 1975 as the first female commissioner in Hollywood. She is now the longest-serving commissioner in our history. Among the many honors that she has accumulated in the nearly three decades she has served her community is her designation as Hollywood's official historian. She has, for many years, been a generous donor to our collections and an ardent supporter and promoter of the city's history. It is to her that this volume is formally dedicated.

Contents

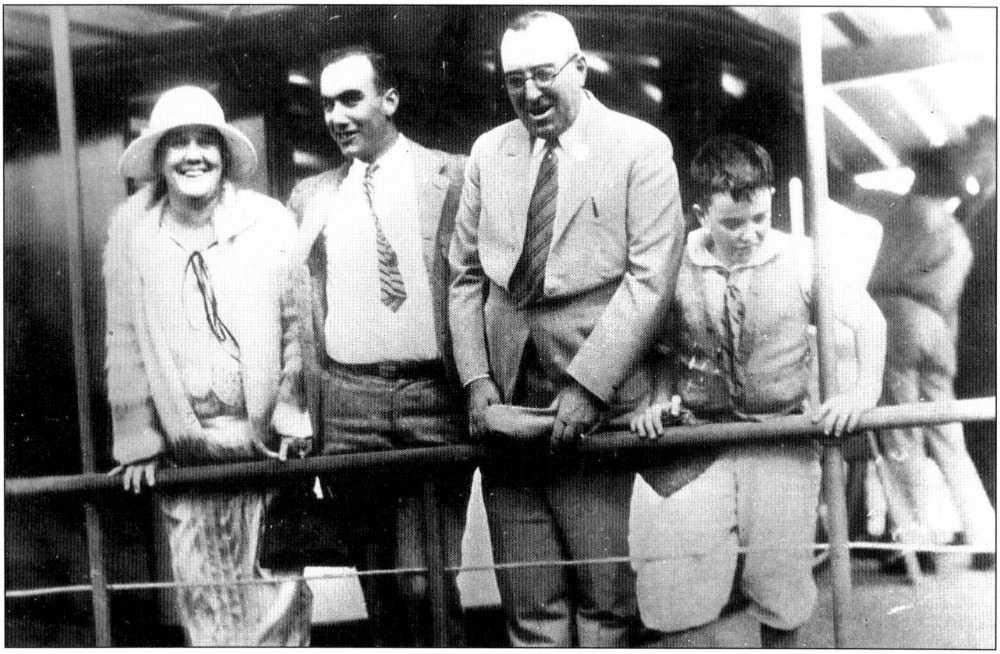

The Young family sails aboard the newly finished yacht *Jessie Faye* in 1924. The $200,000 mahogany vessel was 102 feet long and carried a crew of 10. Pictured from left to right are Mrs. Jessie Faye Young, John M. "Jack" Young, Joseph W. Young, and William J. "Billy" Young. (General Collection.)

ACKNOWLEDGMENTS

This volume is the result of many years of collecting and cataloging historical photographs of Hollywood by the staff of the Records and Archives Division, a division of the Office of the City Clerk, with which I am proud to be associated as director. First, my thanks are extended to everyone in the division for their help and patience in seeing this project through. My special thanks go to Terry Cairns, who selected the cover photograph and provided support and assistance, and to Philip Gioco, who has been the primary cataloger in the archives for nearly two years. Both played a bigger part in the successful completion of this work than either will ever realize. I would also like to thank the many donors who graciously contributed photographs and other historical materials to document the history of our community.

Thanks are also in order for the continuing support of the Hollywood City Administration, including City Manager Cameron D. Benson, City Clerk Patricia A. Cerny, and our mayor, Mara Giulianti, along with City Commissioners Cathleen A. Anderson, Beam Furr, Sal Oliveri, Keith Wasserstrom, Fran Russo, and Peter Bober.

Introduction

This book presents a pictorial history of the City of Hollywood from its early 1920s inception as Joseph Wesley Young's dream city in Florida, to the 1960s when the city reached its corporate limits. In Young's vision, Hollywood would "be a city for everyone—from the opulent at the top of the industrial and social ladder to the most humble of working people." In many ways, his vision was realized, but not before he died at 51 in his Hollywood mansion in February 1934.

The story of Hollywood is not particularly unique in the annals of South Florida. It was begun as a city to compete with other more established (though not by much) municipalities hoping to lure northern visitors and new residents to the balmy climes of the region. Timing, unfortunately, was not in the city's best interest. Less than one year after its incorporation in 1925, the area was devastated by a hurricane that nearly destroyed the city before it could firmly establish itself as a destination of choice for wealthy visitors. The economic blow was more than Joseph Young could reasonably recover from, and his company eventually fell into receivership. Company properties were auctioned off at a sheriff's sale on the courthouse steps while Young lost control of his company to his creditors. The collapse of the stock market and the ensuing depression in the United States left Hollywood, like so many other cities, desperately clinging to survival in a world where the economic cards were stacked against it.

Despite its rocky start, Hollywood held on against the odds and managed to function, if not thrive, throughout the 1930s and 1940s. In the wake of Young's financial collapse and death, two of his principal creditors formed new corporations in an attempt to renew the growth of Hollywood. Led by Hollywood, Inc., a slow but perceptible growth was re-ignited during the decade of the 1930s. Construction began on a new federal highway, and in 1932, the Hollywood Hills Inn in the city's westernmost circle was converted into the winter quarters of the Georgia-based Riverside Military Academy. Orangebrook Golf and Country Club opened, and Dowdy Field, a baseball park that later became the temporary spring training home of the Baltimore Orioles, was completed. In the 1940s, World War II came to Hollywood. Riverside Military Academy was taken over and converted into the United States Naval Air Gunners School; the Hollywood Beach Hotel became the United States Naval Indoctrination and Training School; and the Hollywood Golf and Country Club became an entertainment and recreation center for United States servicemen. With the end of the war, the facilities were returned to their former uses. The population began a steady climb, and even two hurricanes in the fall of 1947 failed to deter the city's renewed vigor.

Continuing growth in the 1950s, the city passed a bond referendum to finance the construction of Hollywood Memorial Hospital, providing a major medical facility for southern Broward County. In 1952, Gen. Joseph Watson became Hollywood's city manager, a post he would hold for the next 18 years, no small accomplishment considering that, in the 27 years preceding his appointment, the city had hired 21 city managers. In 1954, Hollywood Boulevard was extended from State Road 7 westward to U.S. 27 along the eastern edges of the Everglades, triggering the westerly expansion of the city. In 1958, Hollywood celebrated the opening of the Diplomat Hotel on the beach and for years, the Diplomat was renowned as one of the world's first-class resorts.

By the time the city began its fifth decade in the 1960s, a final, massive growth spurt had increased its boundaries into newer, unincorporated areas to the west, north, and south. From a population of nearly 23,000 in 1955, Hollywood grew to 35,237 in 1960, almost doubling to 67,500 in 1965, and expanding to nearly 107,000 residents by the end of the decade. Much of that growth resulted from the incorporation of West Hollywood into the city proper.

The particular emphasis of this volume is on the early development of the community as well as on Port Everglades, one of the largest ports on the East Coast. Joseph Young originally envisioned the port, and although it is now more popularly thought of as Fort Lauderdale's port, 80 percent of the facility lies within the corporate boundaries of the City of Hollywood. The most striking images in our collections are those associated with the early development of the city and Port Everglades, the damage caused by the 1926 hurricane, and the evolution of the city's most valuable asset, its beach.

It is impossible in a book of this size to include photographs of every significant person or event that has contributed to the ultimate success of the city during its first three-quarters of a century. In fact, a special effort was made to do just the opposite—to document the daily lives of those everyday men, women, and children, who, in their day-to-day living, helped shape the history we now look back upon. That is why in many photographs, the subjects are unidentified; nonetheless, they remain important to our community. Readers who can connect names to faces are encouraged to contact the Records and Archives Division so that our catalog records can be updated.

All of the images included in the book can be found in the City's Records and Archives Division, the official historical repository for city government records. Each photograph used herein is identified in its caption by the specific collection from which it was drawn. Most of the photographs were donated by individuals or companies with long ties to the community; others are official government photos. The division actively seeks to enhance the collection with additional images and is eager to expand the scope of the collection with a new emphasis on the contributions of the African-American and Hispanic communities, whose importance in Hollywood history has been sadly neglected. For those interested in more historical photographs of Hollywood, the division has provided internet access to 4,000 images on its web site. All royalties from the sale of this book will be used to enhance the programs and services of the Records and Archives Division.

One

The 1920s

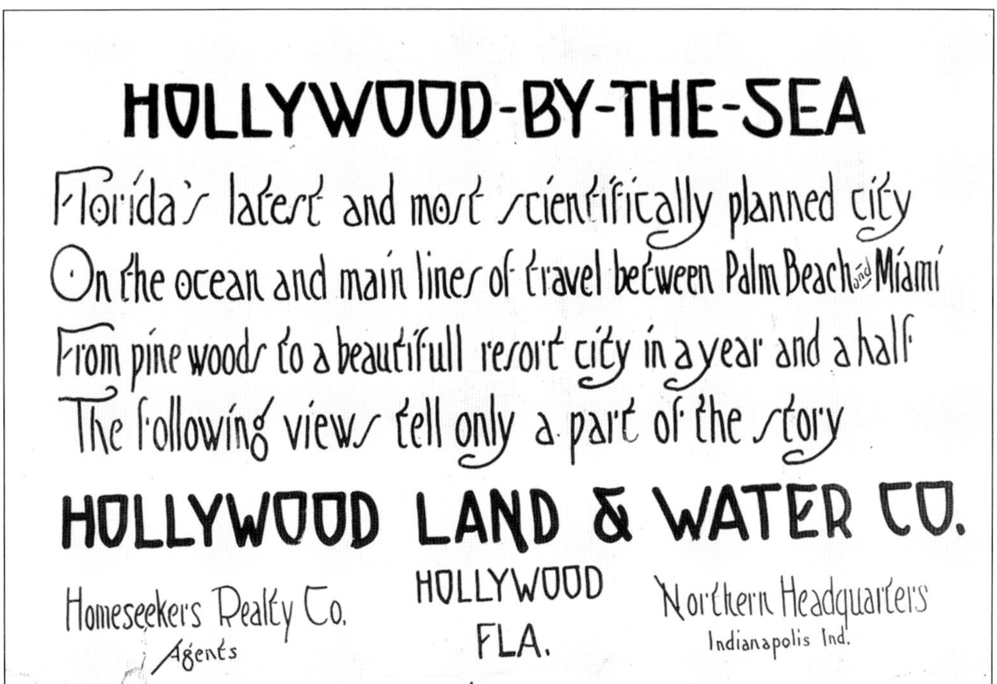

This is an example of one of Joseph Young's advertising techniques. Information brochures like this one were mailed across the country and included photographic views of the new city in all its glory. (General Collection.)

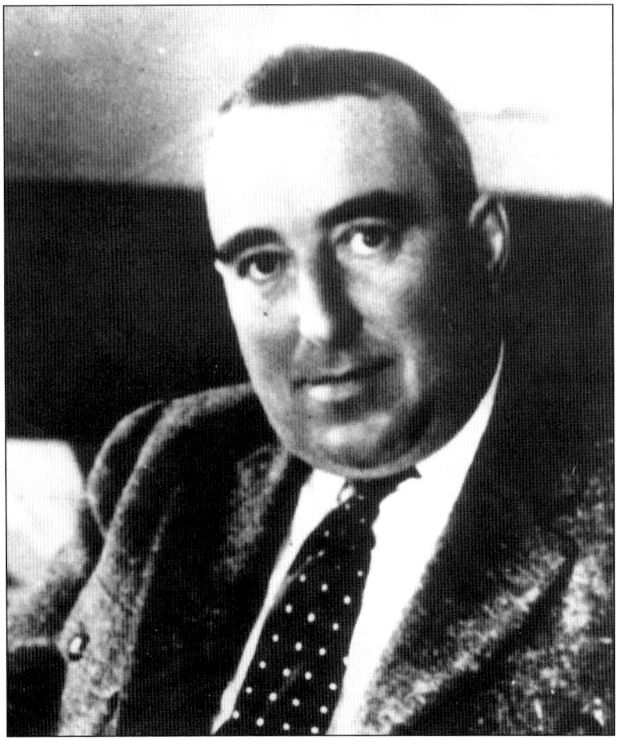

This portrait of Joseph Young was taken at his desk in the executive offices of his company's administration building. Young began building his new city in 1921 after coming to Florida from California, where he was enamored with Hollywood, California. (Elsie Johns Collection.)

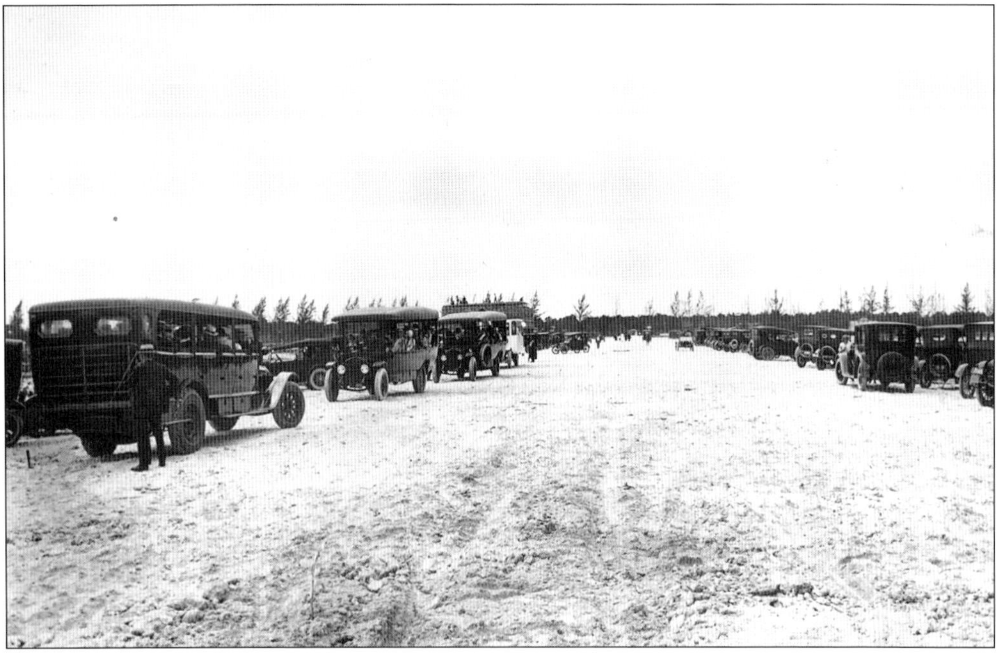

Another of Young's sales techniques was the use of buses to transport prospective buyers to the construction sites in Hollywood. Later editions of the buses were white with a script "Hollywood" logo painted on them. This photograph was taken along a still-under-construction Hollywood Boulevard. At the time of its completion, Hollywood Boulevard was thought to be the widest in Florida. (General Collection.)

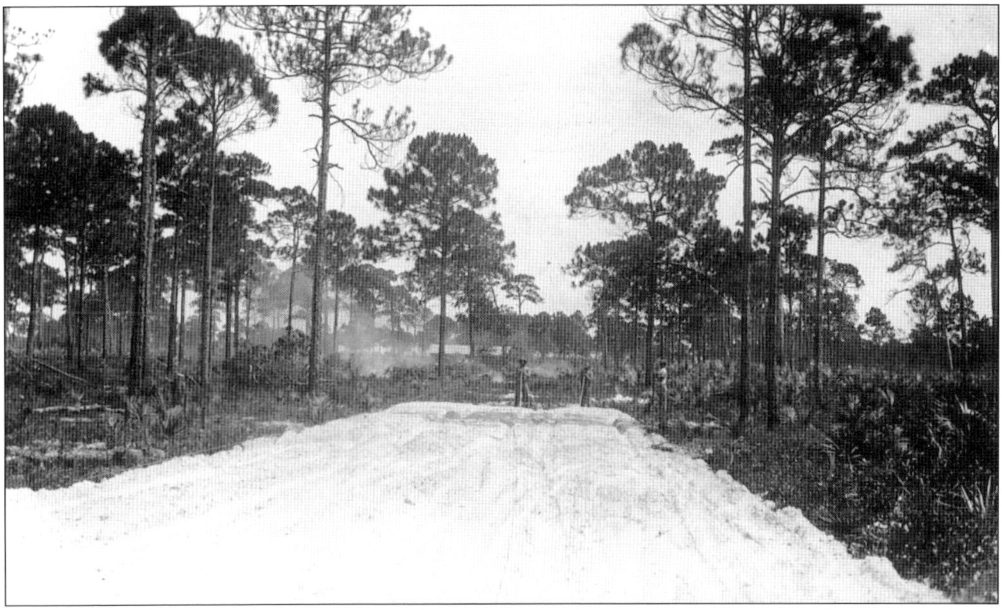

Road construction was obviously one of the Young company's first priorities. This road was being built into the Liberia area of Hollywood, an isolated community established by Young to house the African-American laborers hired by his company. (Patricia Smith Collection.)

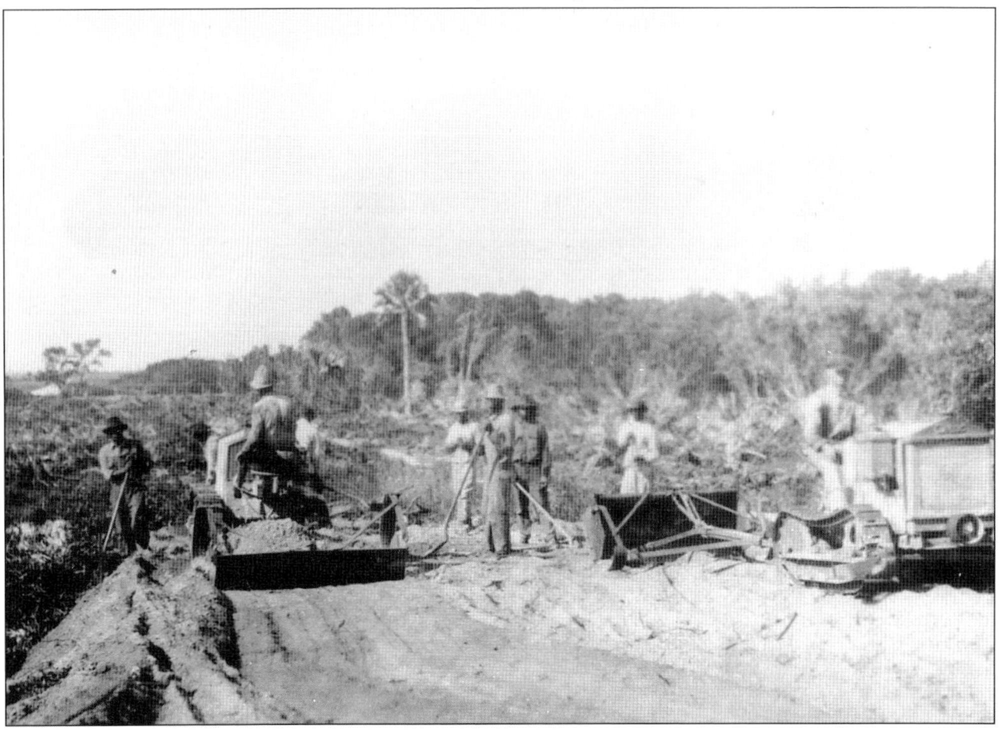

The site of this road construction is unknown, but it is an excellent example of the landscape Young faced as he created a new city from the pine scrubs of South Florida. Young's purchase of the property that would soon become Hollywood cost him approximately $175 per acre. (General Collection.)

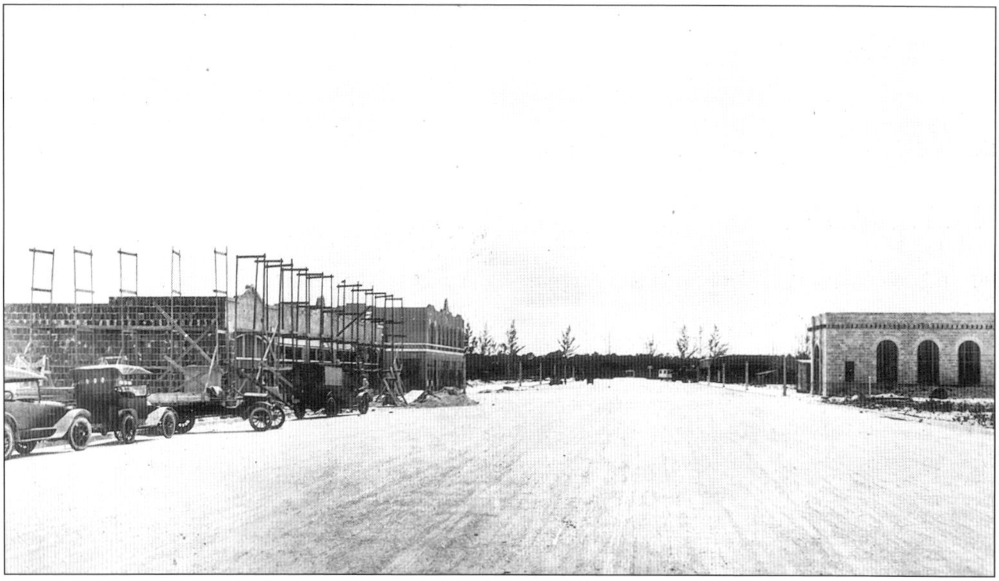

This view of an unpaved Hollywood Boulevard was taken looking west near what would soon be the intersection of Twentieth Avenue. The building in the left background is the Young company headquarters; the building across the boulevard on the right is the Hollywood State Bank. The Bastian Building is under construction in the left foreground. (Whitson Collection.)

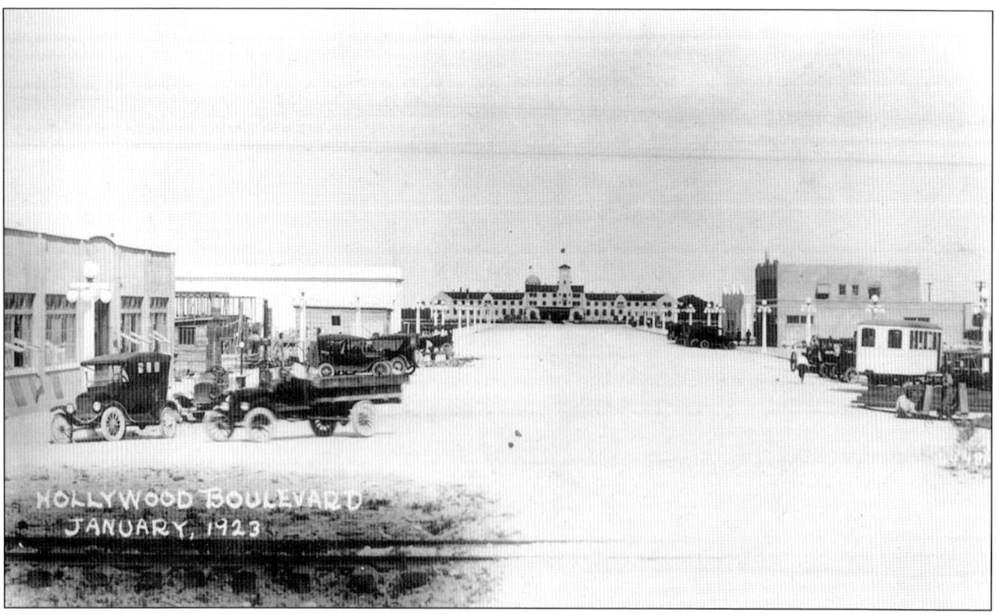

This 1923 image illustrates a developing Hollywood Boulevard. Very faintly in the foreground are the tracks of the Florida East Coast Railroad along Twenty-first Avenue. This eastward view looks down the boulevard across Harding (now Young) Circle to the Hollywood (later Park View) Hotel, which is now the site of a supermarket and drug store. (General Collection.)

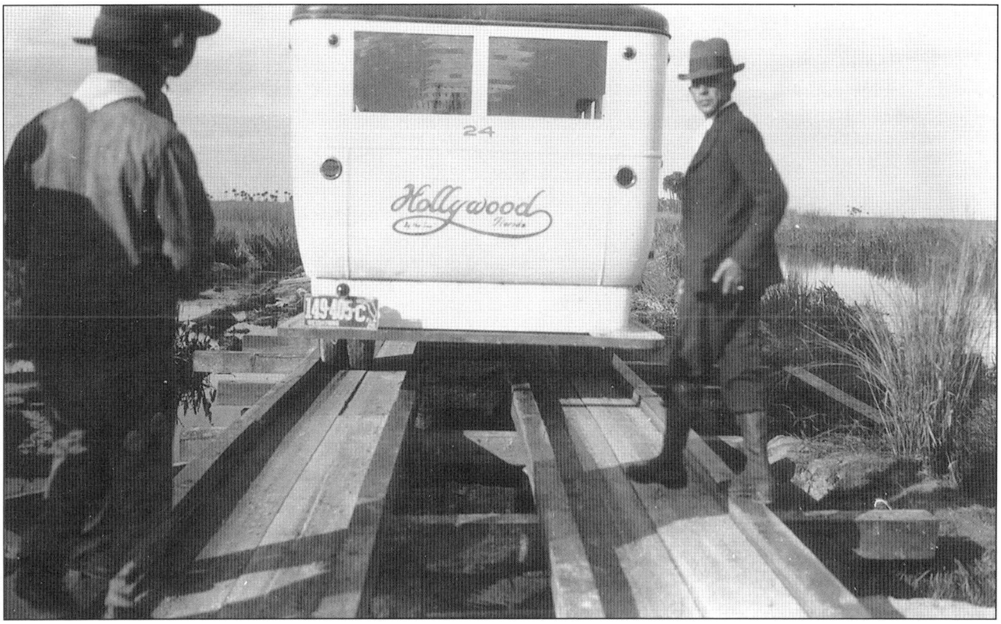

Several men stand behind one of the new Hollywood Land and Water Co. touring buses. The buses traveled along wooden plank tracks in the wet, undeveloped areas of the city. (General Collection.)

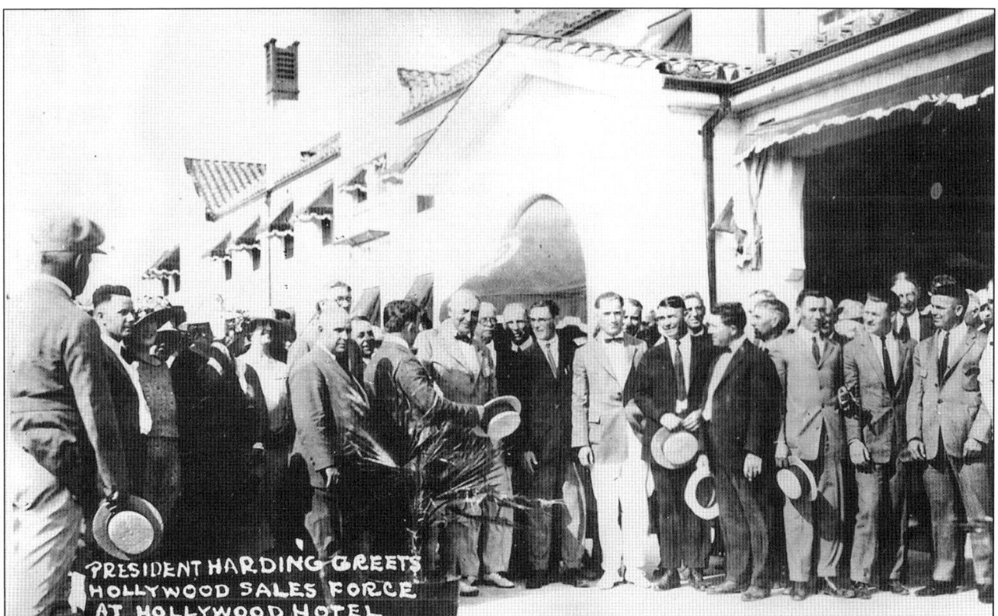

President Warren G. Harding, left of center in bow tie, greets the Hollywood Co. sales force at the Hollywood Hotel on March 13, 1923. Harding was a guest of Joseph Young and toured the new city. Harding, president from 1921 to 1923, was honored with having the city's major traffic circle and park named for him. (General Collection.)

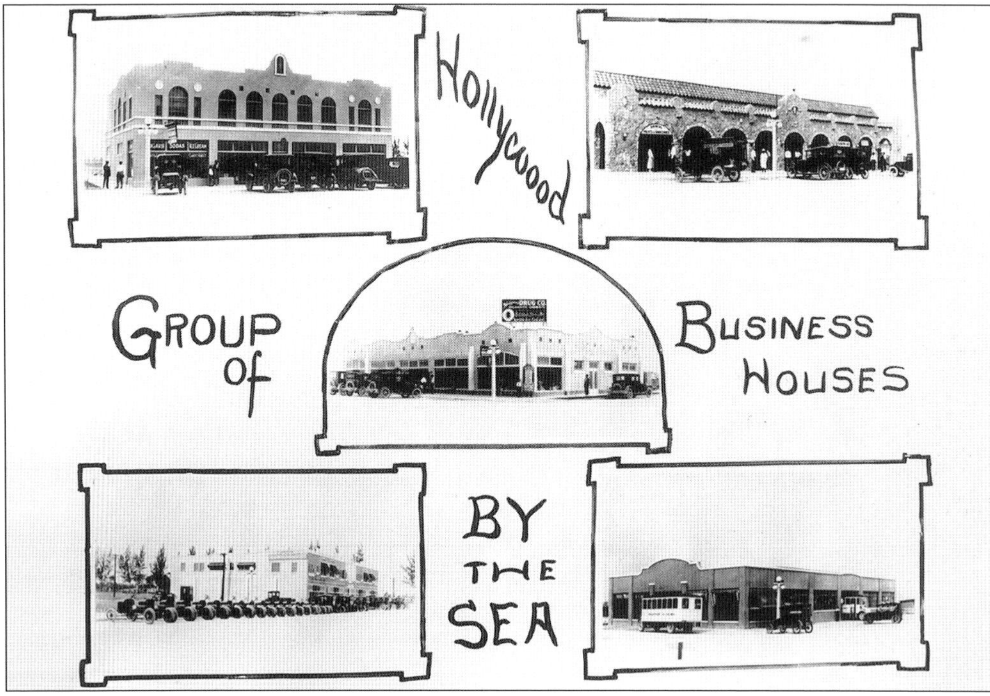

One part of Joseph Young's illustrated sales brochure touted the fine selection of business buildings available to small business owners. (General Collection.)

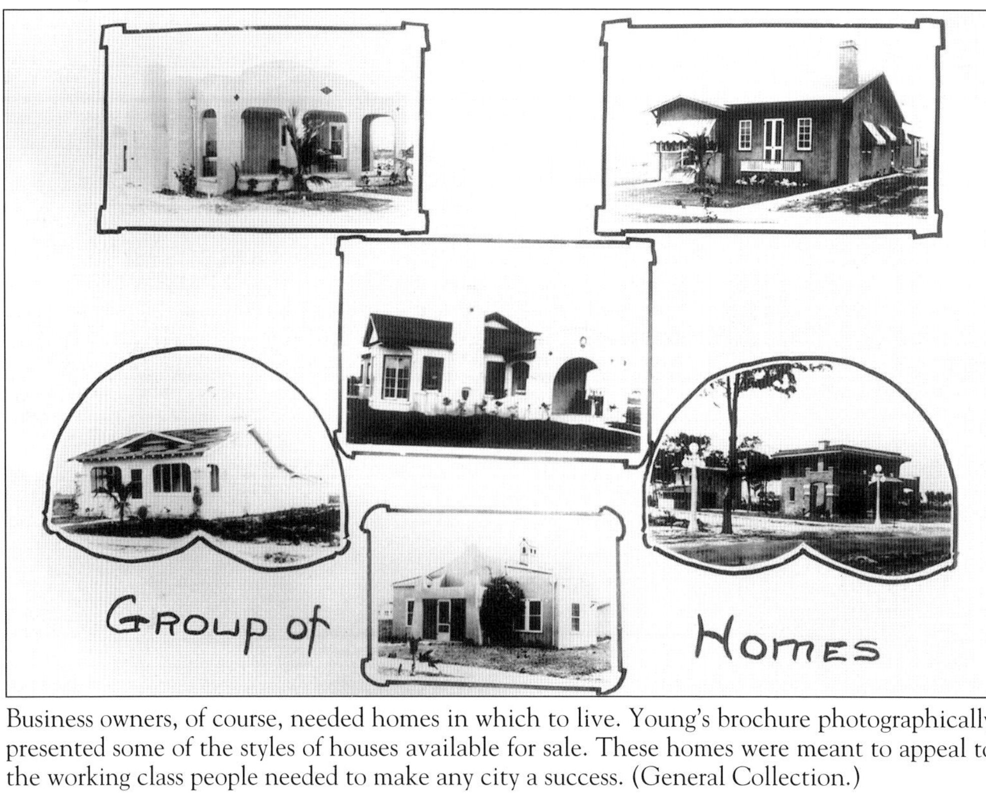

Business owners, of course, needed homes in which to live. Young's brochure photographically presented some of the styles of houses available for sale. These homes were meant to appeal to the working class people needed to make any city a success. (General Collection.)

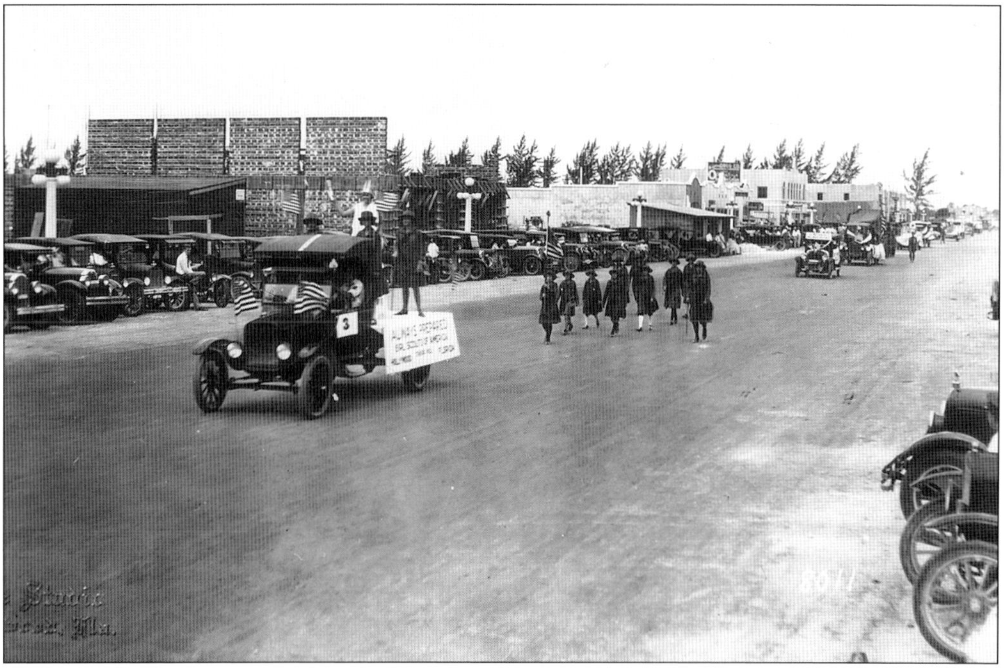

Troops of Girl Scouts march along Hollywood Boulevard during an Independence Day parade on July 4, 1925. In this view looking southwest, the sign for the Hollywood Drug Co. at the corner of Twentieth Avenue is visible just to the right of center. (General Collection.)

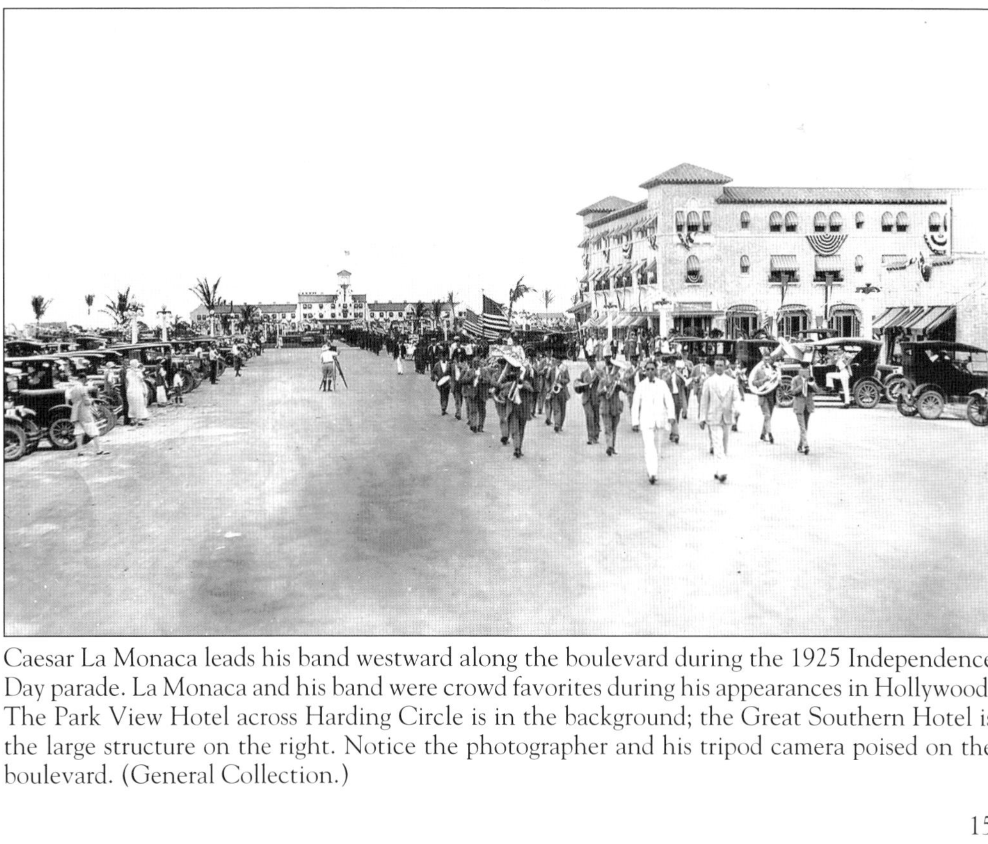

Caesar La Monaca leads his band westward along the boulevard during the 1925 Independence Day parade. La Monaca and his band were crowd favorites during his appearances in Hollywood. The Park View Hotel across Harding Circle is in the background; the Great Southern Hotel is the large structure on the right. Notice the photographer and his tripod camera poised on the boulevard. (General Collection.)

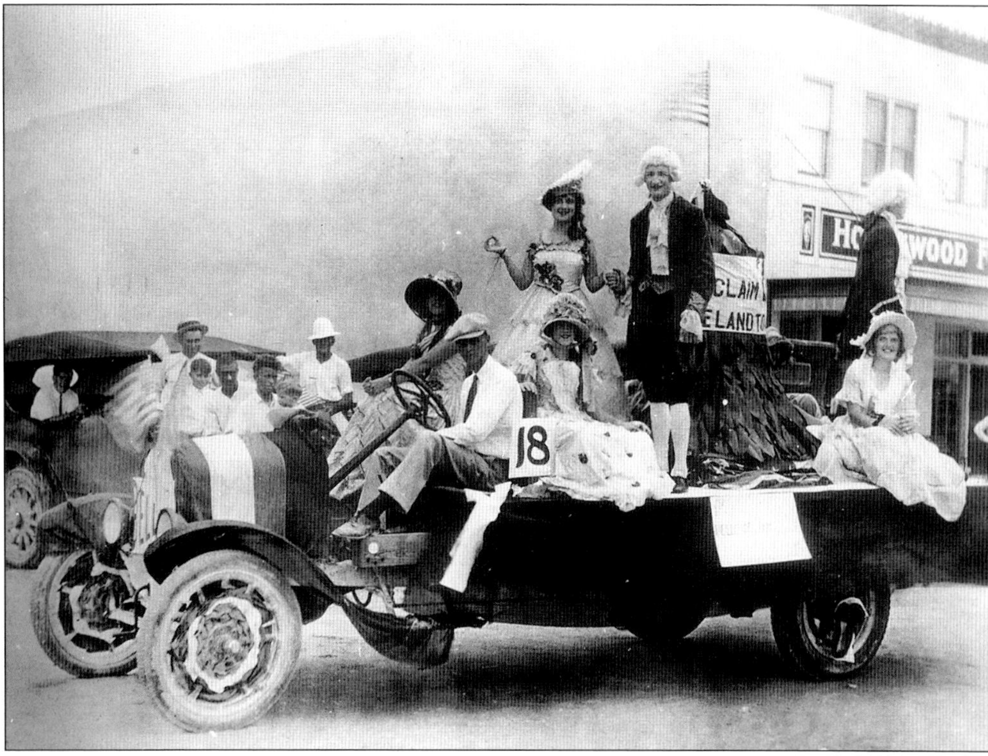

The Hollywood Woman's Club float, *Belles and Beaux of 1776*, won first prize in the 1925 parade. From left to right are (standing) Josephine Hurt, Thomas Mitchell, and Arthur Scott; (seated) Virginia Elliott, an unidentified driver, Anne Hurt, and Betty Garrison. (General Collection.)

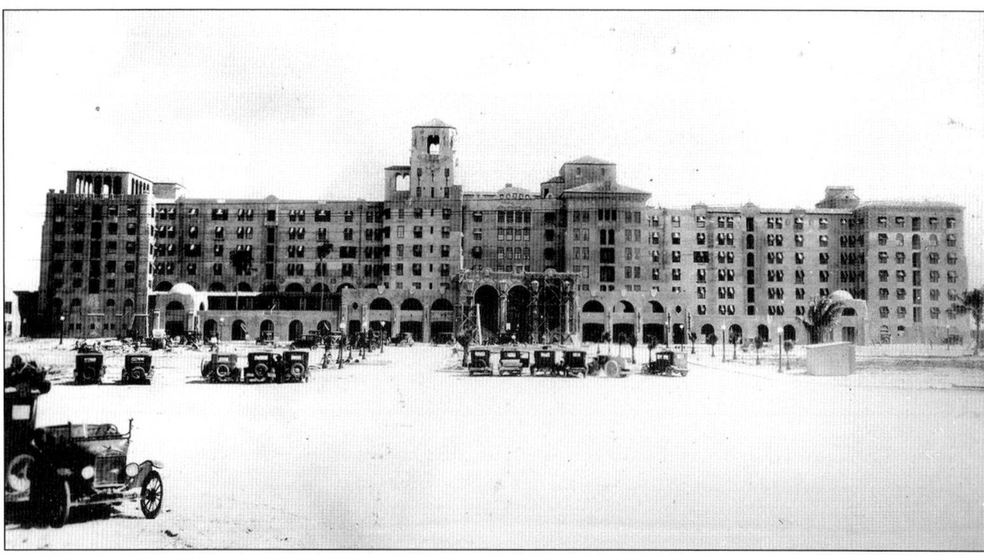

The Hollywood Beach Hotel nears completion in this 1925 photograph. The hotel opened in February 1926 and included 500 rooms with private baths, the world's largest solarium, and private wire connections to the New York Stock Exchange. It cost $3 million to build and quickly became the center of the winter social scene on the beach. (Peracchio Collection.)

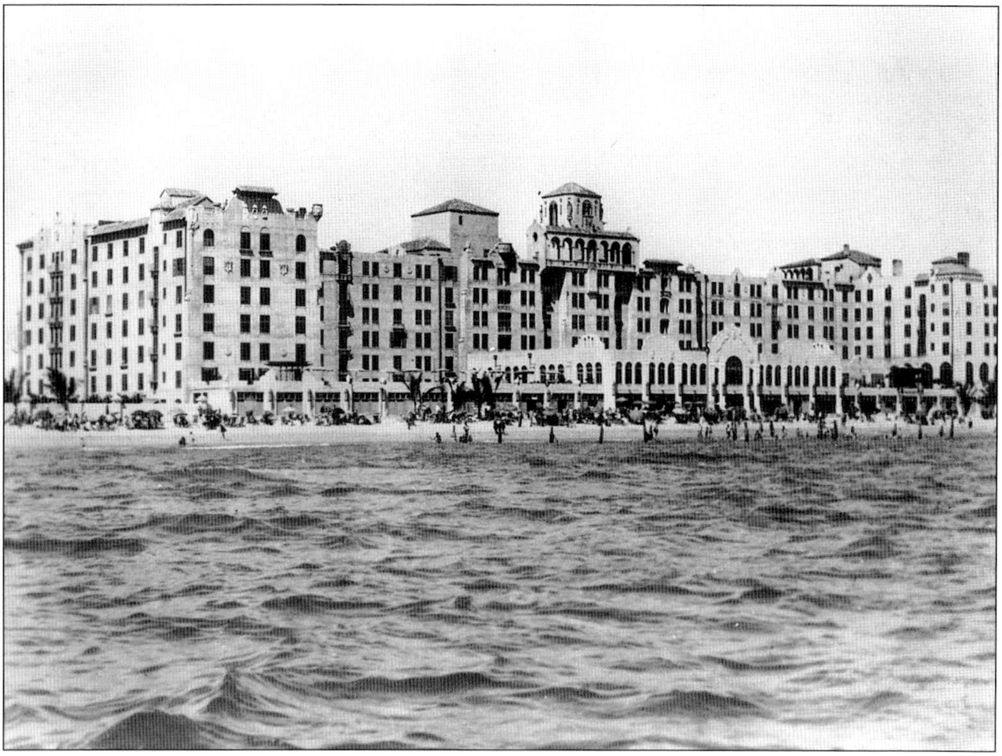

The Hollywood Beach Hotel, seen here from the ocean, was an instant success. It was referred to as the "90-Day Wonder" for the speed with which it was built. The hotel occupied an 800-foot expanse of oceanfront property at the terminus of Hollywood Boulevard. (Elsie Johns Collection.)

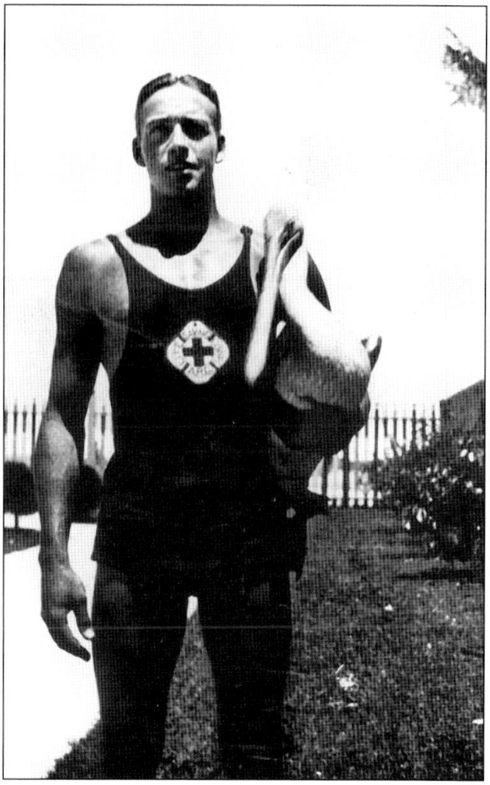

One of the lifeguards at the Hollywood Beach Hotel cradles a pelican known to residents of the area as "Old Bill." This photograph was taken in 1926 shortly before a major hurricane hit the area. The lifeguard safely reached cover at the hotel during the storm. "Old Bill's" fate remains a mystery. (Martha Rose Scott Collection.)

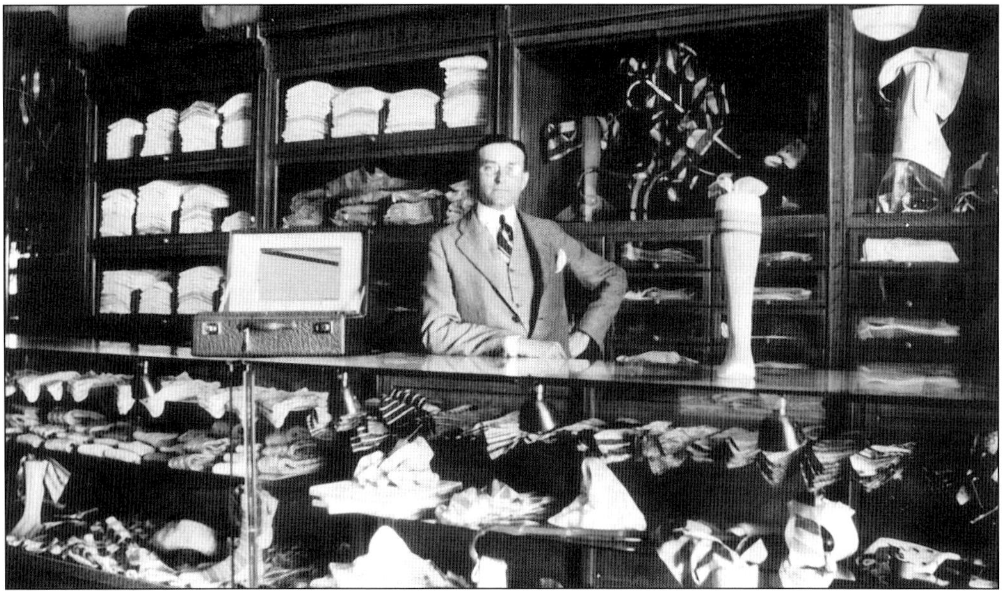

Harold Leroy Scott displays his wares in the Smartclad Men's Shop located in the concourse of the Hollywood Beach Hotel. Scott, originally from Indianapolis, came to Hollywood with his wife and 12-year old daughter, Martha Rose, during the summer of 1926 to manage the shop. (Martha Rose Scott Collection.)

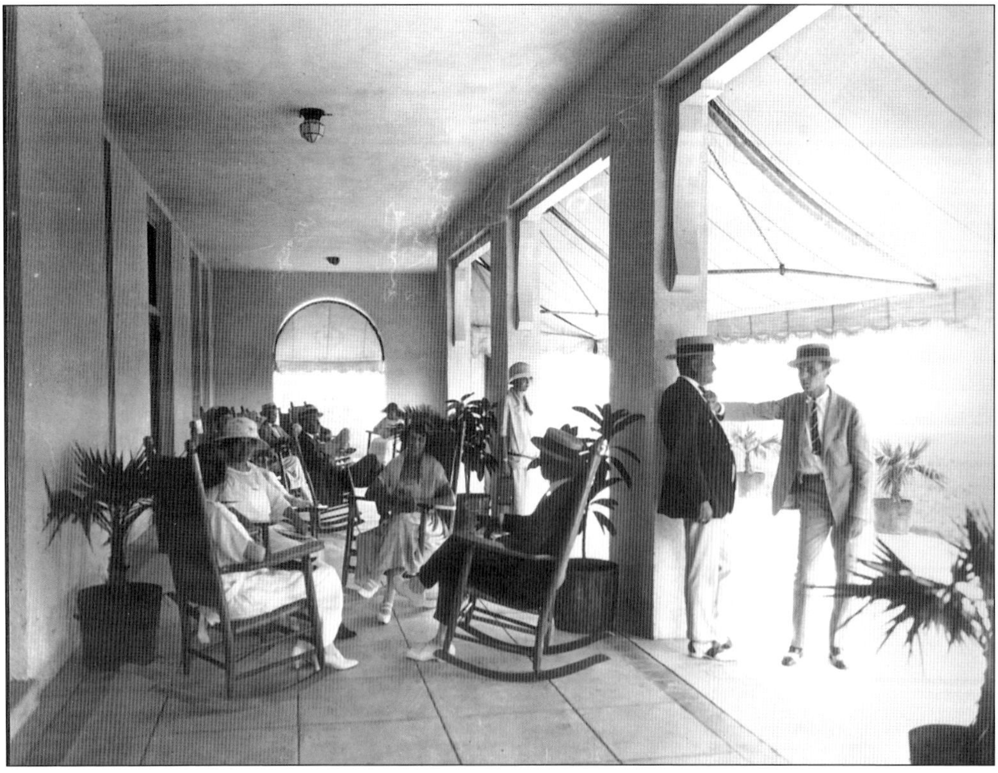

Hollywood Beach Hotel guests enjoy the quiet life and ocean breezes on the porch of the hotel. (General Collection.)

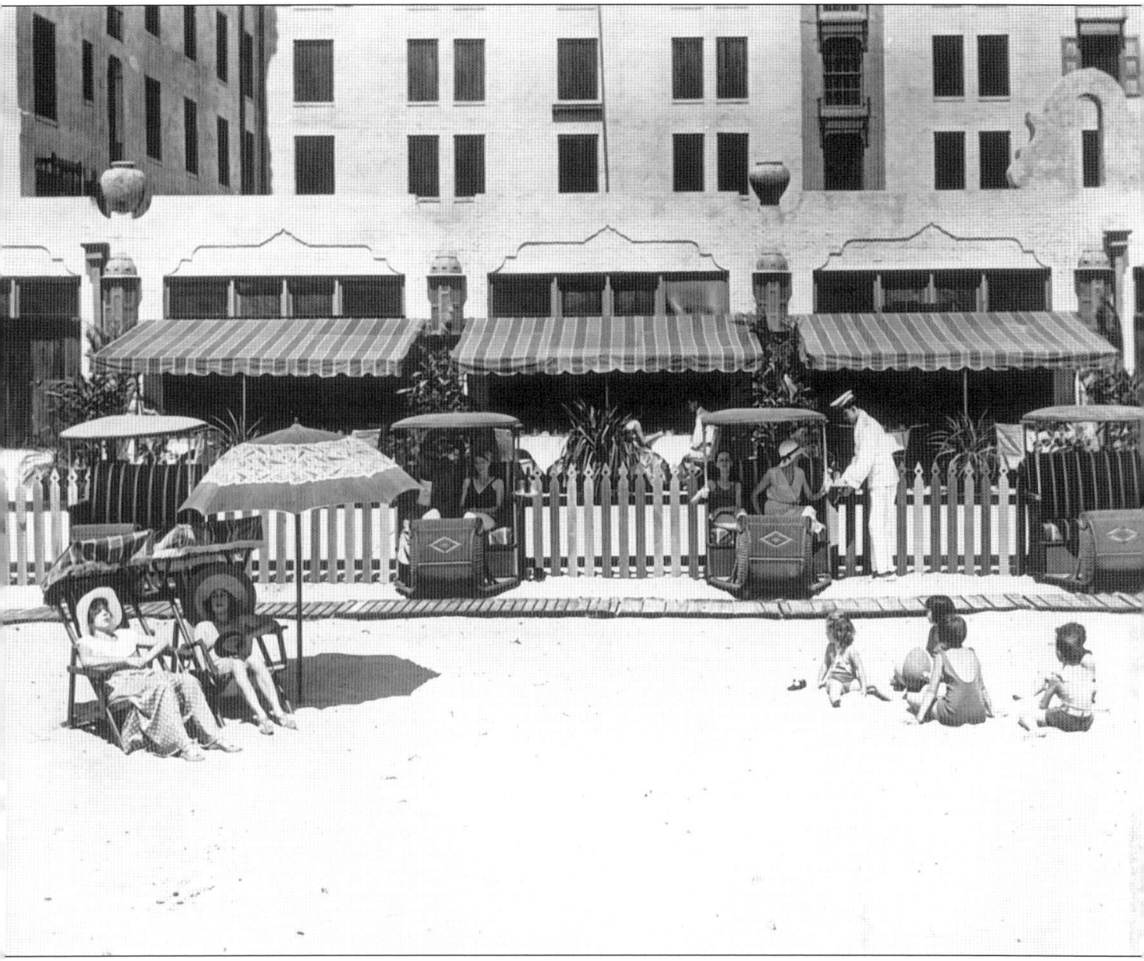

An equipped staff pampered hotel guests. The perambulators, wicker-wheeled chairs, were either pushed along the Broadwalk by strolling employees or parked along the beach for a more sedentary view of the Atlantic. (General Collection.)

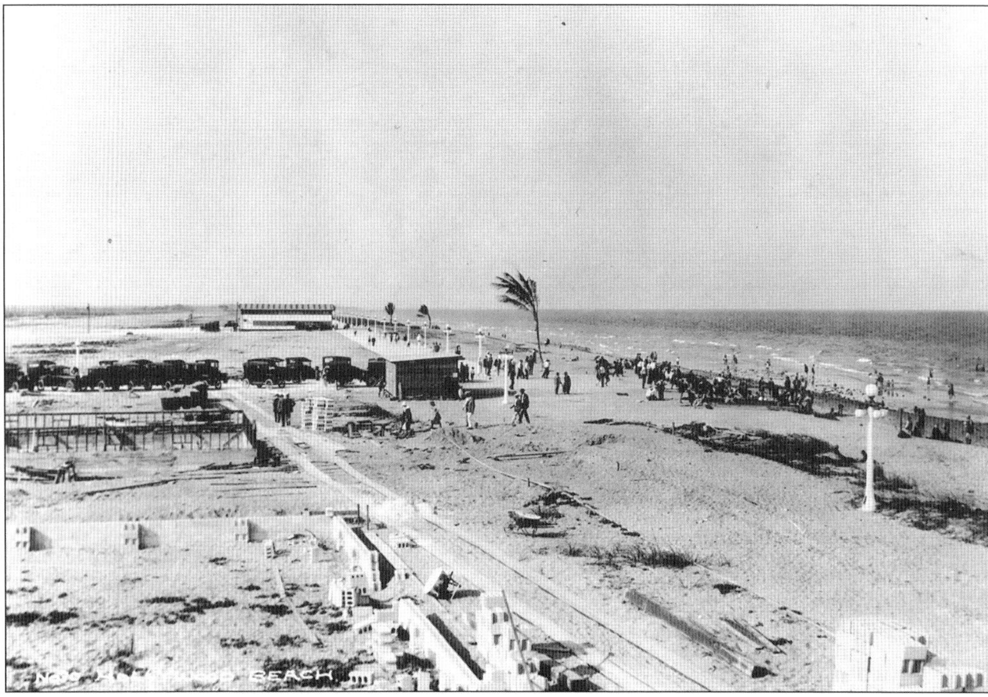

In addition to the activities offered to Hollywood Beach Hotel guests, Joseph Young also envisioned a facility where others could enjoy the beauties of the beach. The Hollywood Beach Casino was built along the Broadwalk, a 1.5-mile long concrete promenade. When completed, the casino would be the largest and best-appointed bathing pavilion in Florida. The two-story structure in the background is a Young company sales office. (Whitson Collection.)

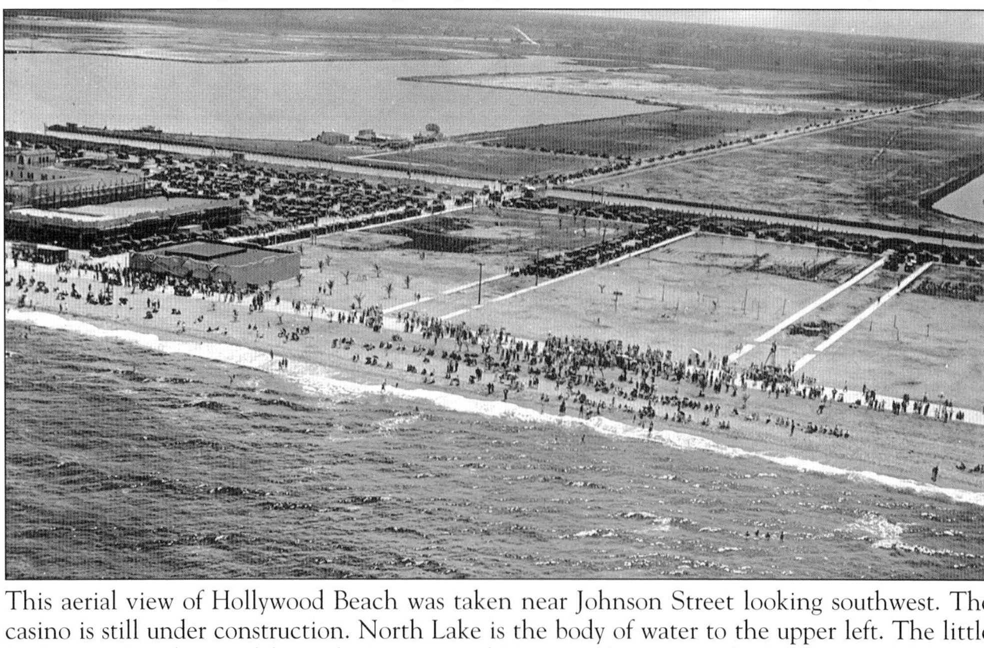

This aerial view of Hollywood Beach was taken near Johnson Street looking southwest. The casino is still under construction. North Lake is the body of water to the upper left. The little bridge crossing the canal (now the Intracoastal Waterway) connects the beach side of Johnson Street with the mainland side. (General Collection.)

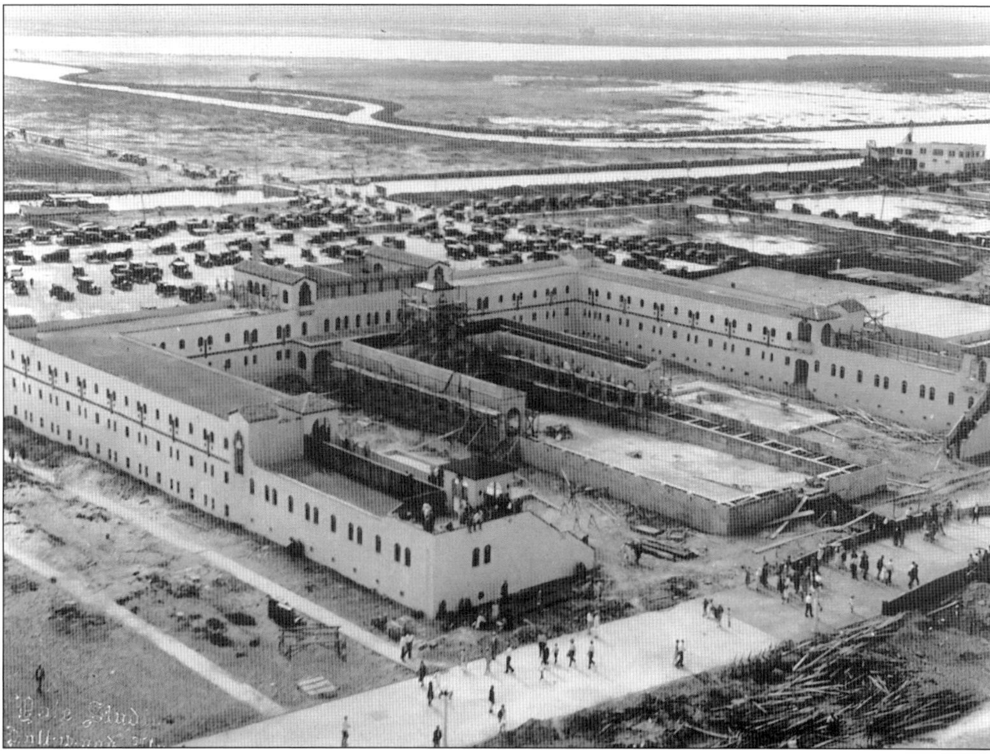

As the casino begins to take shape, curious strollers along the Broadwalk check out the progress being made. The structure in the center of the building is the pool, which would be fed by seawater pumped from the Atlantic. (General Collection.)

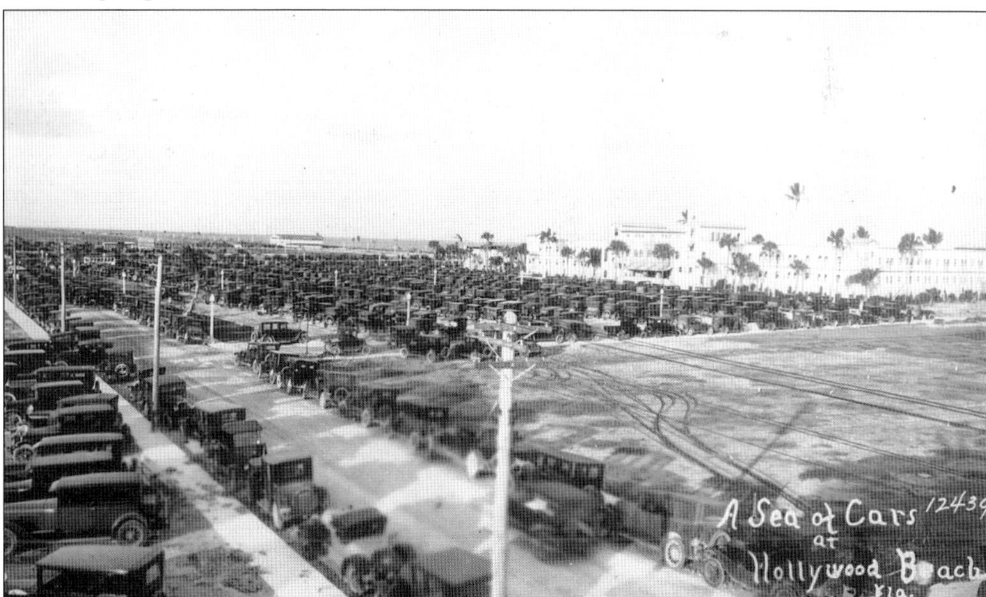

The Casino, which opened to the public in the autumn of 1924, proved to be a favorite attraction to residents and visitors to the area, drawing hundreds of cars on a regular basis. (General Collection.)

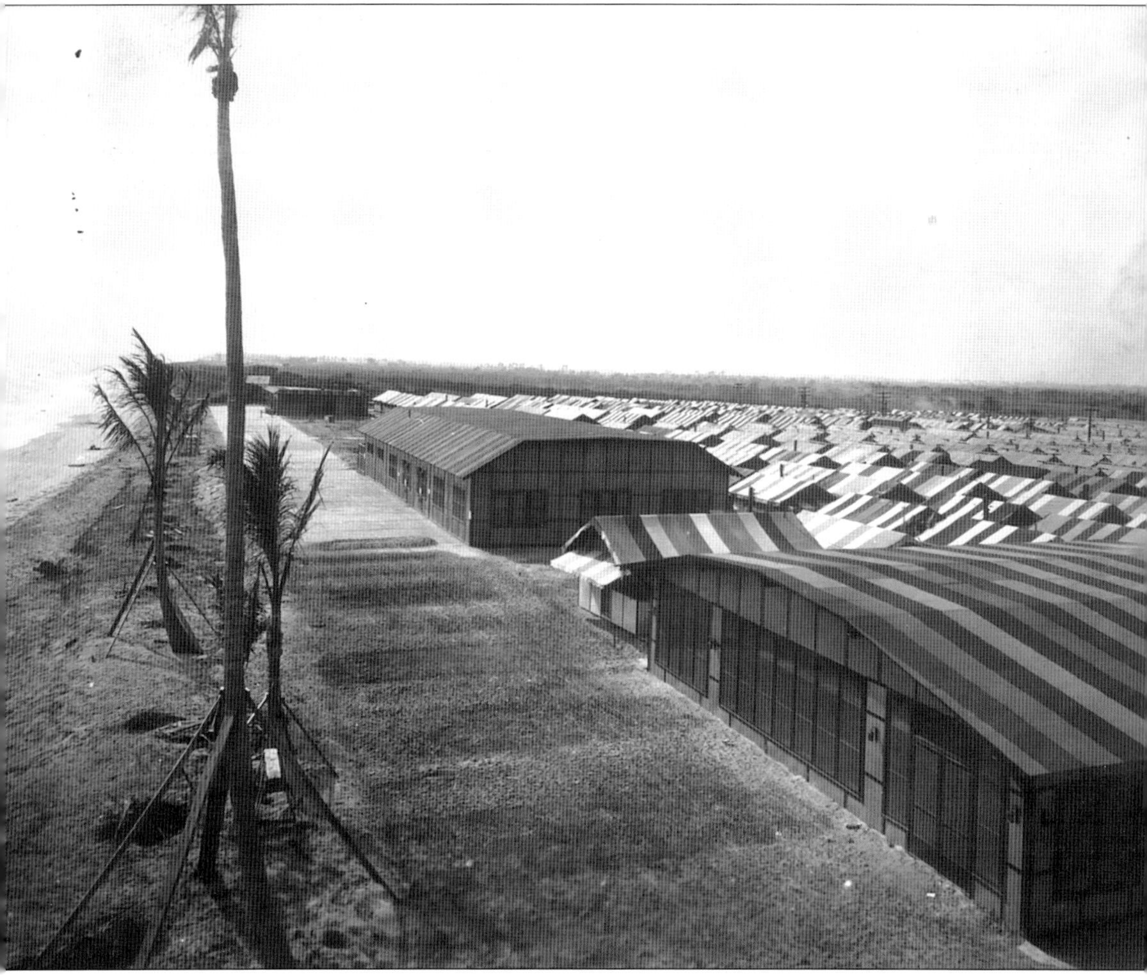

Tent City, located on Hollywood Beach at Washington Street and the Broadwalk, was under construction and completed at the same time as the Hollywood Beach Hotel. Units consisted of furnished living rooms and bedroom and bath suites. Many had kitchenettes, each in its own tent. The cottage-like structures had wood frames and floors, with screened upper walls. The roofs were of colorfully striped canvas with matching awnings over the entrances. Maid service and other amenities were provided at a level comparable to the best hotels of the day. Tent City was opened and filled to capacity during the 1925–1926 tourist season, but it was destroyed by the 1926 hurricane and never rebuilt. (General Collection.)

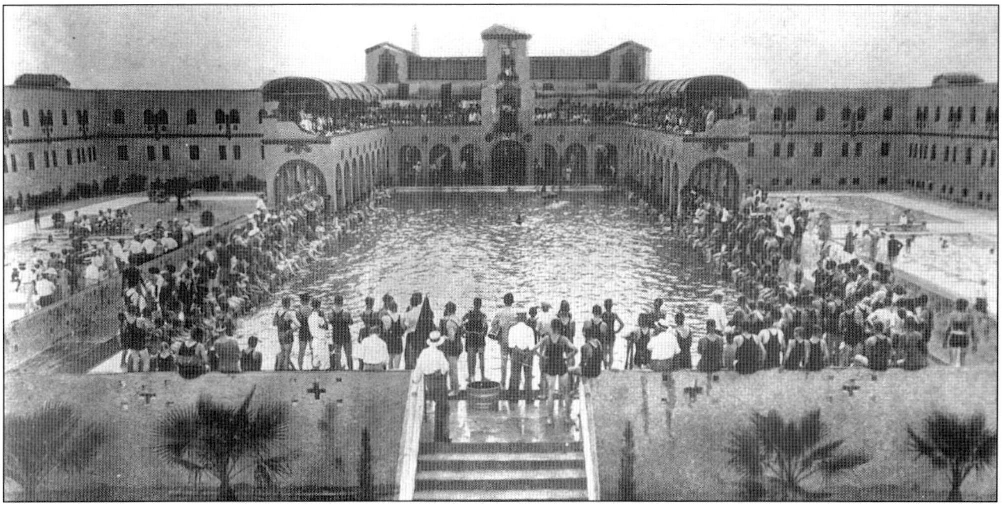

A crowd gathers at the Casino pool. The Casino was built at a cost of $250,000 and included 824 dressing rooms, 80 shower/baths, a shopping arcade, and of course, an Olympic-size swimming pool—everything a family needed for a long day at the beach. This photograph was one of many published in Joseph Young's sales brochures. (Al Vessella Collection.)

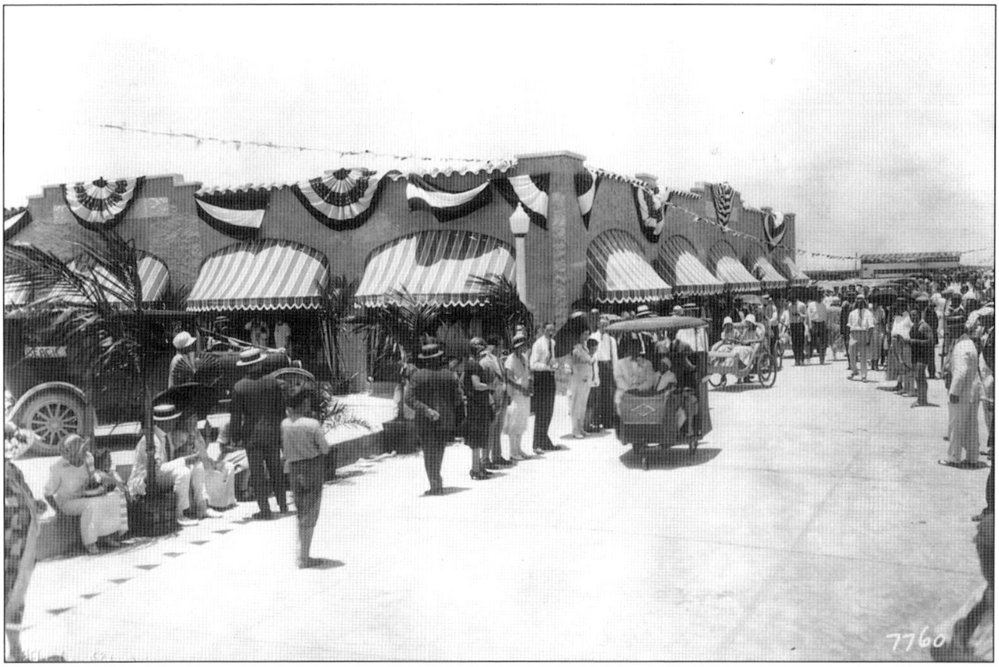

The Tangerine Tea Room, across Johnson Street from the Casino, was the most popular center of entertainment for the younger set. It served lunch and dinner daily and was noted for its nightly dances. An almost identical photograph was published in a brochure produced by Hollywood, Florida Tours, Inc. and identified as being taken on Thanksgiving Day. The year was not indicated, but it was likely 1925. (General Collection.)

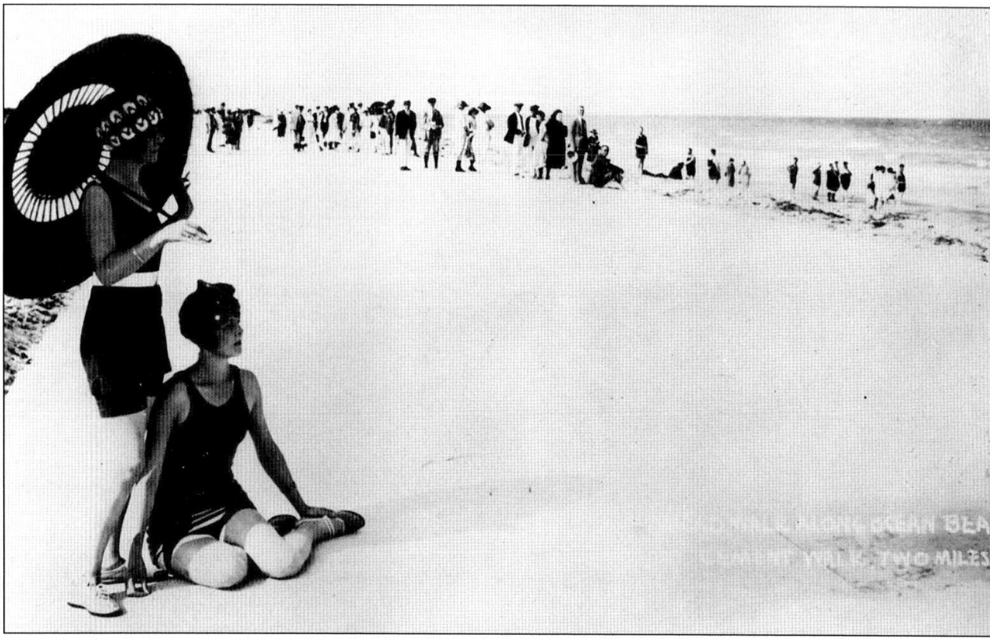

Two bathing beauties strike a serene pose on the beach. The inscription in the photograph's lower right corner reads, "Broadwalk along ocean beach. Cement walk two miles long." (Whitson Collection.)

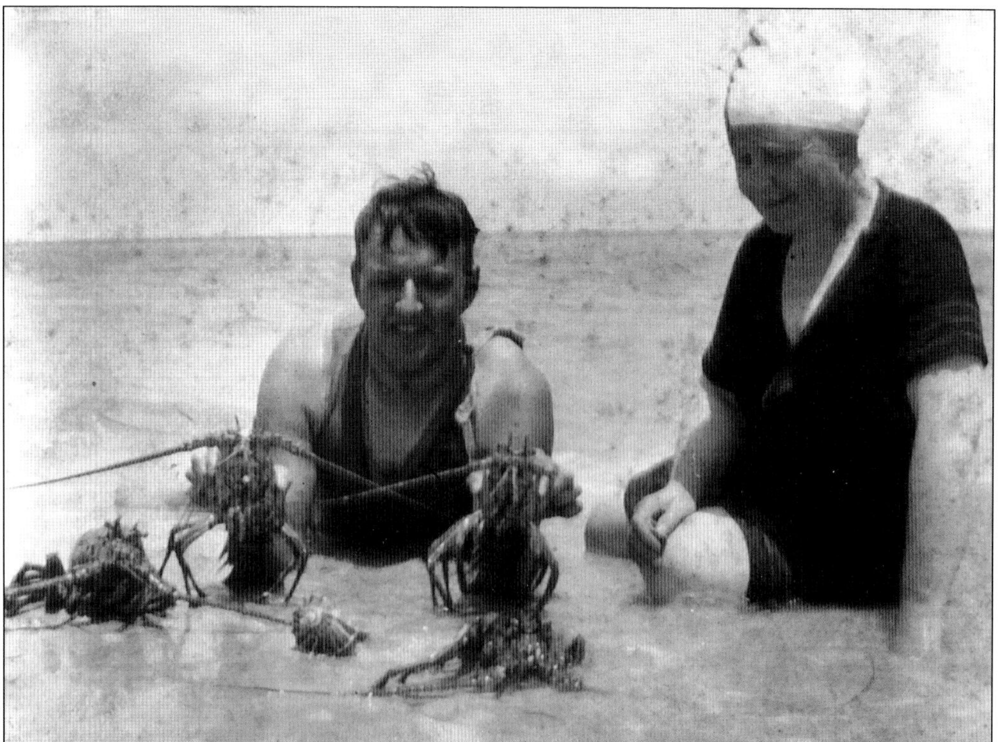

In this photo, beachgoers display four lobsters and a shell along the edge of the Atlantic. (Whitson Collection.)

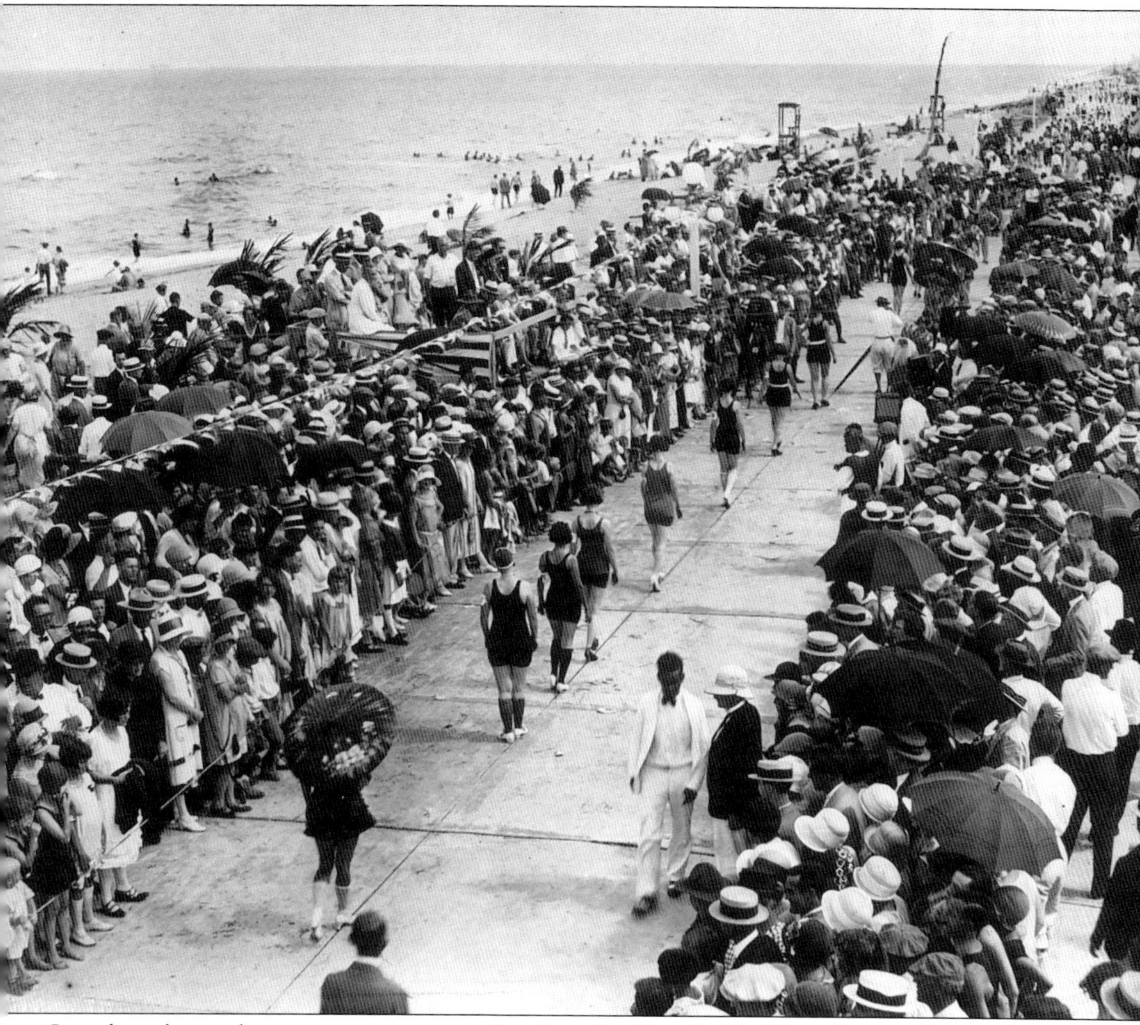

Crowds gather as beauty contestants parade along the Broadwalk. This photograph was also included in the Hollywood, Florida Tours, Inc. brochure and was identified as taking place on Thanksgiving Day. (General Collection.)

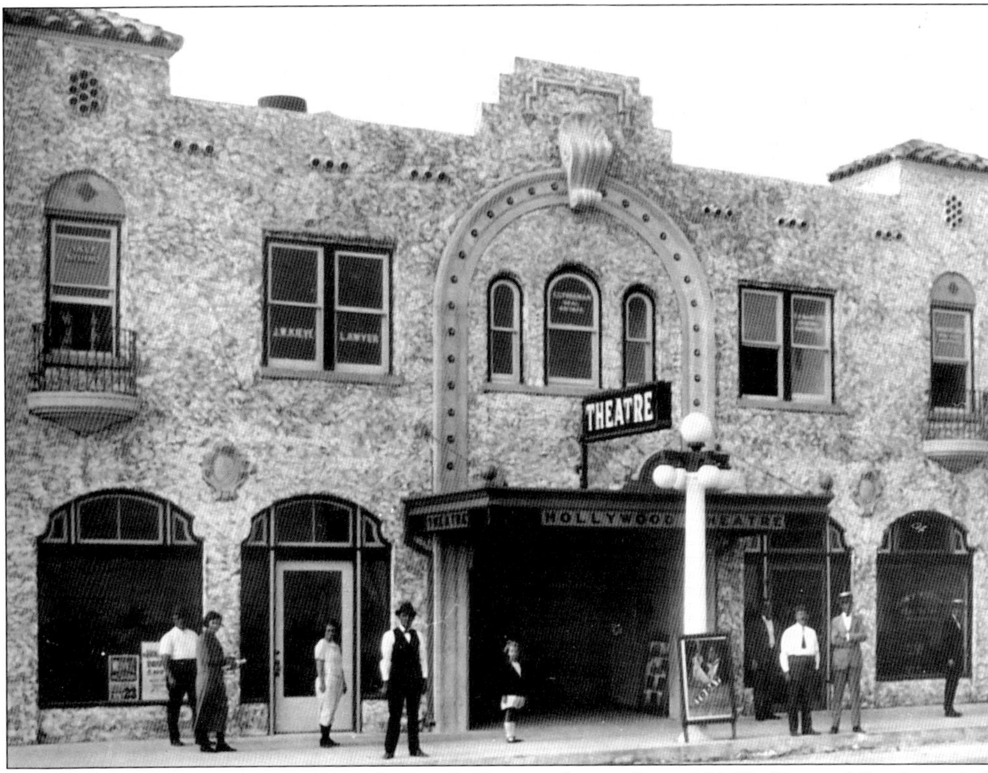

Several people stand about the Hollywood Theatre, located at 1921 Hollywood Boulevard. It was built in early 1924 by contractor Thomas M. McCarrel. Arthur Enos was the owner and manager. (General Collection.)

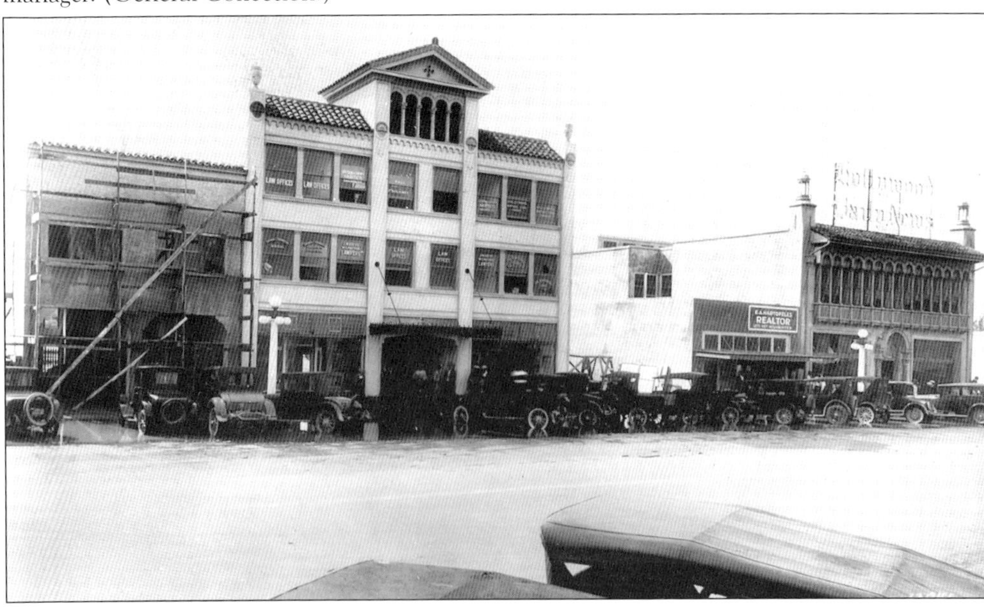

The Morse Arcade and the *Hollywood Daily News* buildings were two of the earliest buildings along Hollywood Boulevard. The Morse Arcade is located at 1926 Hollywood Boulevard and the Daily News Building is at 1932 Hollywood Boulevard. (General Collection.)

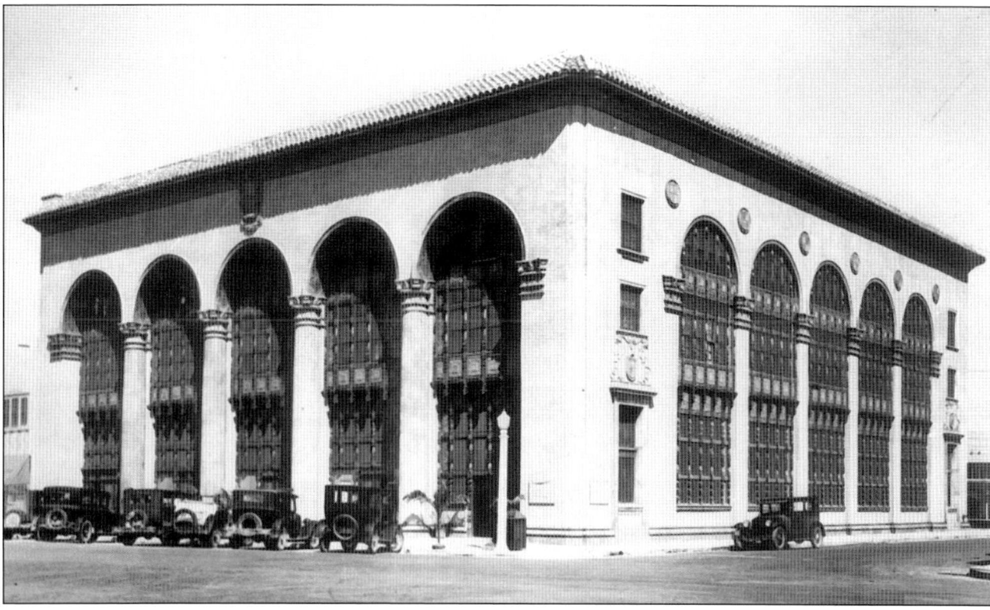

The Hollywood State Bank Building was one of the largest commercial buildings in early Hollywood. The building was designed by Joseph Young's personal architects, Rubush and Hunter of Indianapolis, Indiana, and it was constructed on the corner of Hollywood Boulevard and Twentieth Avenue. The building also served as the city's post office from 1926 to 1950. (General Collection.)

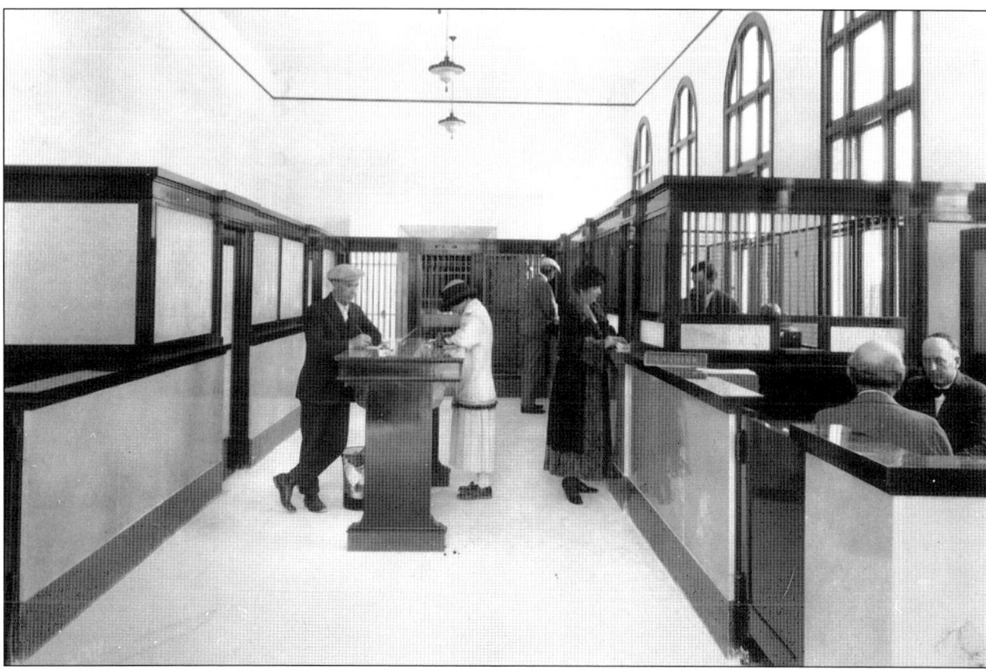

In this 1924 photograph, customers of the Hollywood State Bank prepare their transactions for the cashier. Head cashier E.K. Bowie is seated to the right. The building still serves Hollywood as a financial center and Sun Trust Bank now occupies the site. (General Collection.)

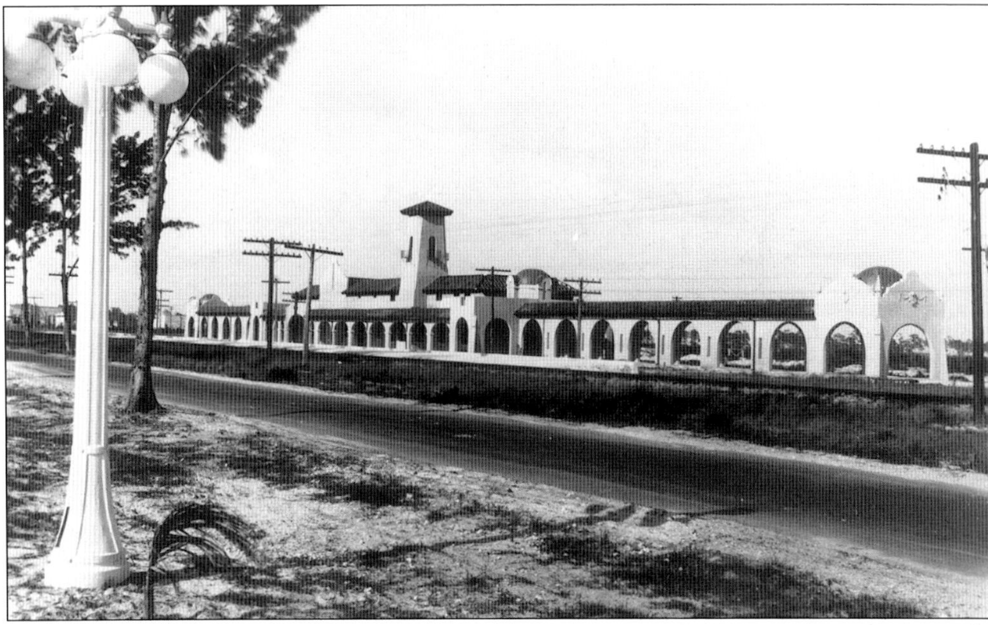

Joseph Young built Hollywood's first railroad station from October 1923 to March 1924. The station, designed in Spanish mission style for service on the Florida East Coast Railroad line, was 425 feet long and located at 420 North Twenty-first Avenue. The first passenger train to stop at the new station, the *Floridian*, was greeted by a large group of company officials and residents on April 6, 1924. Regular stops began on August 20 that year. The station was razed in 1967. (General Collection.)

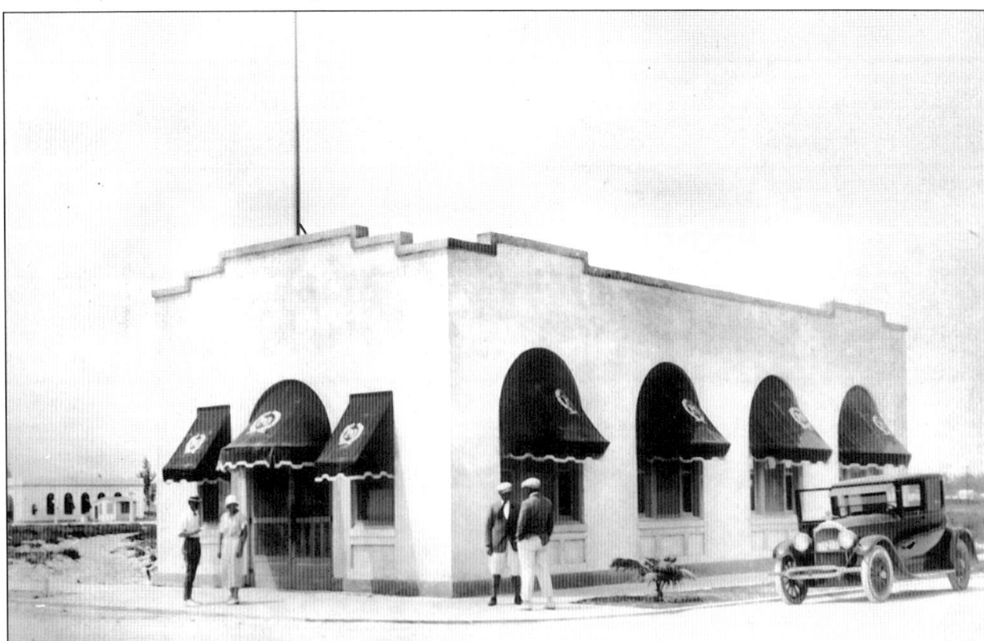

The city's first permanent post office was built on the northwest corner of Harrison Street and Nineteenth Avenue. Paul R. John Sr. was Hollywood's first postmaster. The building was destroyed in the 1926 hurricane. (General Collection.)

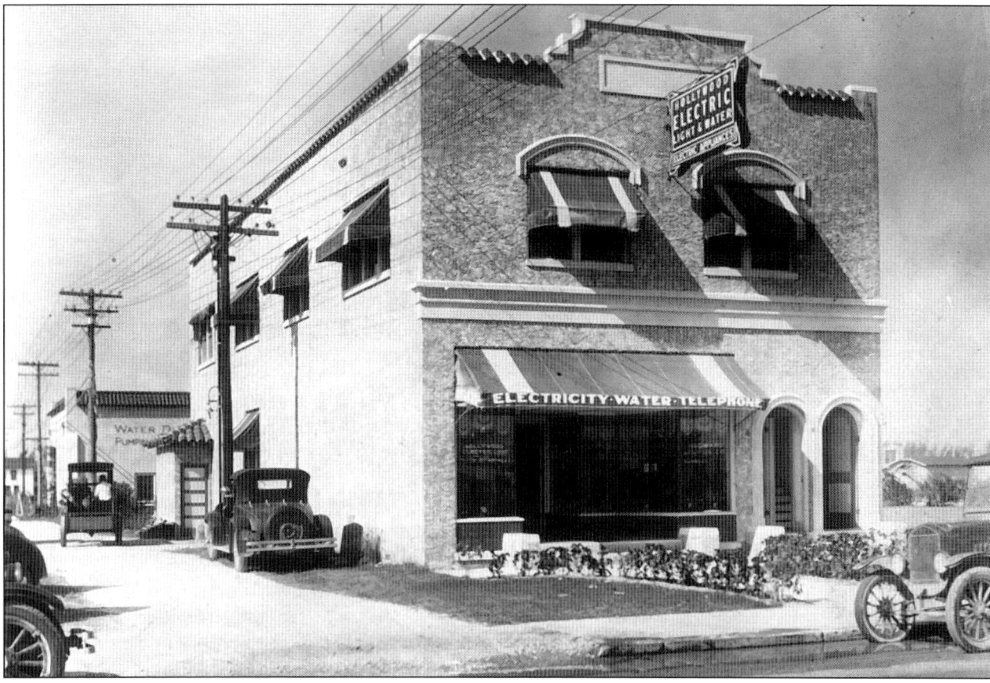

The Hollywood Electric Light and Water Dept., a Joseph Young company, shared space with Broward Utilities, which provided telephone service to the area. The building was located on Eighteenth Avenue between Polk and Tyler Streets. The water department's pumping facility is behind the utilities building. (Whitson Collection.)

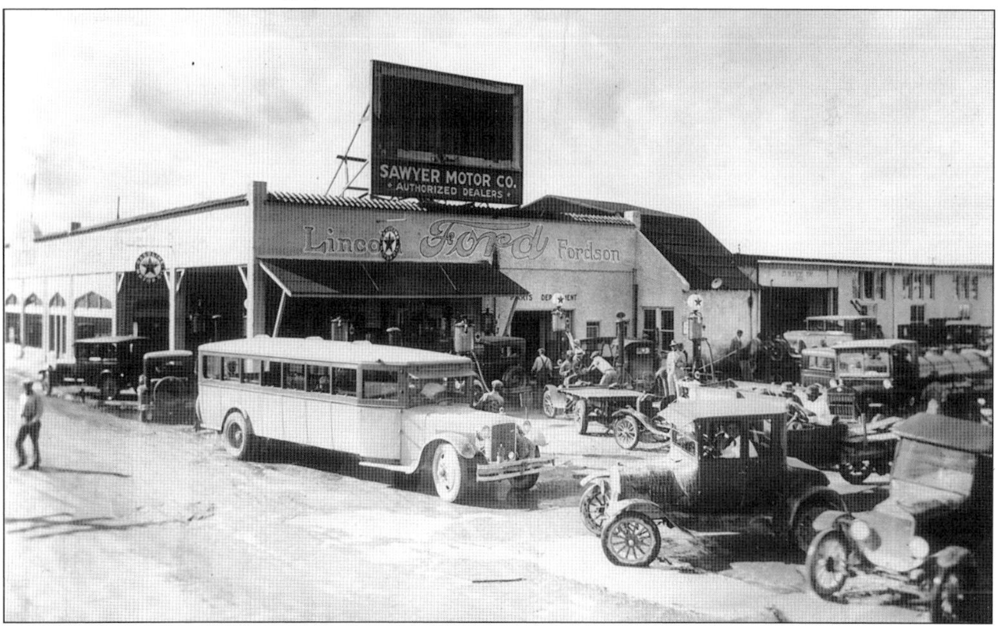

The Sawyer Motor Co. was one of the earliest auto dealerships in the area, selling Lincolns, Fords, and Fordson tractors. The garage, gas station, and showroom were located on Harding Circle. One of the white Hollywood Land and Water Co. tour buses is filling up in this view. (Whitson Collection.)

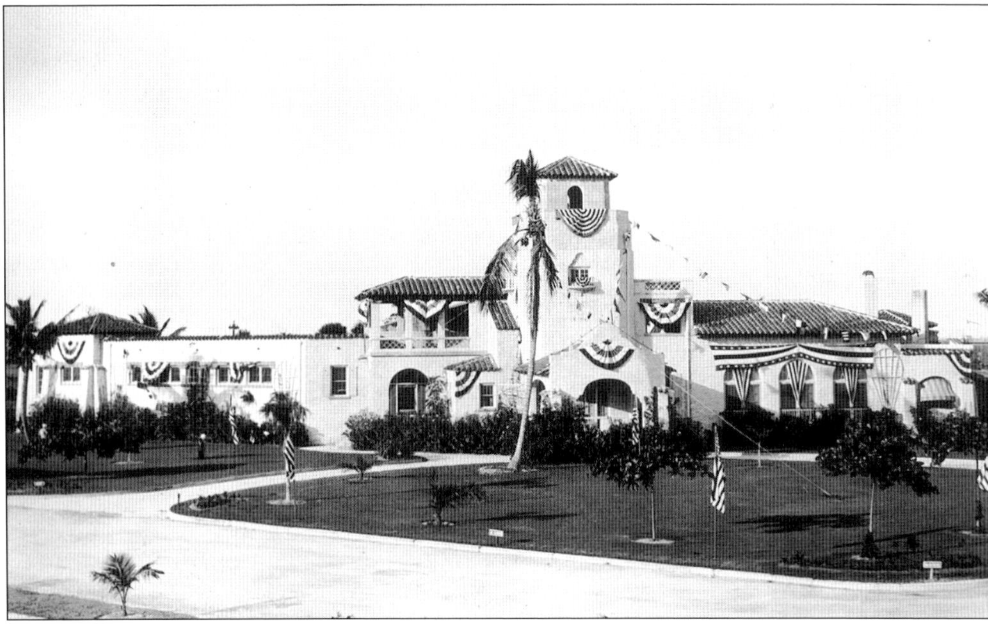

The Hollywood Golf and Country Club at Polk Street and Seventeenth Avenue opened with grand festivities on January 19, 1924, and quickly became another elegant venue for social occasions. (General Collection.)

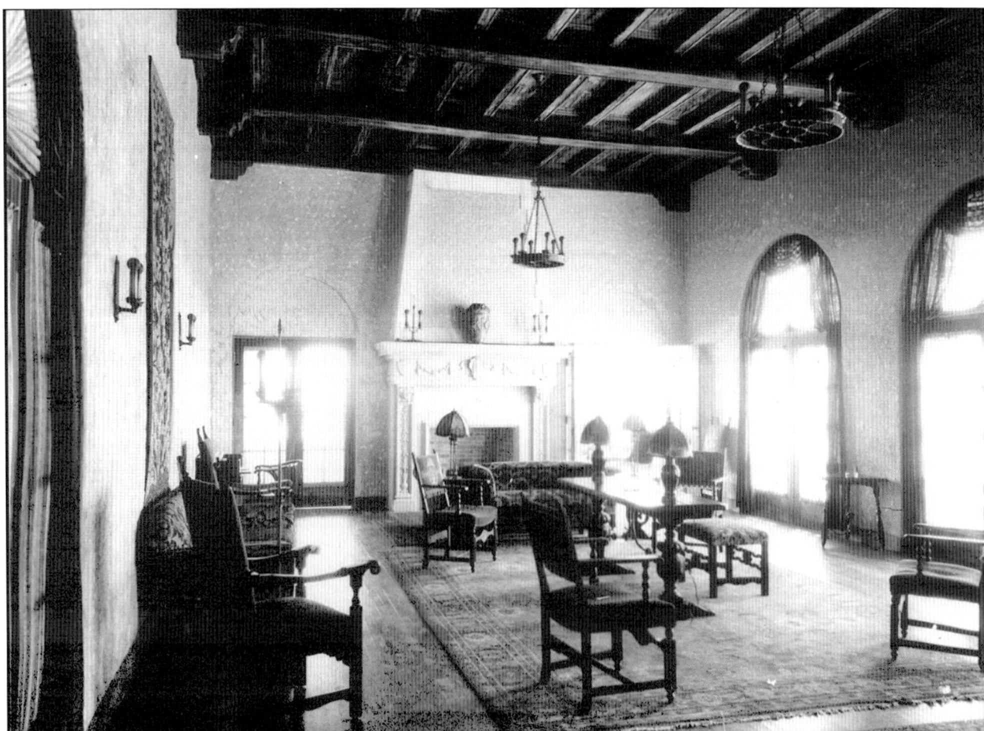

No expense was spared in constructing the country club. Hardwood floors, cypress ceilings, tapestries, and a large fireplace dominated the lounging area of the club. (Whitson Collection.)

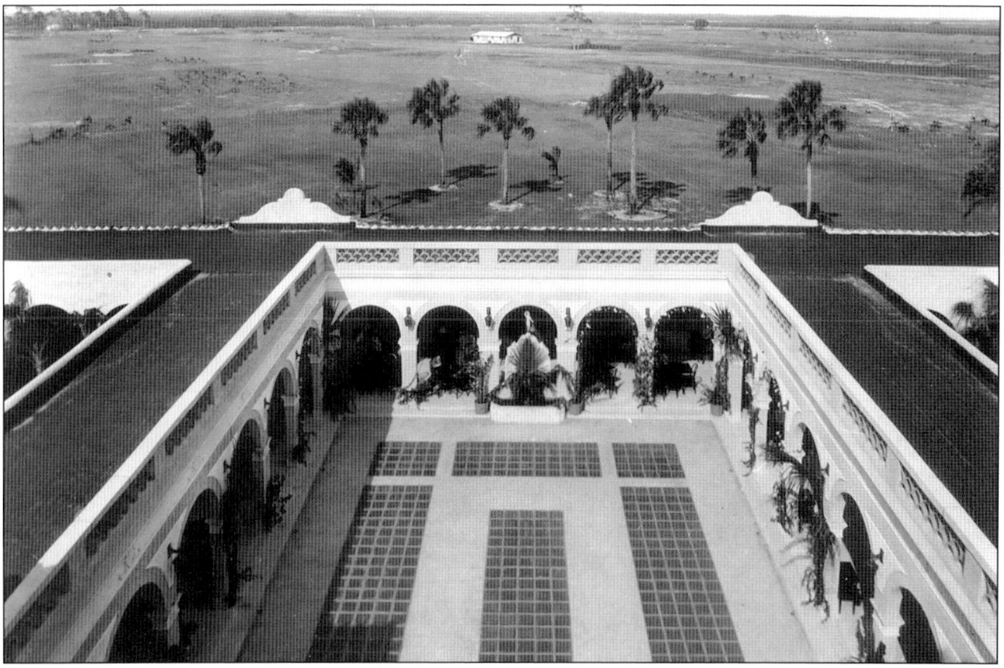

What many would guess to be the Golf and Country Club's pool is actually the club's patio, which served as a ballroom. A retractable roof, shown rolled away, could be opened or closed depending on the weather. Evening dances under the stars were popular. (Whitson Collection.)

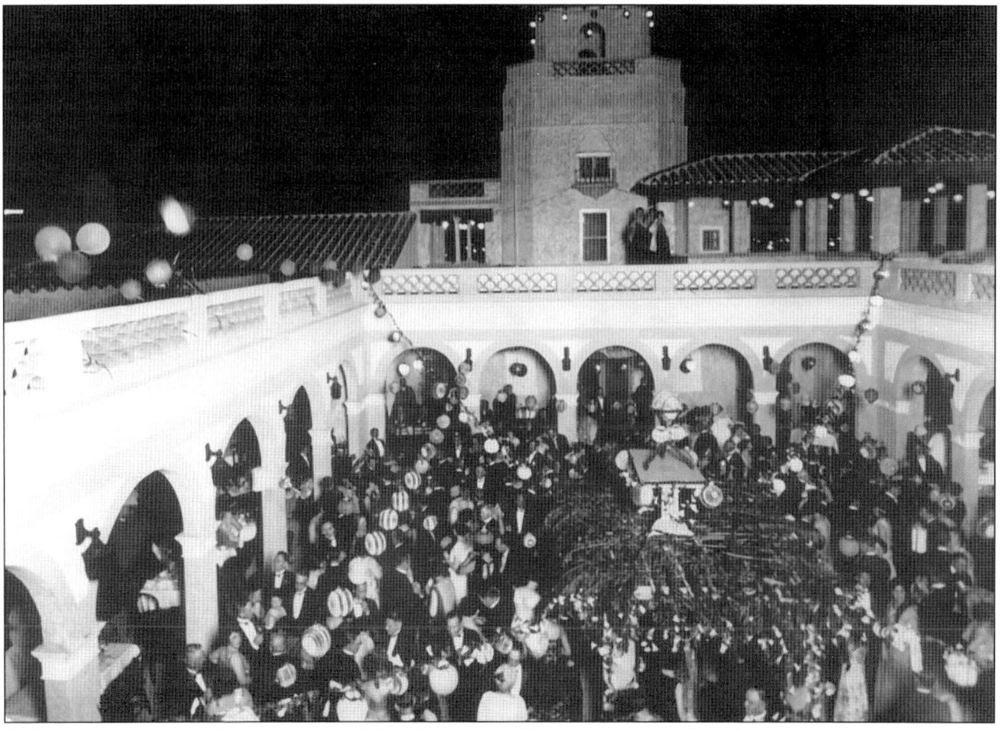

A festive crowd in formal attire fills the dance floor of the Golf and Country Club during a dinner dance with a Japanese theme on Saturday, February 23, 1924. (General Collection.)

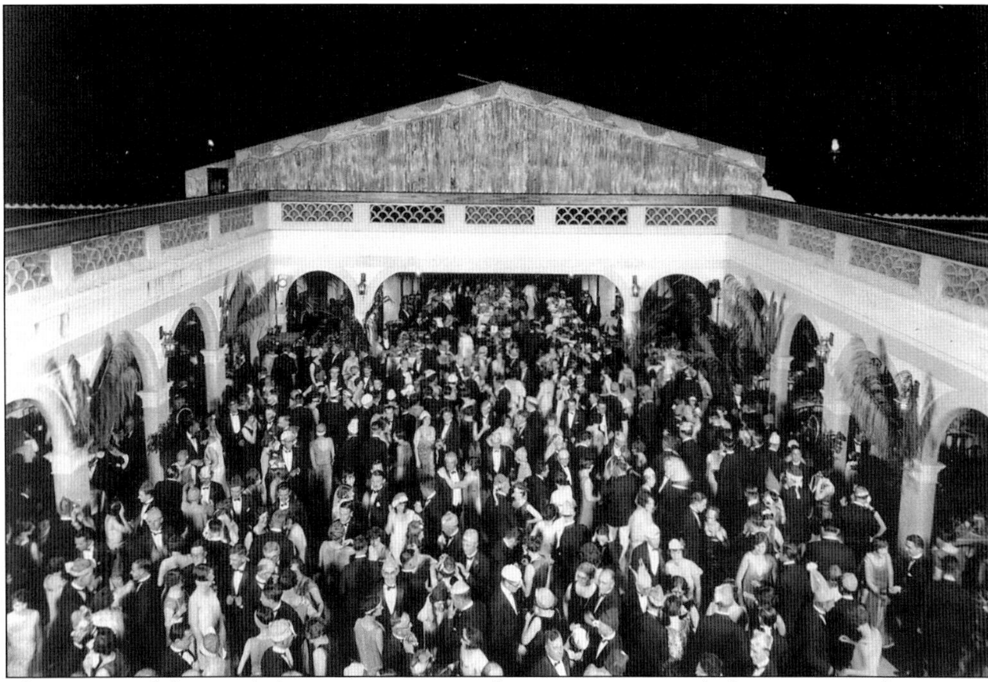

The country club provided a constant source of entertainment, including concerts, dances, and formal balls. The dance floor was state-of-the-art—it was built with glass blocks lit from within, much like many disco floors from a considerably later age. (Whitson Collection.)

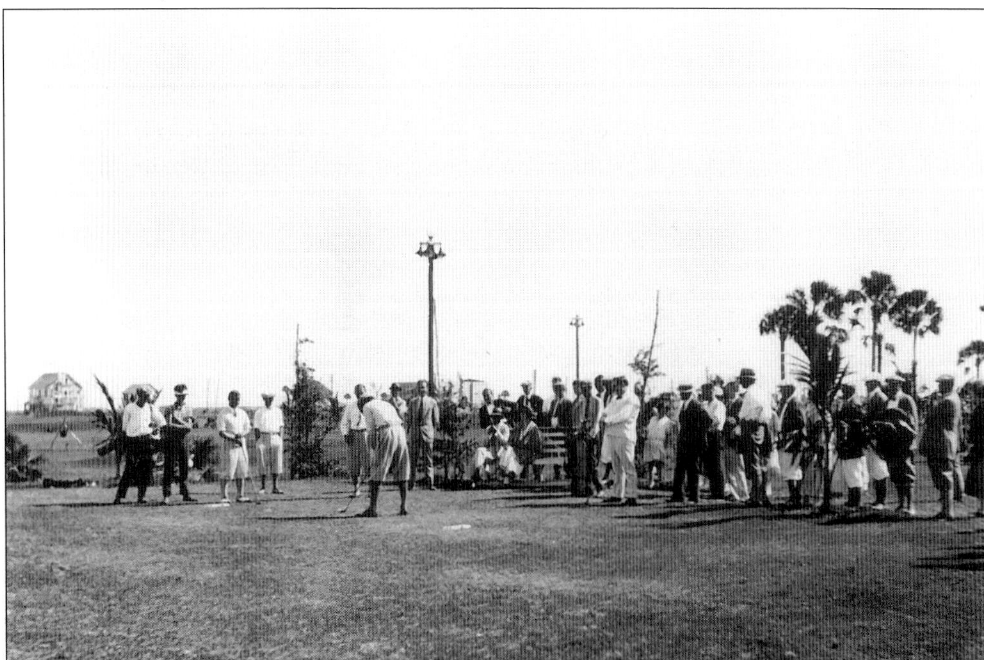

Of course, dancing and partying weren't the only attractions residents and visitors could find at the Hollywood Golf and Country Club. Between rounds of parties, some members actually played golf (Whitson Collection.)

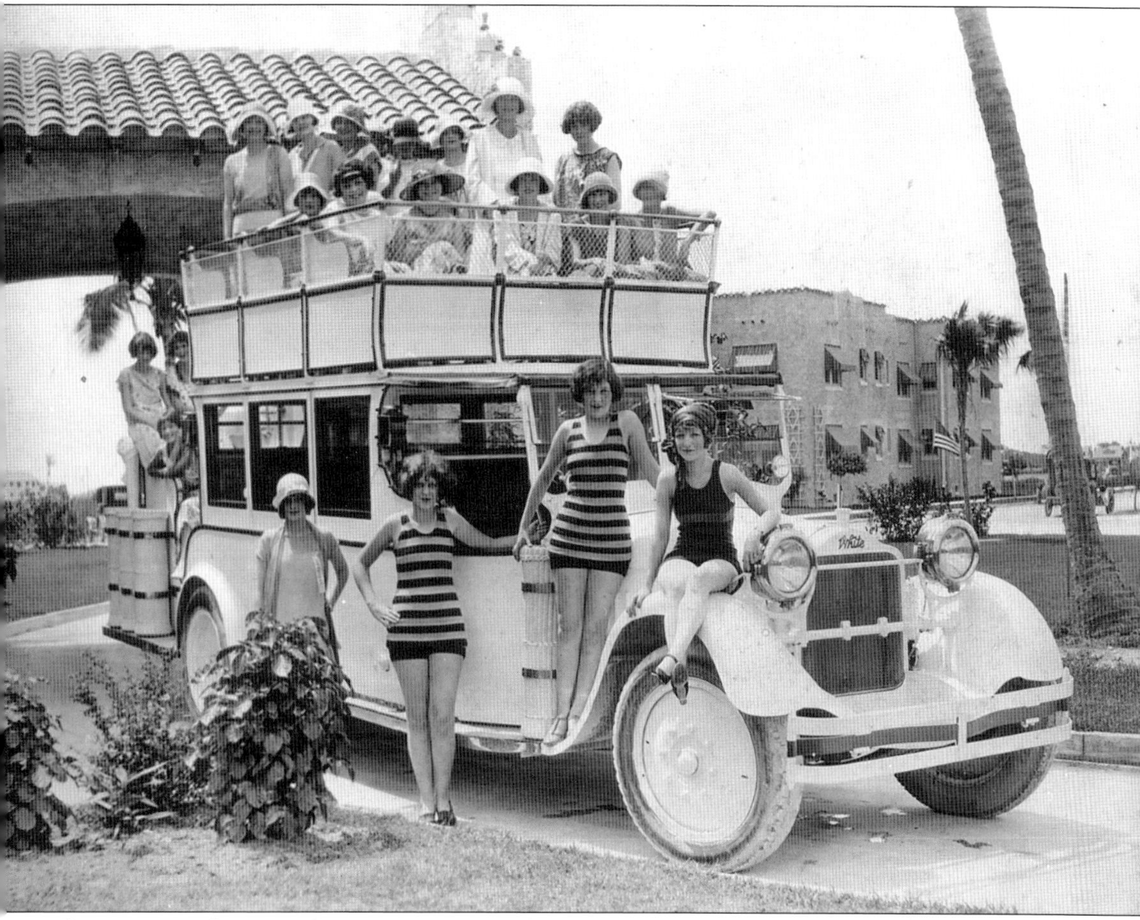

The concept of sex in advertising is not new, contrary to many contemporary thinkers. This view is enhanced by a bevy of fetching young beauties posing outside the Golf and Country Club aboard one of the tally-ho wagons used by the club to transport guests to the links. The Flora Apartments appear in the background. (General Collection.)

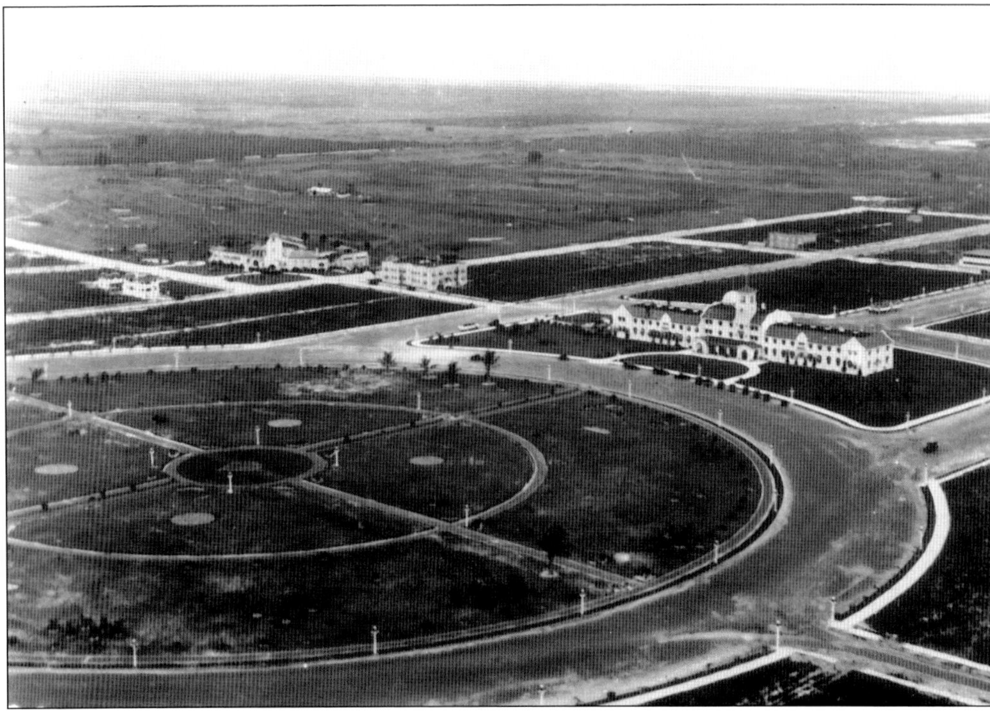

This early aerial view of Harding Circle shows a largely undeveloped Hollywood. The three major structures beyond the circle are the Hollywood Golf and Country Club on the corner of Polk Street and Seventeenth Avenue, the Flora Apartments at 1656 Polk Street, and the Hollywood (later Park View) Hotel. (Whitson Collection.)

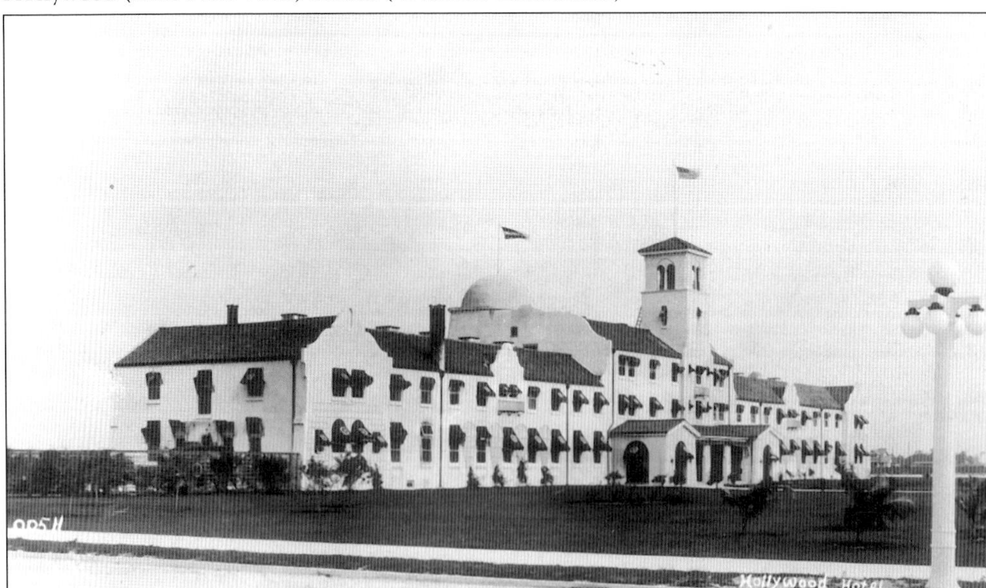

The Hollywood Hotel, which opened in February 1923, was built to accommodate prospective land buyers. The name was changed in 1925 to the Park View Hotel, and later to the Town House Hotel. A grocery store now occupies this site. (Whitson Collection.)

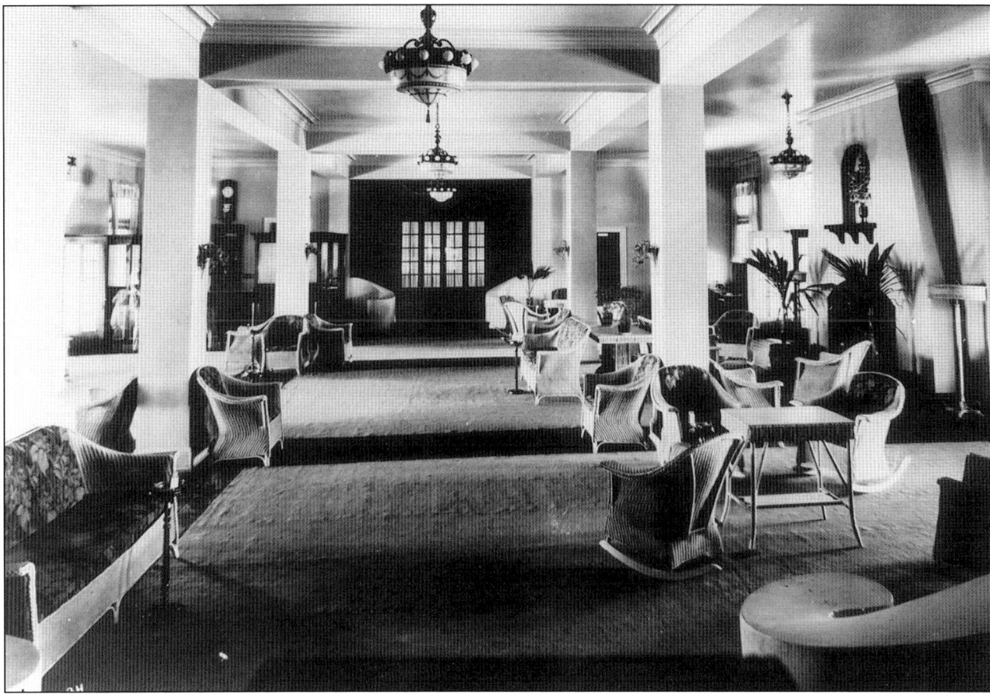

The Hollywood Hotel was the first hotel to open in Hollywood, two years before the city was incorporated. The lobby of the Hollywood Hotel was fashionably furnished with wicker. (Whitson Collection.)

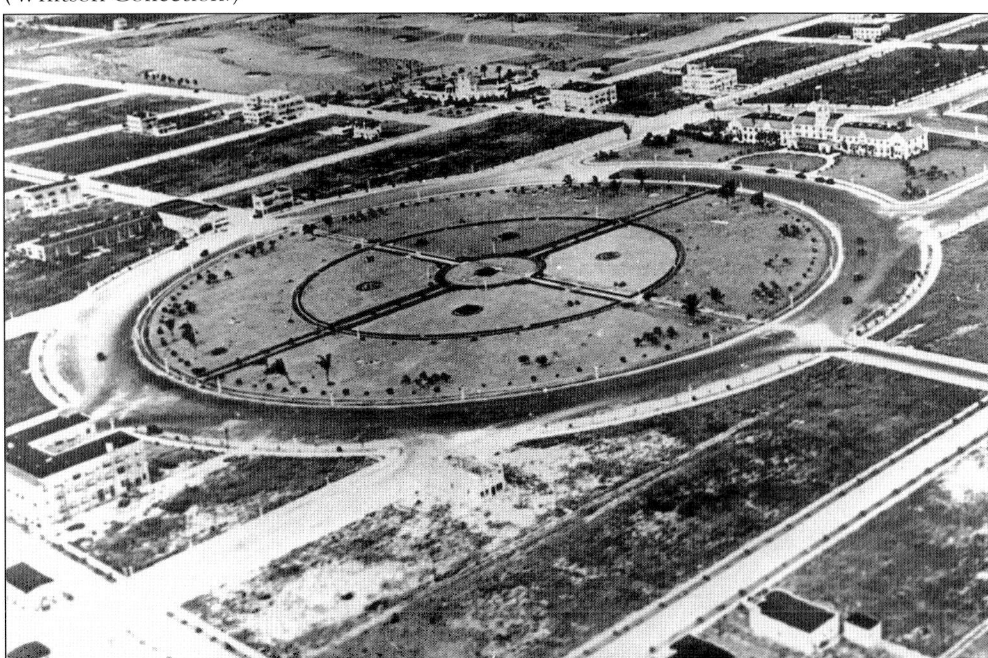

This aerial of Harding Circle, dated April 1924, shows a growing community. At the lower left are the Great Southern Hotel and the post office. At center left are the telephone company building and the Sawyer Motor Co. (General Collection.)

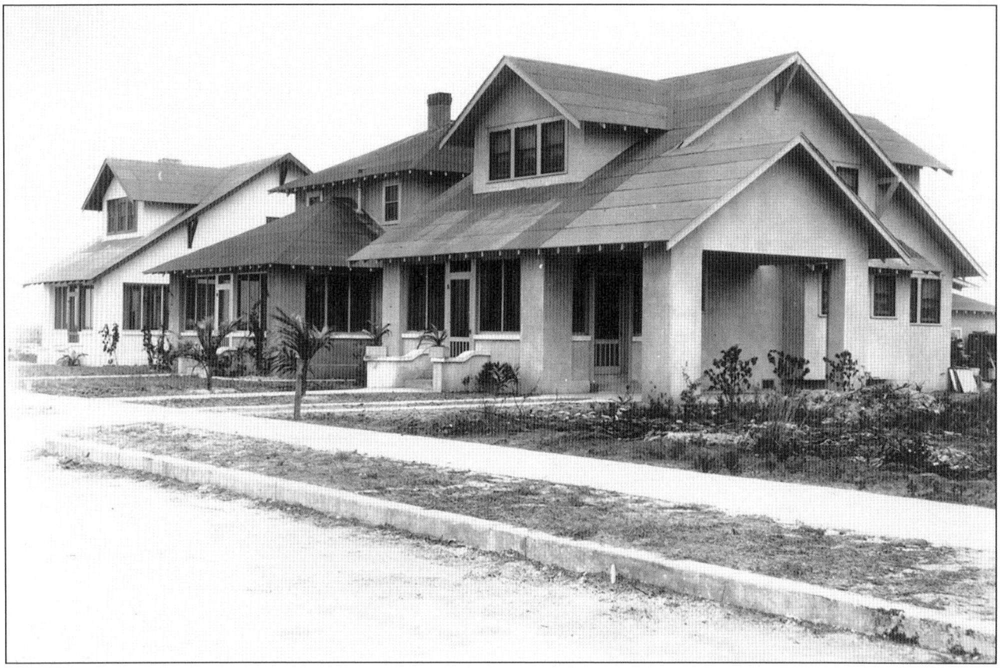

Three newly constructed homes in the 1600 block of Monroe Street await their new owners in April 1924. Mr. and Mrs. Merrill Nevin, Mr. and Mrs. Ollie C. Forbes, and Mrs. E.H. Whitson originally owned the three houses, pictured from left to right. (General Collection.)

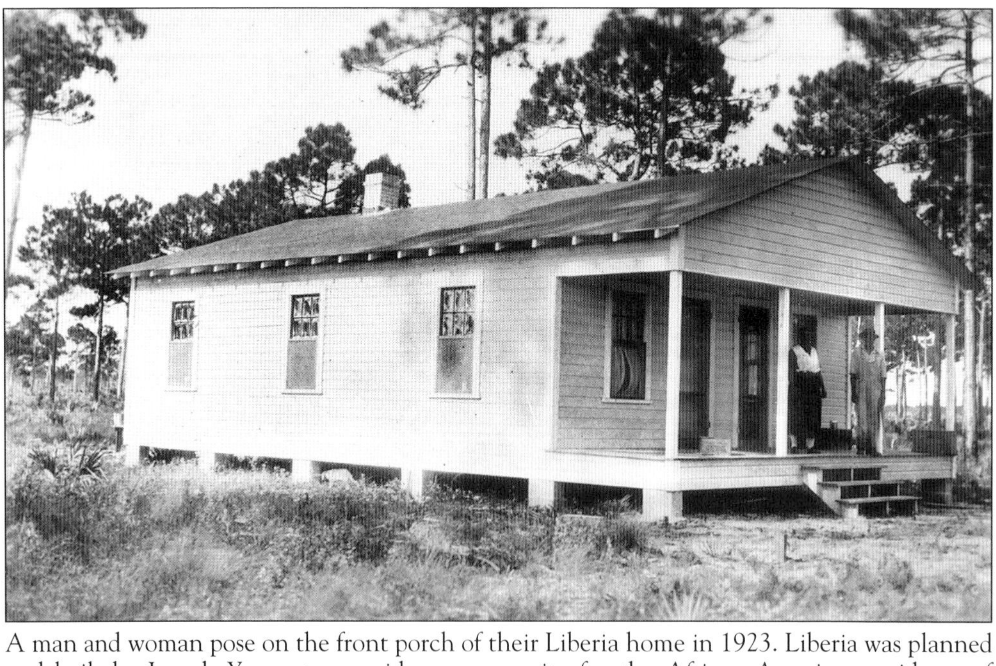

A man and woman pose on the front porch of their Liberia home in 1923. Liberia was planned and built by Joseph Young to provide a community for the African-American residents of Hollywood. Florida, like the other southern states, strictly enforced segregation laws. (Patricia Smith Collection.)

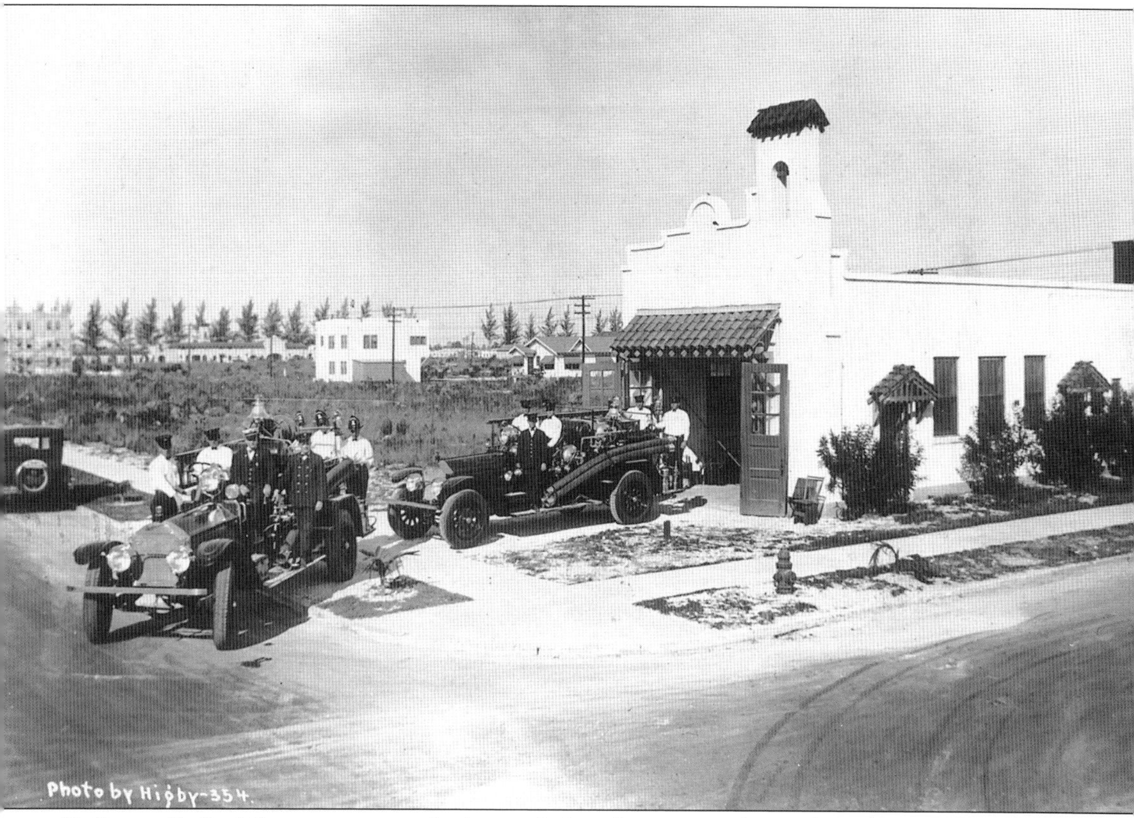

Hollywood's firefighters pose outside the city's first fire station, located on the corner of Polk Street and Nineteenth Avenue. This photo was taken in 1924. The fire station was actually ready for occupancy in September 1923, but its equipment was not delivered until later. (Whitson Collection.)

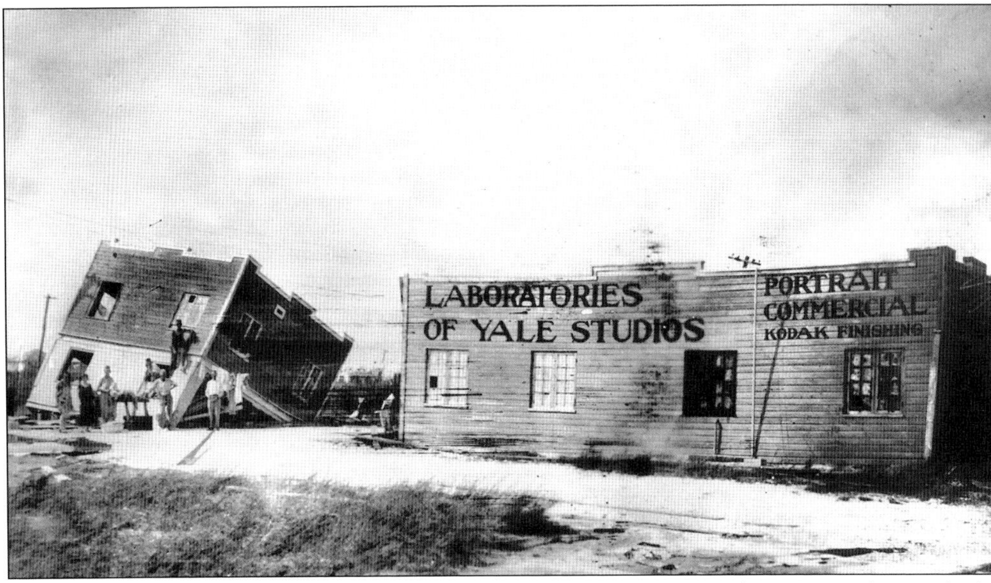

On September 18, 1926, disaster struck Hollywood. A vicious hurricane slammed the coast, claiming 37 lives and flattening or flooding buildings all over town. While he was able to hold on for a few more years, Joseph Young had effectively been wiped out as Hollywood struggled to recover. The building next to Yale Studios was upended from its foundation. (Peracchio Collection.)

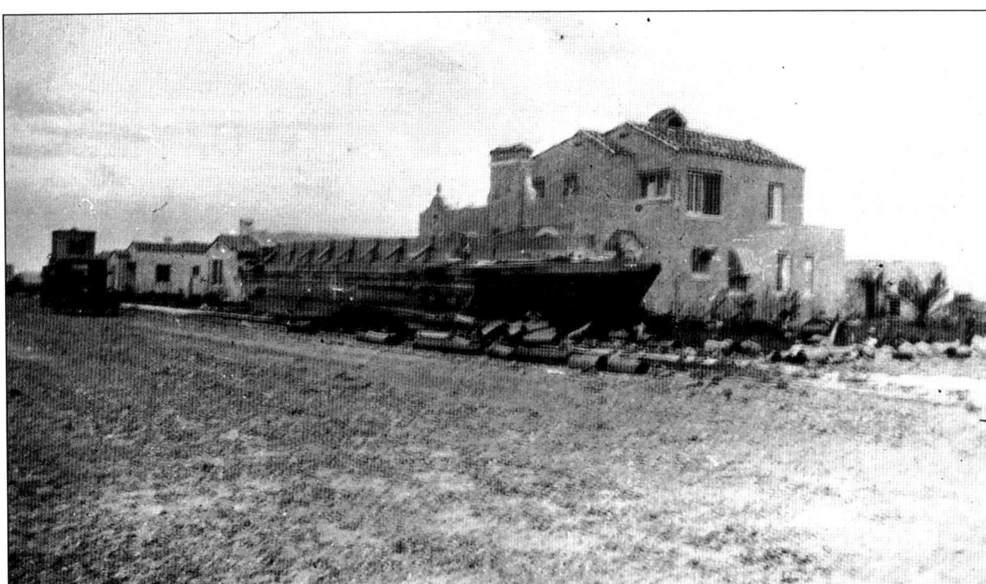

During the storm, a barge broke away from its moorings and was swept away by raging floodwaters. It eventually "beached" itself on the front lawn of a home at 1025 Tyler Street. (Martha Rose Scott Collection.)

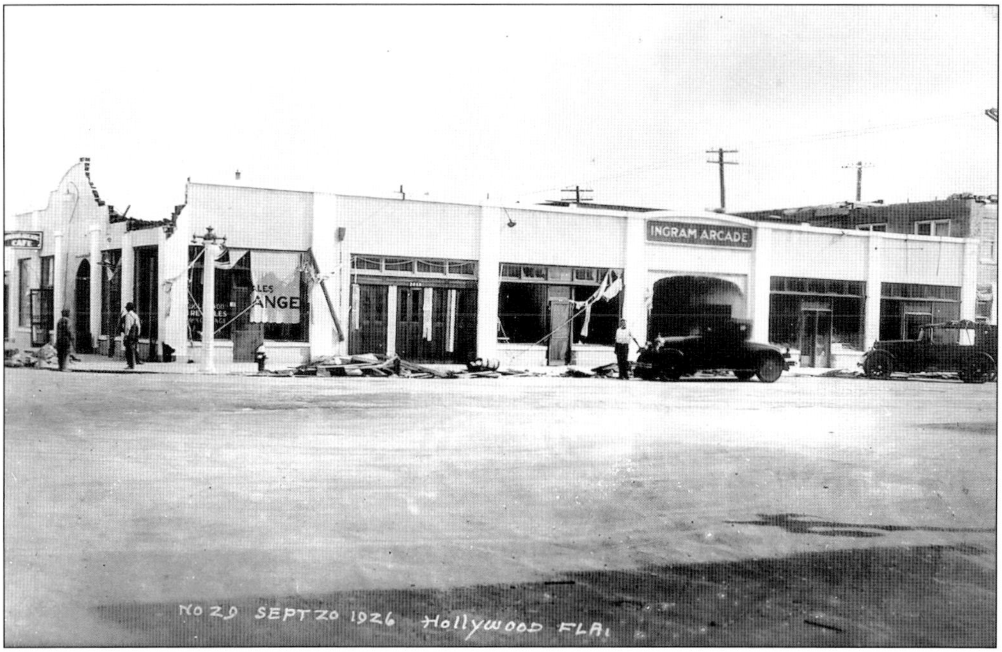

Even buildings of the sturdiest construction were damaged by the hurricane. This building at the northeast corner of Hollywood Boulevard and Twenty-first Avenue was the first building erected by Joseph Young. It served as the city garage from 1921 to 1923, when it was sold and remodeled into the Ingram Arcade. (Peracchio Collection.)

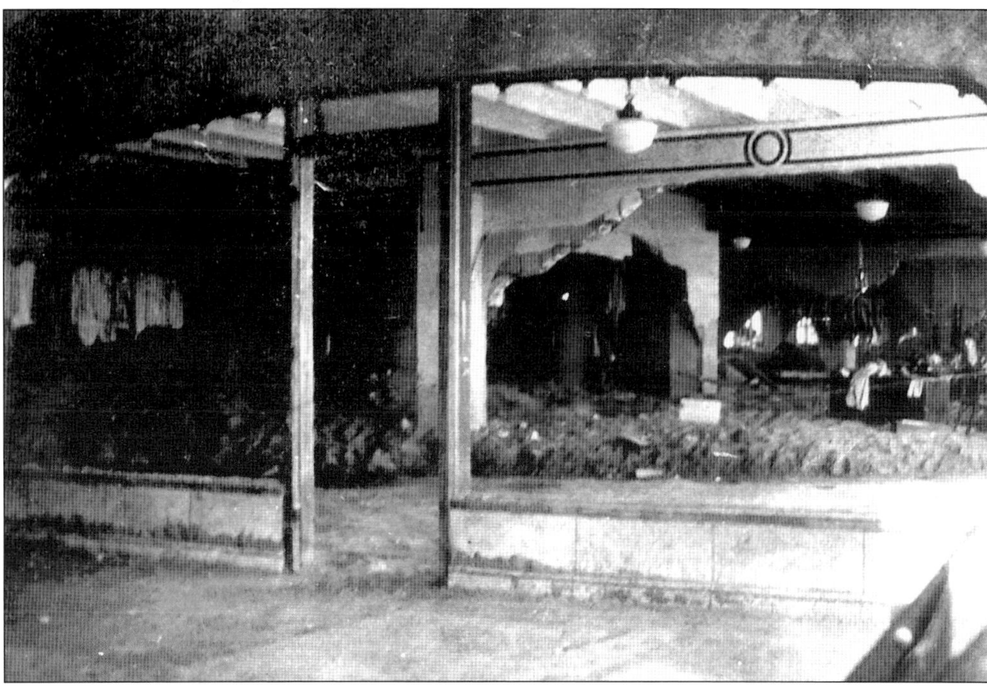

The Smartclad Men's Shop inside the Hollywood Beach Hotel was destroyed by wind and floods during the hurricane. The doors and windows were blown out and sand covered the entire floor space of the shop. (Martha Rose Scott Collection.)

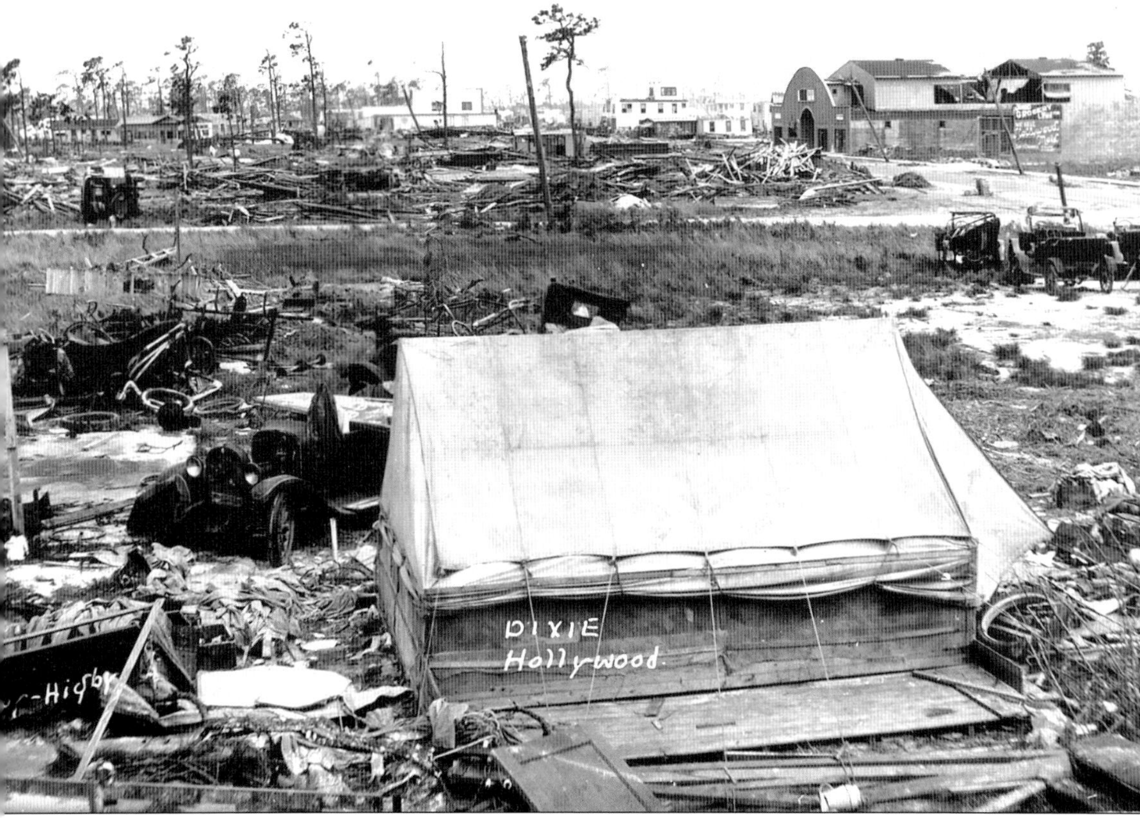

In one of the most dramatic scenes evidencing the ferocity of the 1926 hurricane, this view along Dixie Highway shows the massive devastation suffered by Hollywood. The tent in the center is presumably a shelter for someone amid wrecked cars, leveled trees, and destroyed buildings. (General Collection.)

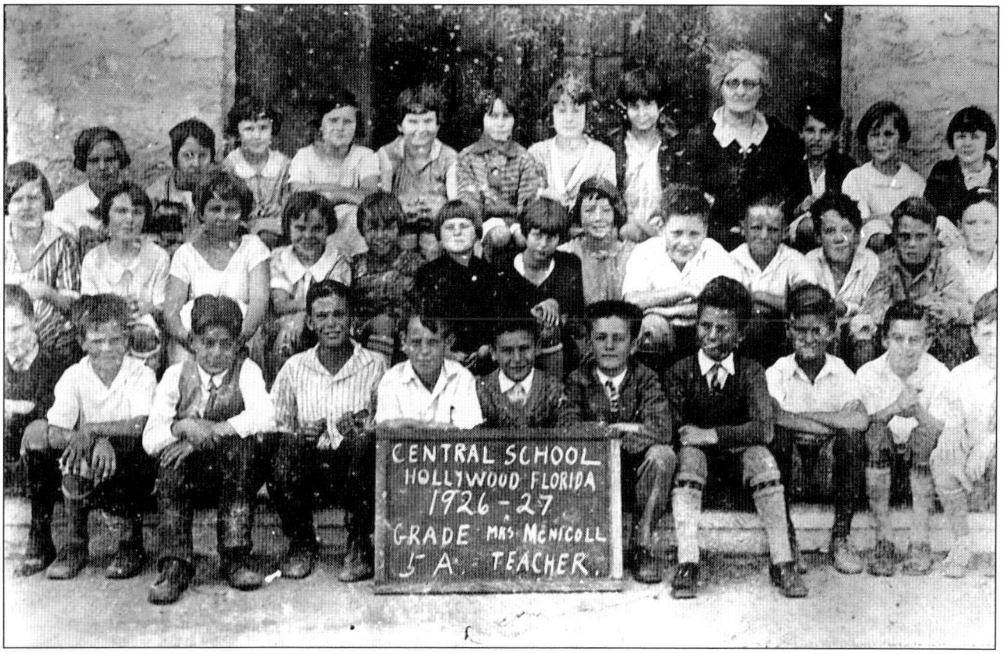

Despite the destruction about them and the reduction in the city's population from 18,000 people to 2,500, Mrs. McNicol's fifth grade class poses for its 1926–1927 school year photograph at Hollywood Central School. (General Collection.)

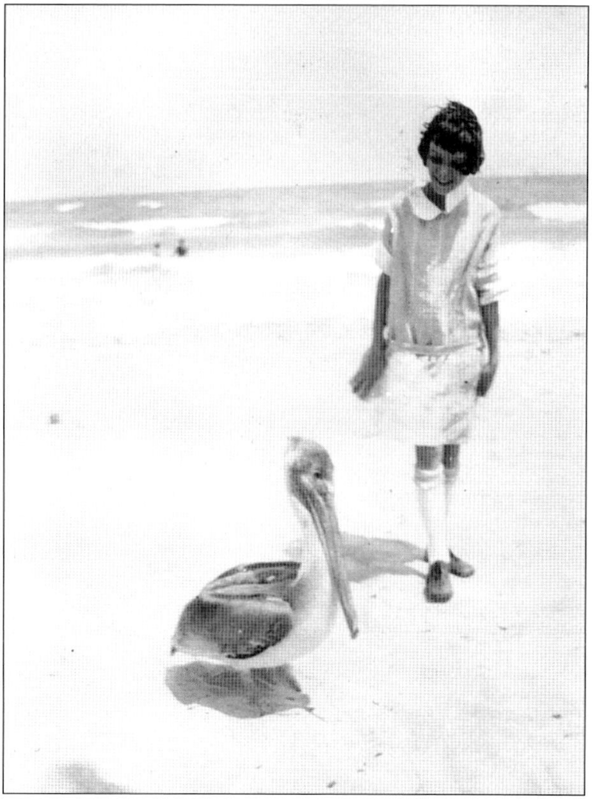

Twelve-year-old Martha Rose Scott, daughter of the men's wear shopkeeper at the Hollywood Beach Hotel, plays along the beach with "Old Bill" during the summer of 1926. Martha and her family survived the hurricane sheltered in the hotel with other employees and guests. Shortly after the storm, she wrote a moving short story about living through the nightmare. Her mother beautifully hand-illustrated and bound the story for her daughter, who later donated the manuscript to the city's archives. (Martha Rose Scott Collection.)

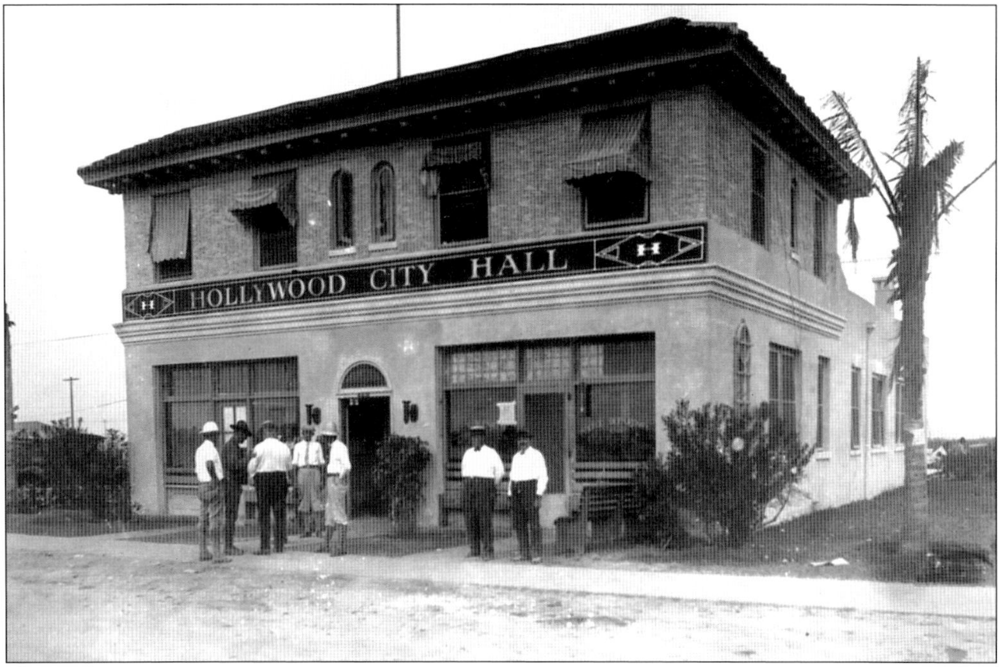

Seven men stand in front the Hollywood City Hall on Twenty-first Avenue. The building was originally constructed as the Young company's printing plant. When the city was incorporated in November 1925, Young donated the structure to the city to serve as its city hall. The building, still standing, has been through many incarnations. (Peracchio Collection.)

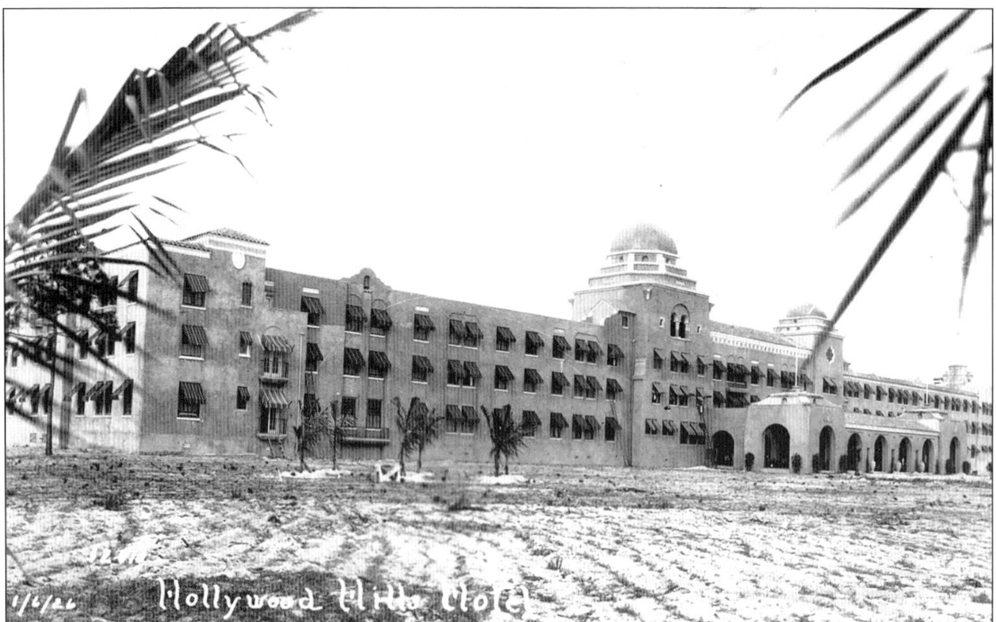

The Hollywood Hills Inn, completed in late 1925, occupied the city's westernmost circle. Never truly successful as a hotel, it became the winter home of the Georgia-based Riverside Military Academy from 1932 to 1985. The building was razed and replaced with the Presidential Circle Building in 1988. (General Collection.)

Two

THE 1930s

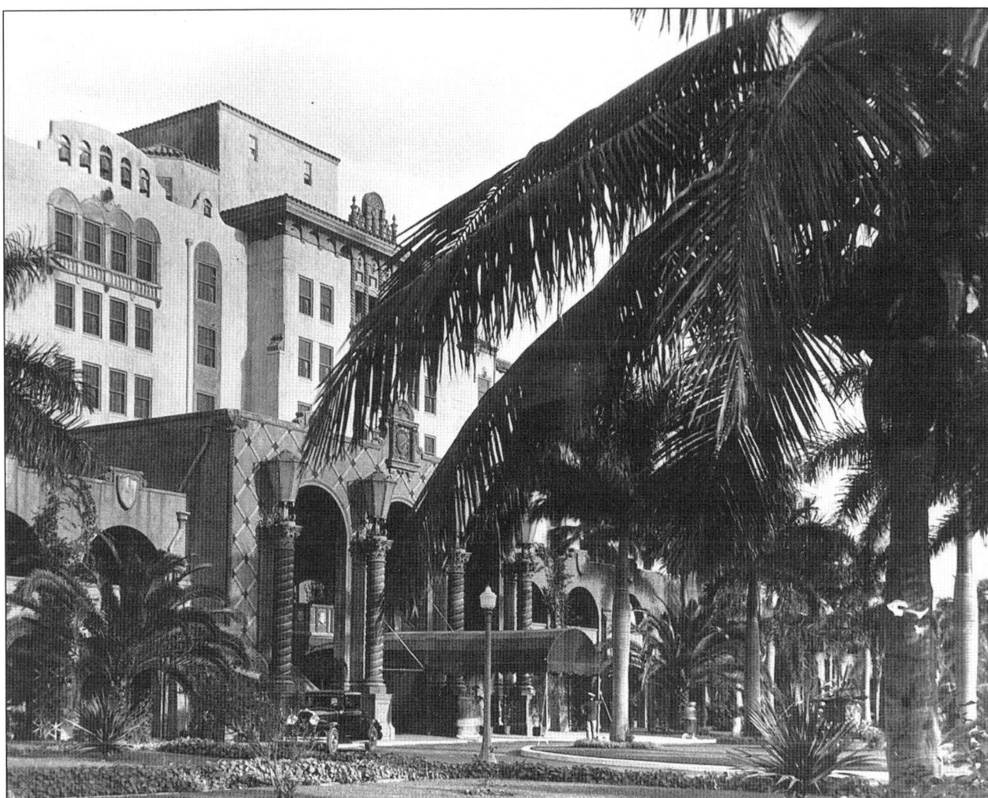

Weathering a hurricane and depression, the Hollywood Beach Hotel continued to draw a substantial clientele of wealthy visitors relatively unscathed by the deepening economic crisis of the 1930s. This is a view of the main entrance of the hotel. (Elsie Johns Collection.)

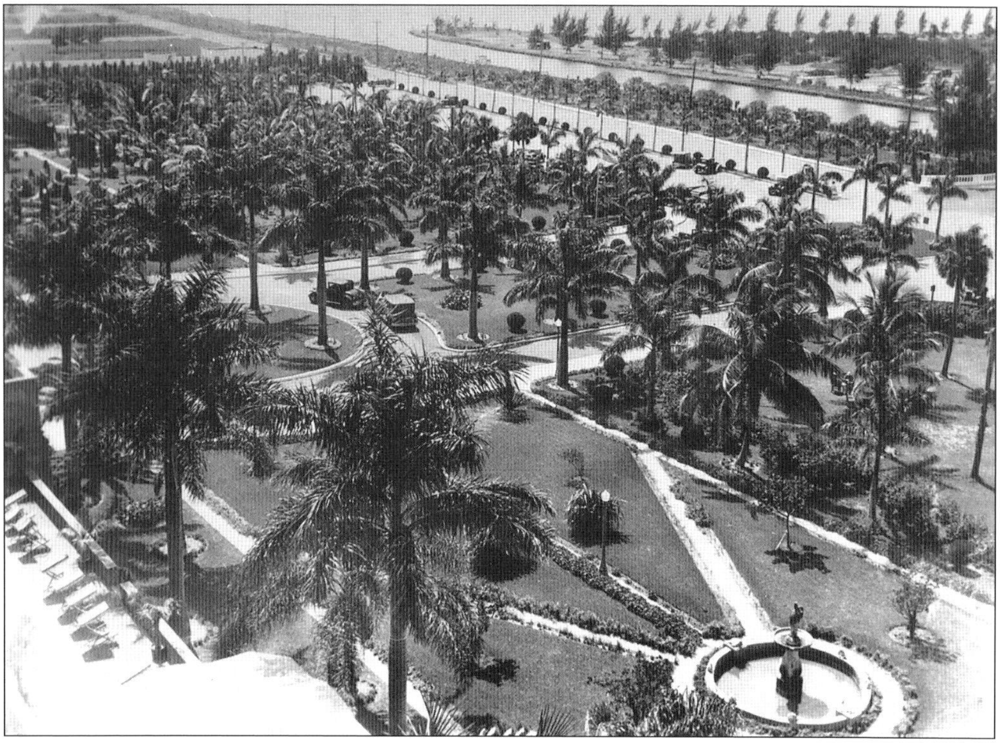

This view is looking southwest from the roof of the Hollywood Beach Hotel. South Lake and the Intracoastal Waterway are in the background. Canopied lounge chairs line the roof in the lower left corner. (Elsie Johns Collection.)

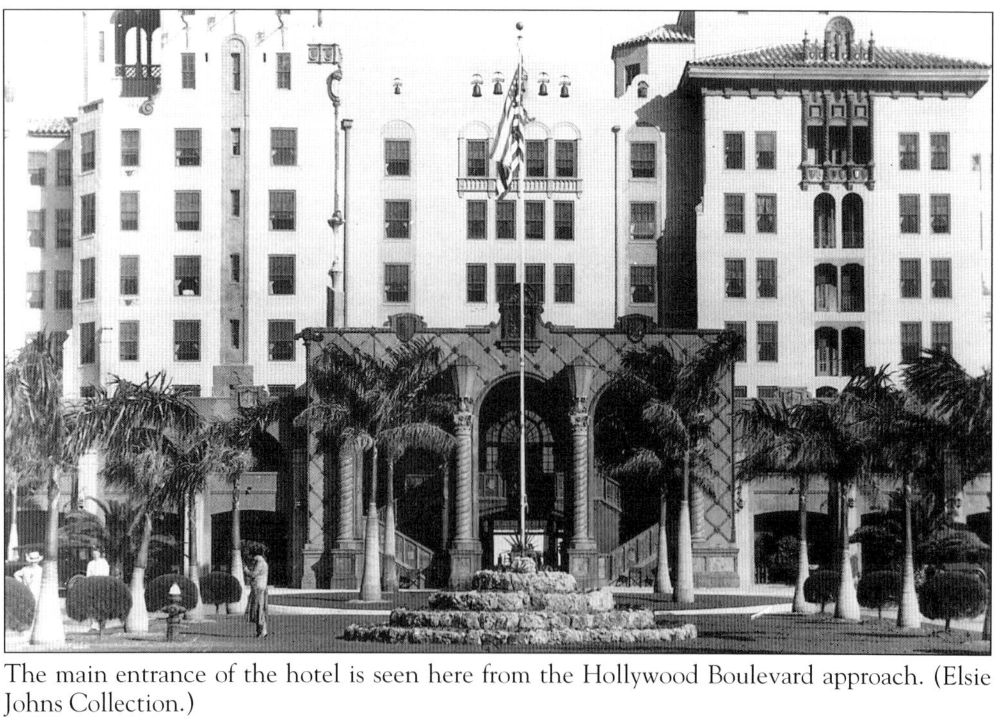

The main entrance of the hotel is seen here from the Hollywood Boulevard approach. (Elsie Johns Collection.)

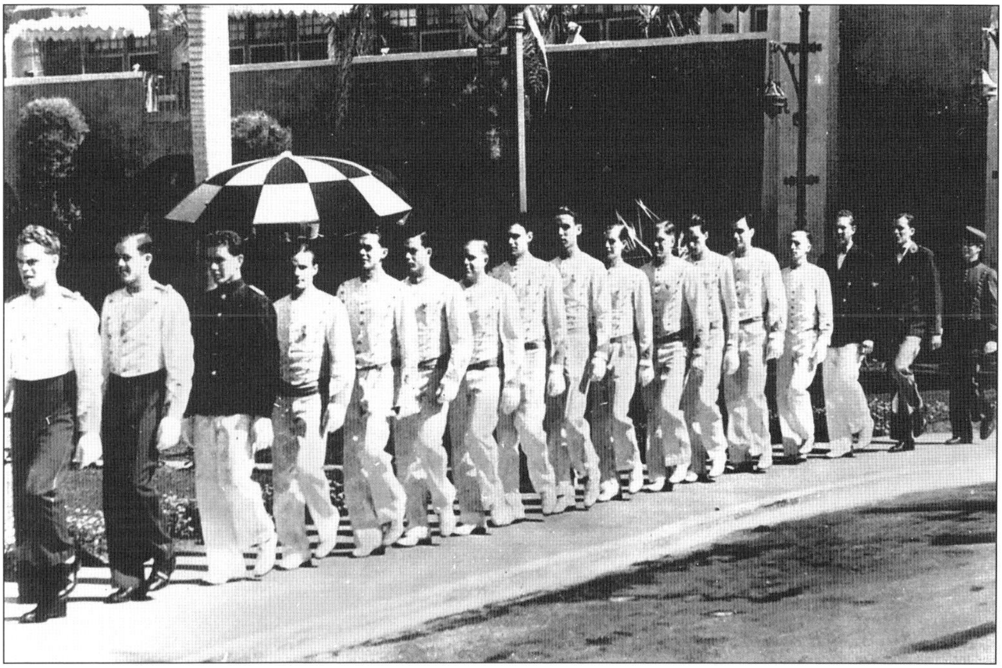

The white-gloved waitstaff march to their posts on the grounds of the Hollywood Beach Hotel. The staff provided amenities to guests on the beach and around the pool. (General Collection.)

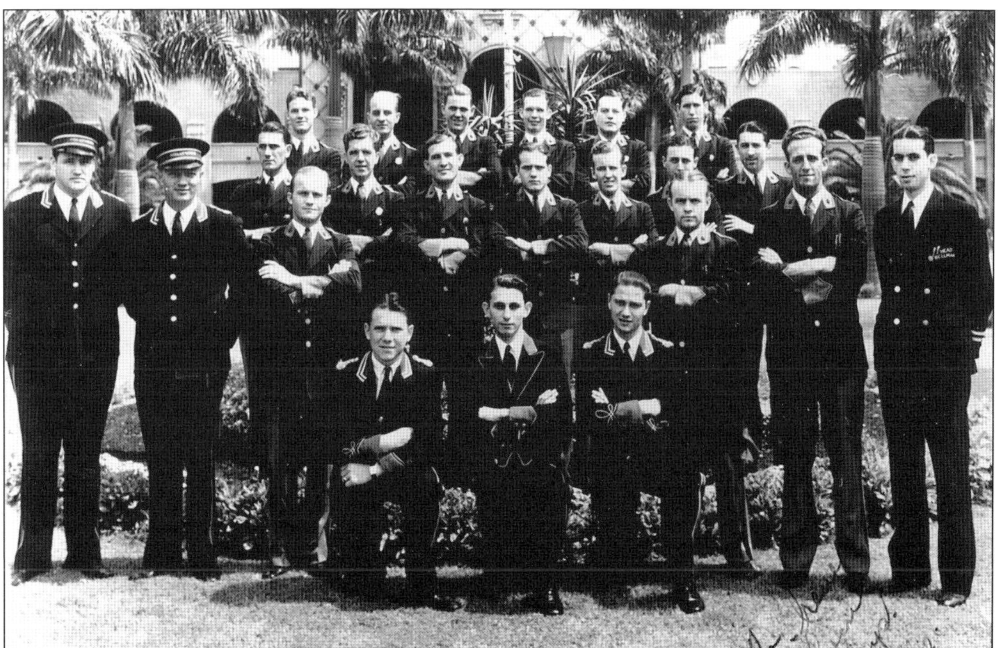

The hotel's bellmen gather for a group photograph outside the main entrance. The head bellman stands on the right in the second row. (General Collection.)

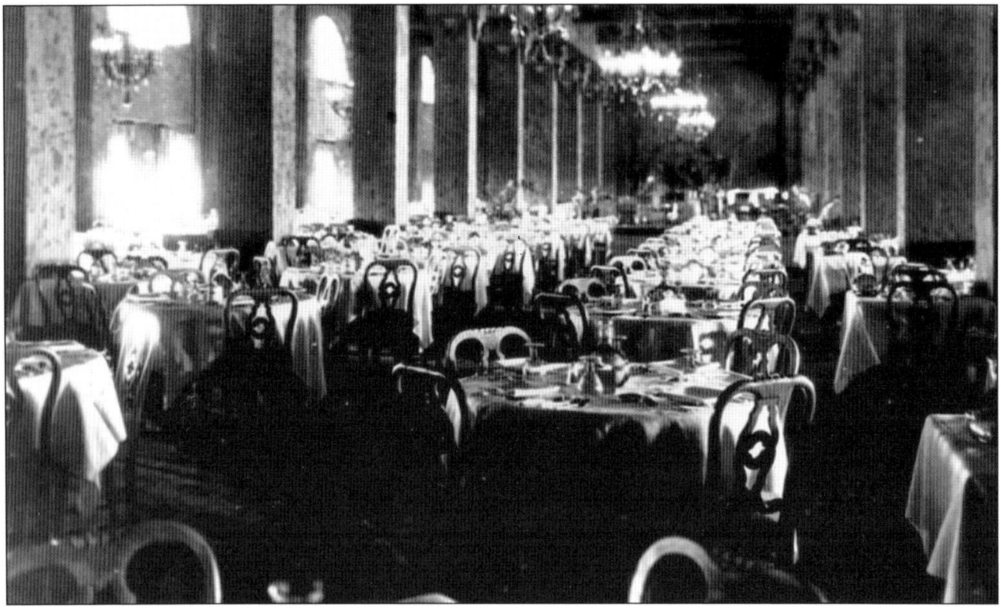

This 1931 image shows the dining room of the hotel as it is prepared for the evening's dinner guests. (Elsie Johns Collection.)

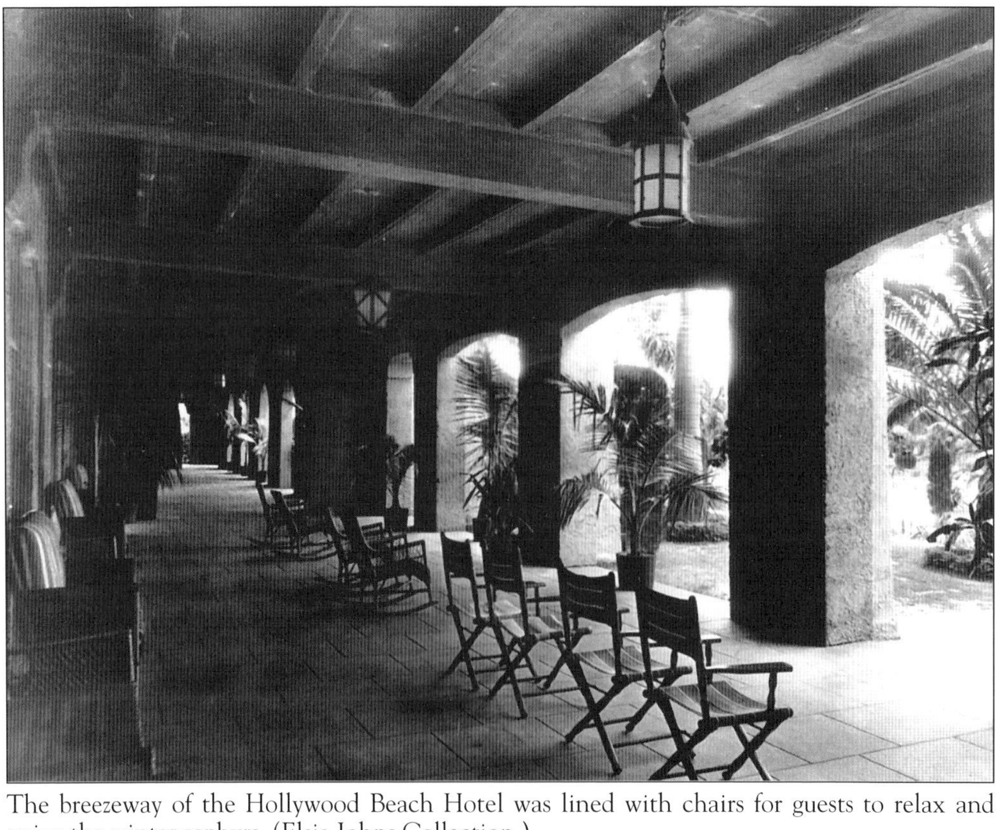

The breezeway of the Hollywood Beach Hotel was lined with chairs for guests to relax and enjoy the winter zephyrs. (Elsie Johns Collection.)

In this photo, two hotel guests display the very latest in fashionable casual attire. (Elsie Johns Collection.)

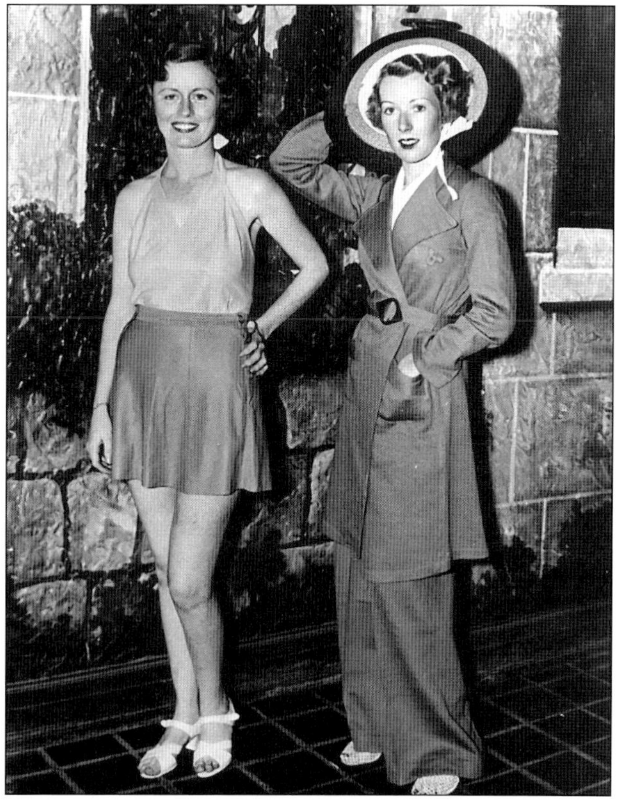

Mr. and Mrs. Eddie Cantor, frequent guests of the Hollywood Beach Hotel, pose beside the beach conditions sign. Eddie Cantor was one of the country's most popular performers. (Elsie Johns Collection.)

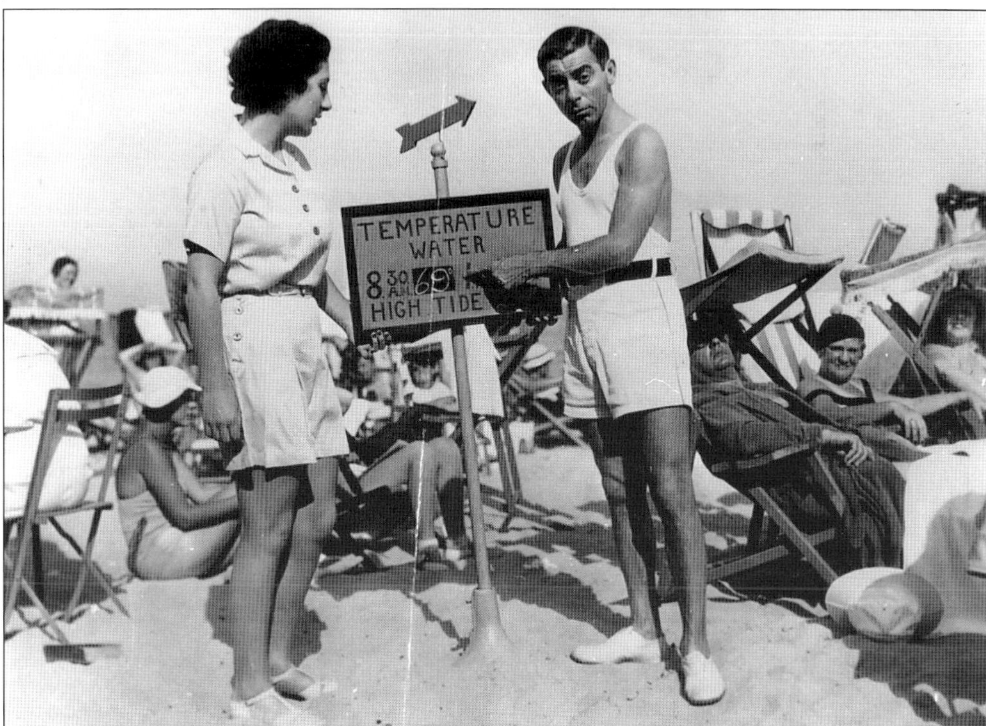

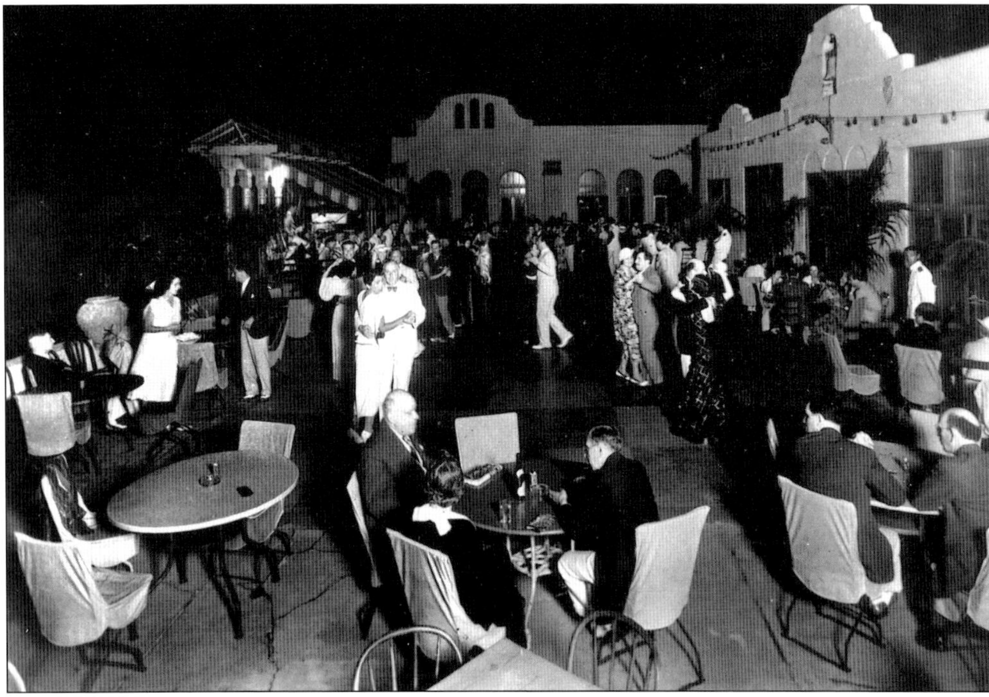

Guests enjoy an evening party on the hotel patio. The orchestra is under the canopy on the left. (Elsie Johns Collection.)

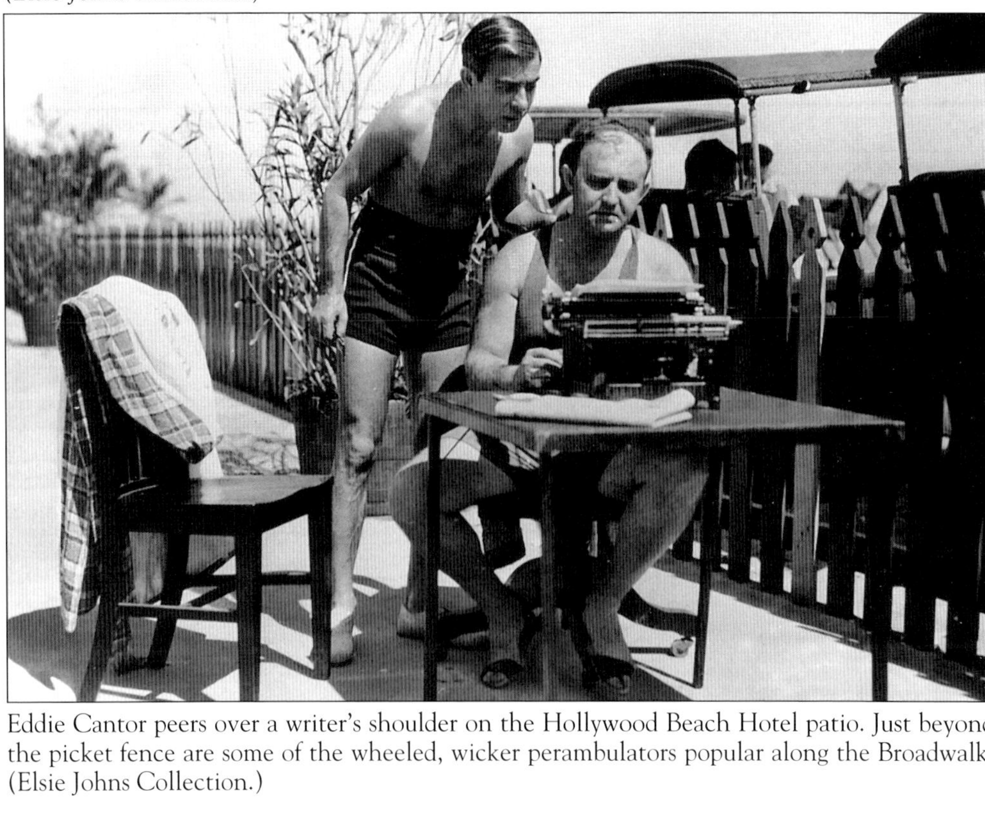

Eddie Cantor peers over a writer's shoulder on the Hollywood Beach Hotel patio. Just beyond the picket fence are some of the wheeled, wicker perambulators popular along the Broadwalk. (Elsie Johns Collection.)

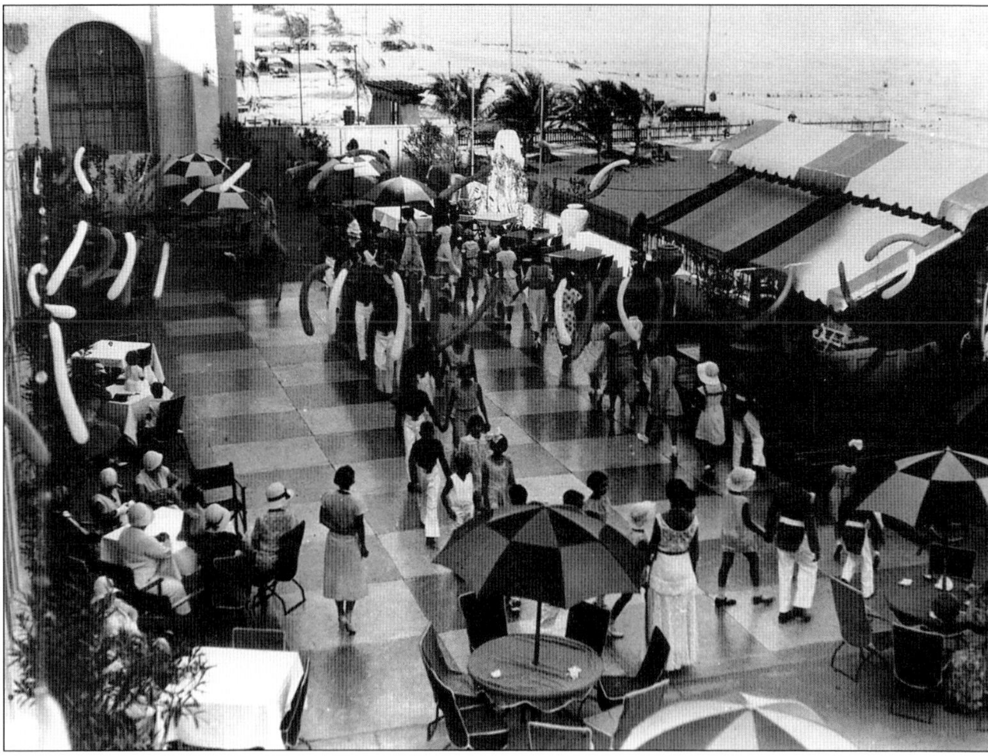

Riverside Military Academy cadets attend a social function on the patio. The cadets appear to be escorting young ladies in a dance rondure. (Elsie Johns Collection.)

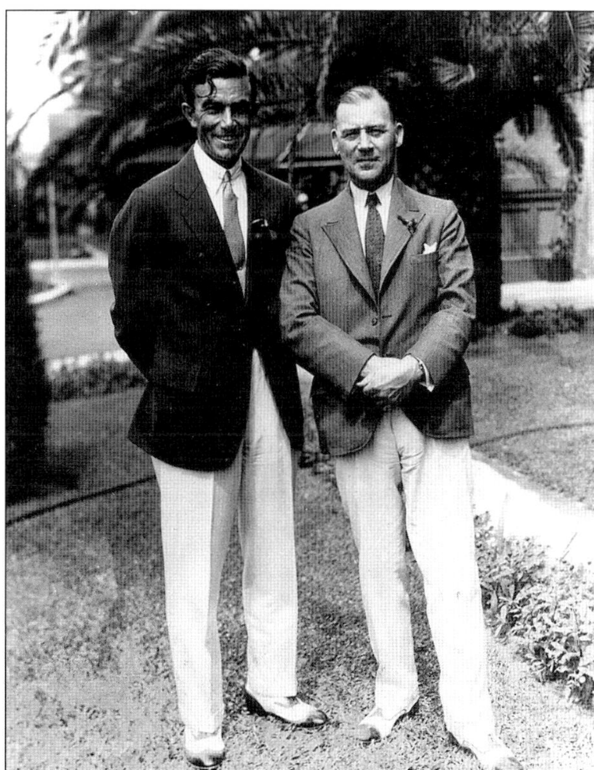

Two well-attired gentlemen pose outside the main entrance of the hotel. (Elsie Johns Collection.)

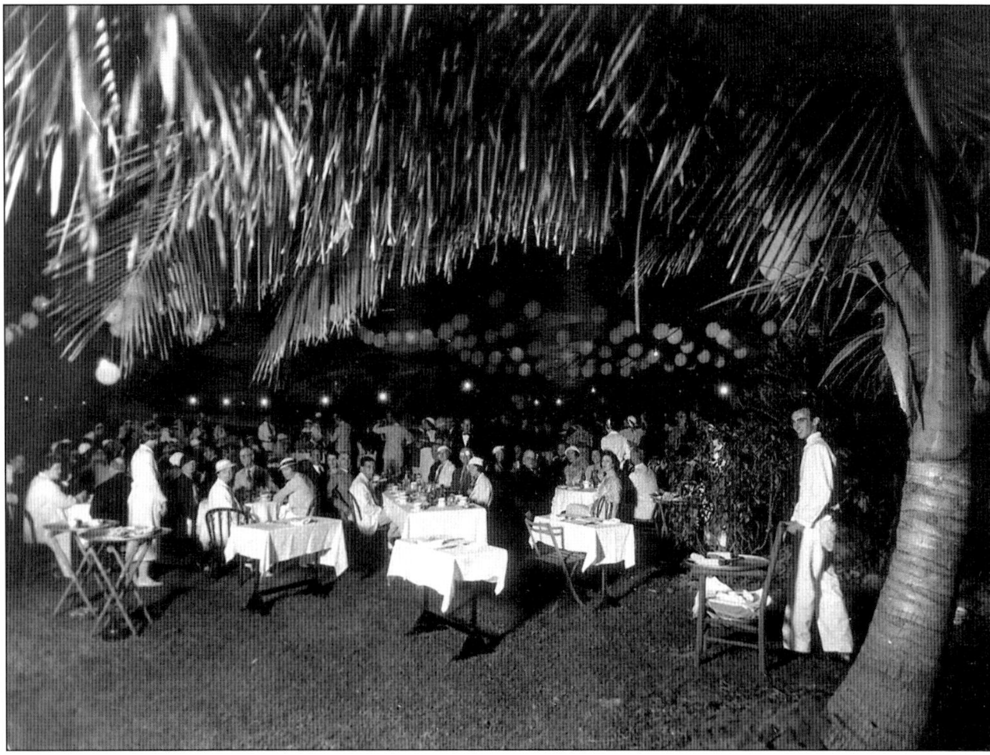

Hollywood Beach Hotel guests enjoy a pleasant evening dining al fresco at a "Beefsteak" party on the hotel grounds, November 8, 1934. (Elsie Johns Collection.)

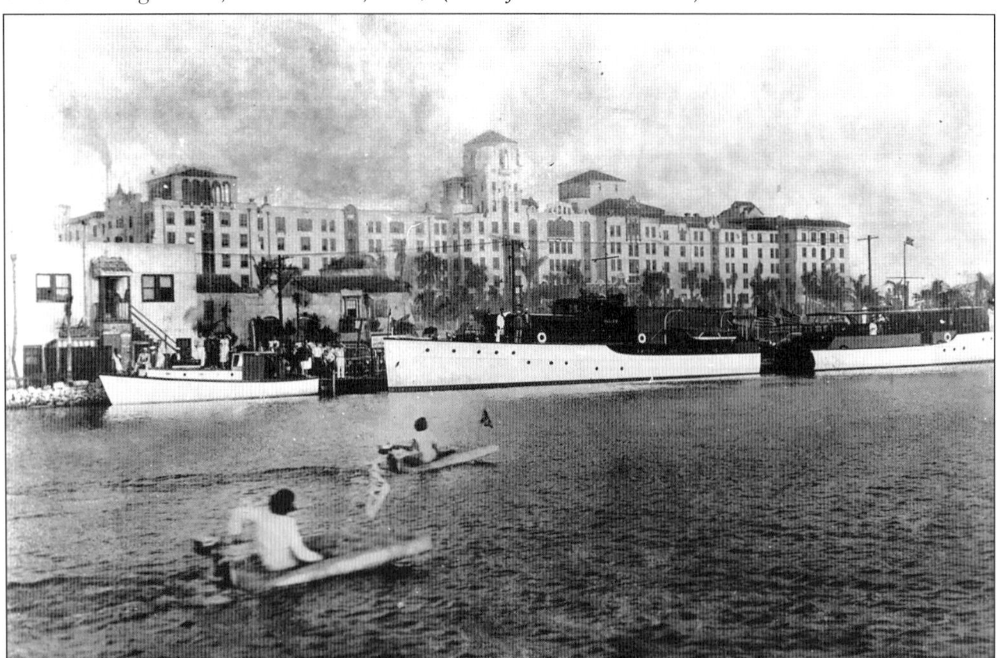

The hotel looms large in the background of this view showing yachts docked along the Intracoastal Waterway. (General Collection.)

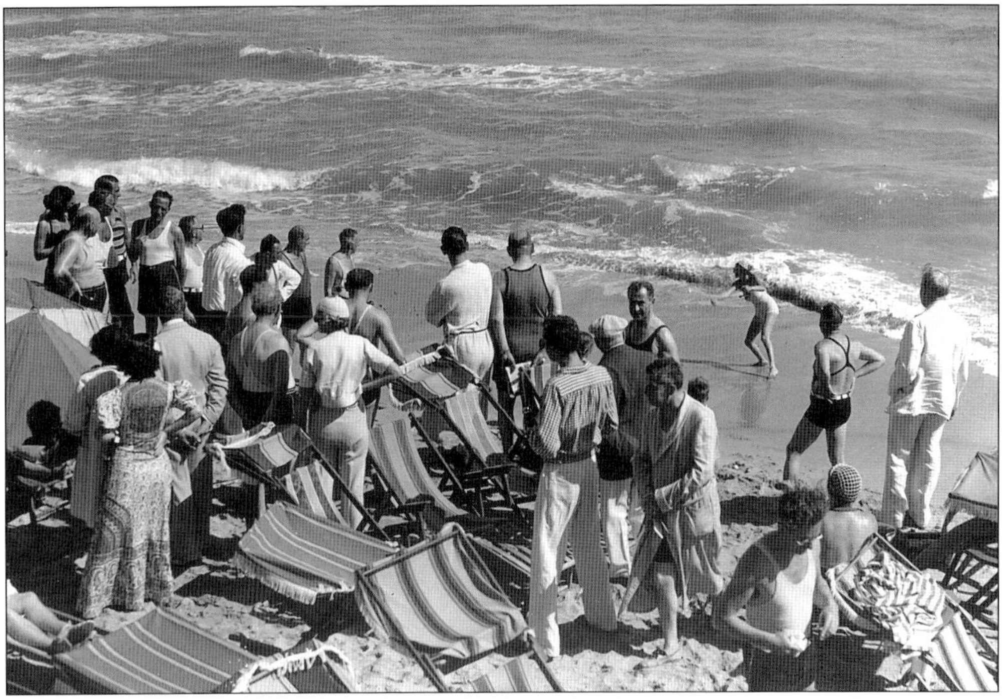

A crowd gathers along the shore, apparently watching a young woman engaged in a game of paddleball. (General Collection.)

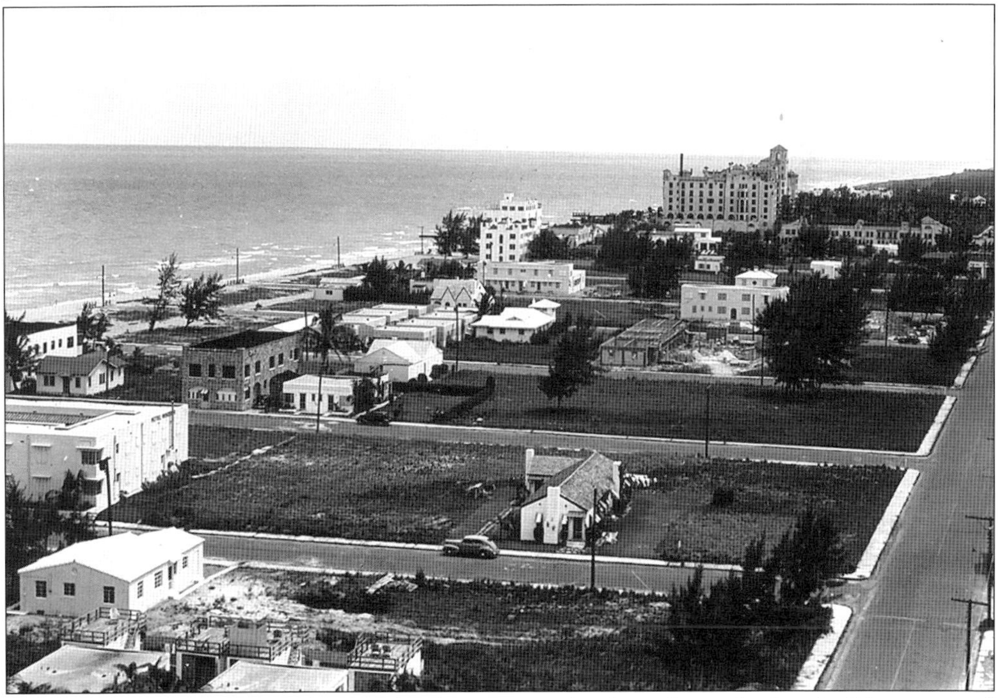

During the 1930s, more and more development took place along the beach. Houses, small hotels, and apartment buildings began to blossom up and down the shore. The large structure in the background is the Hollywood Beach Hotel. (Patricia Smith Collection.)

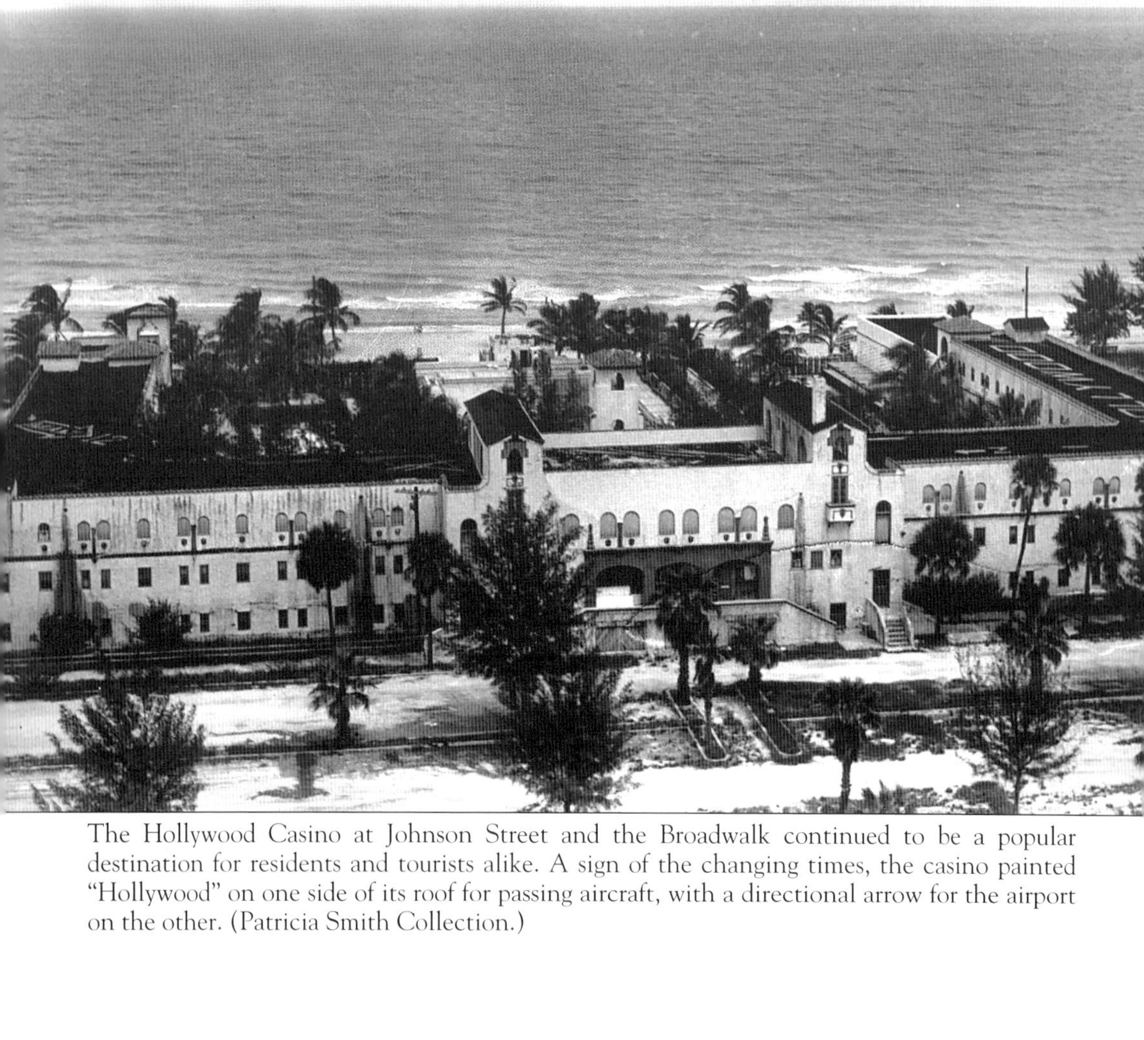

The Hollywood Casino at Johnson Street and the Broadwalk continued to be a popular destination for residents and tourists alike. A sign of the changing times, the casino painted "Hollywood" on one side of its roof for passing aircraft, with a directional arrow for the airport on the other. (Patricia Smith Collection.)

The Hopkins Twins, first names unknown, were championship swimmers who trained at the Hollywood Casino pool. The twins were coached by Mollie Grimshaw, pool manager, and a former professional swimmer and diver. (Patricia Smith Collection.)

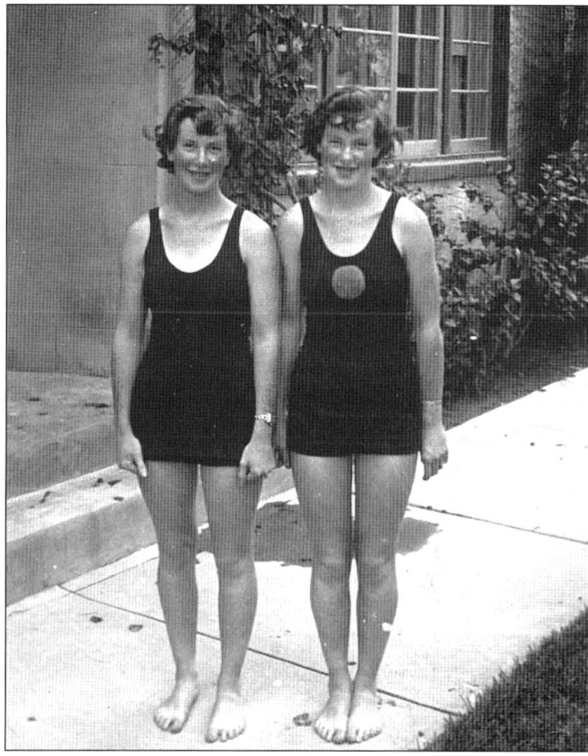

Mollie Grimshaw's casino swim team poses for a group portrait. From left to right are (front row) Joyce Orr, Louis Renn, Ralph Renn, and an unidentified boy; (middle row) Mary Arpin, Gunnard Skoglund, Syble McAlilly, Billy Outten, and Sally Butler; (back row) Derald Hottman, Amos Hall, Roger Brown, Roy Moates, and George I. Williams. (General Collection.)

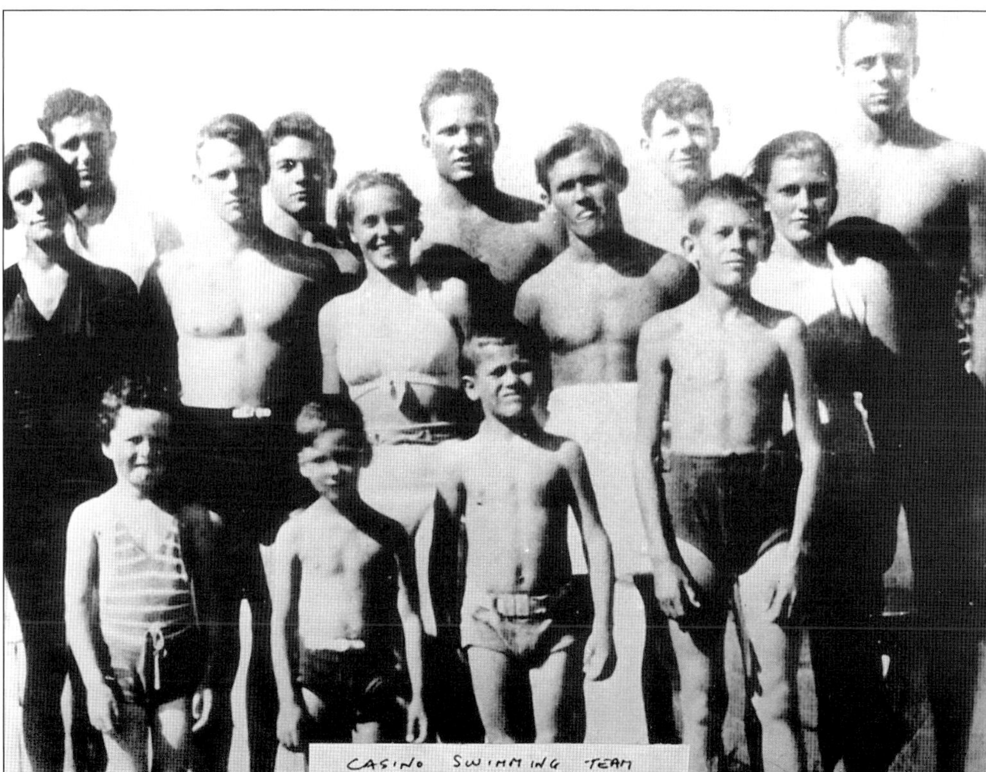

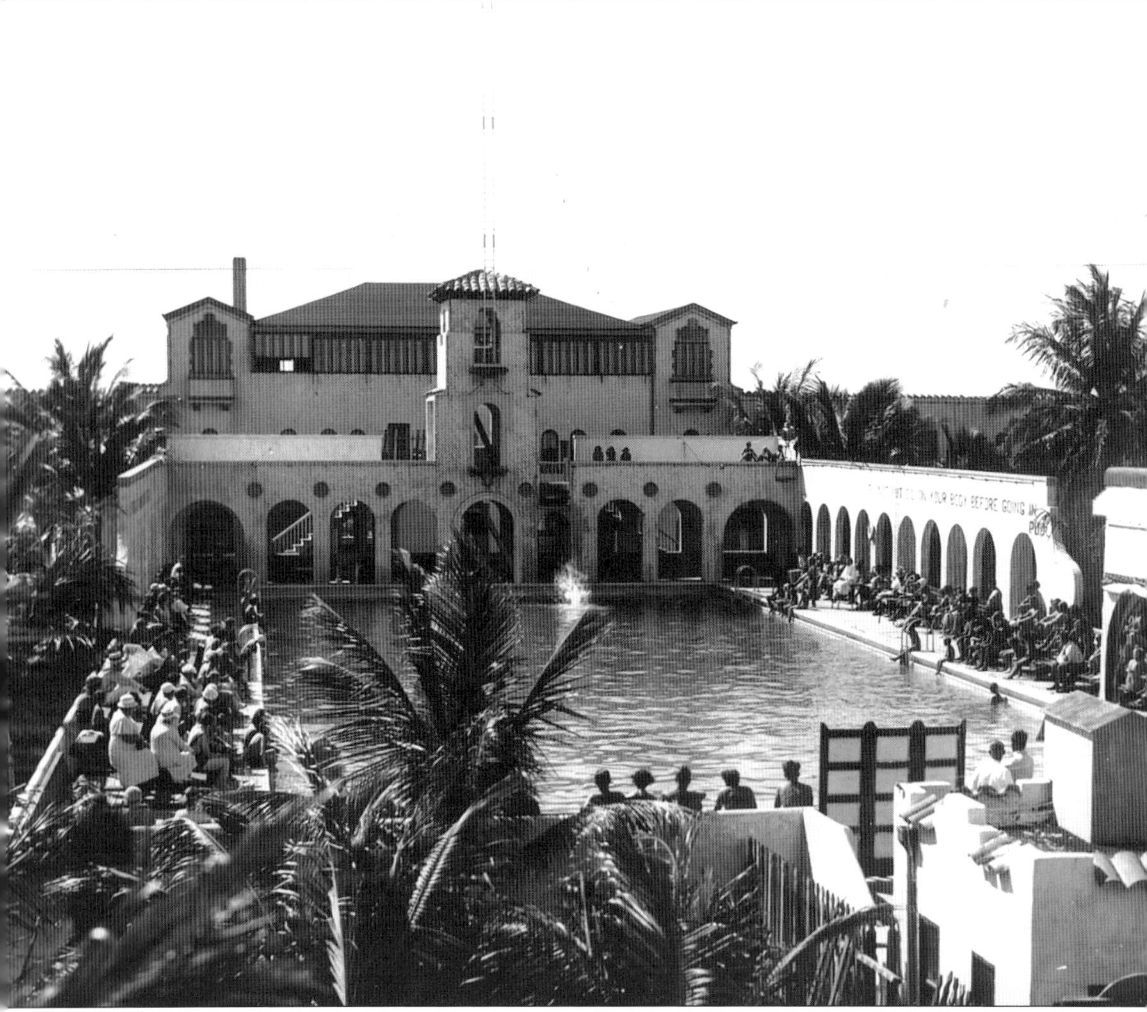

Spectators gather around the casino's pool deck observing a swimming and diving meet. Some casino swimmers, including Amos Hall and Mary Arpin, went on to win a number of state championships. Billy Outten pursued a career as a professional diver. (General Collection.)

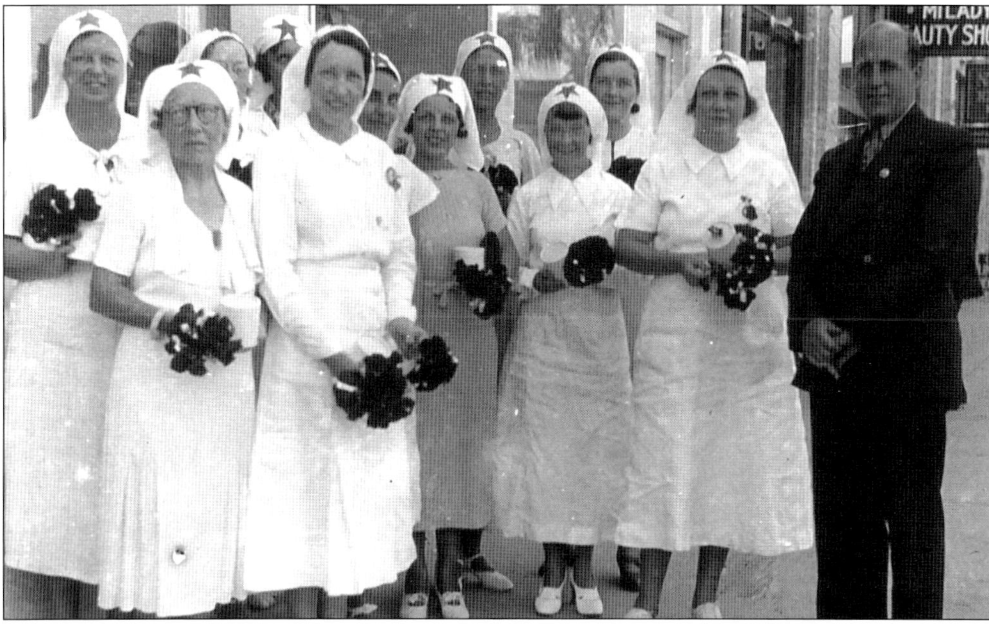

Hollywood's American Legion Auxiliary begins its annual poppy sale along the sidewalks of Hollywood Boulevard. (Patricia Smith Collection.)

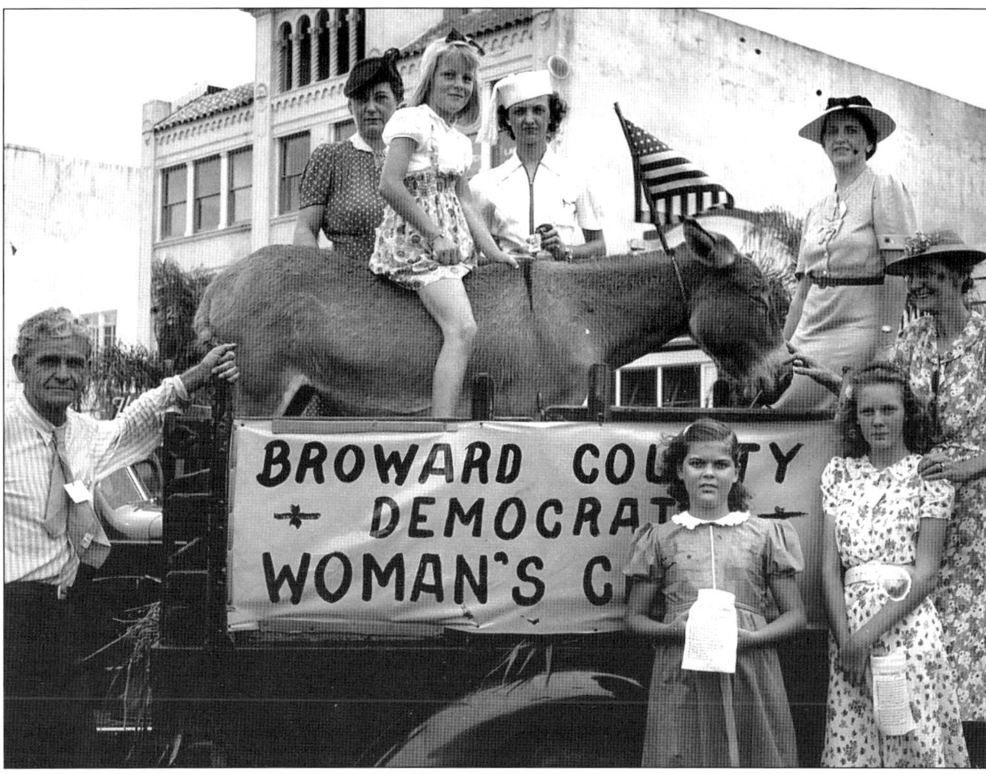

In a float guaranteed to draw attention, the Broward County Democratic Woman's Club solicits donations in front of the Morse Arcade building at 1926 Hollywood Boulevard. (Patricia Smith Collection.)

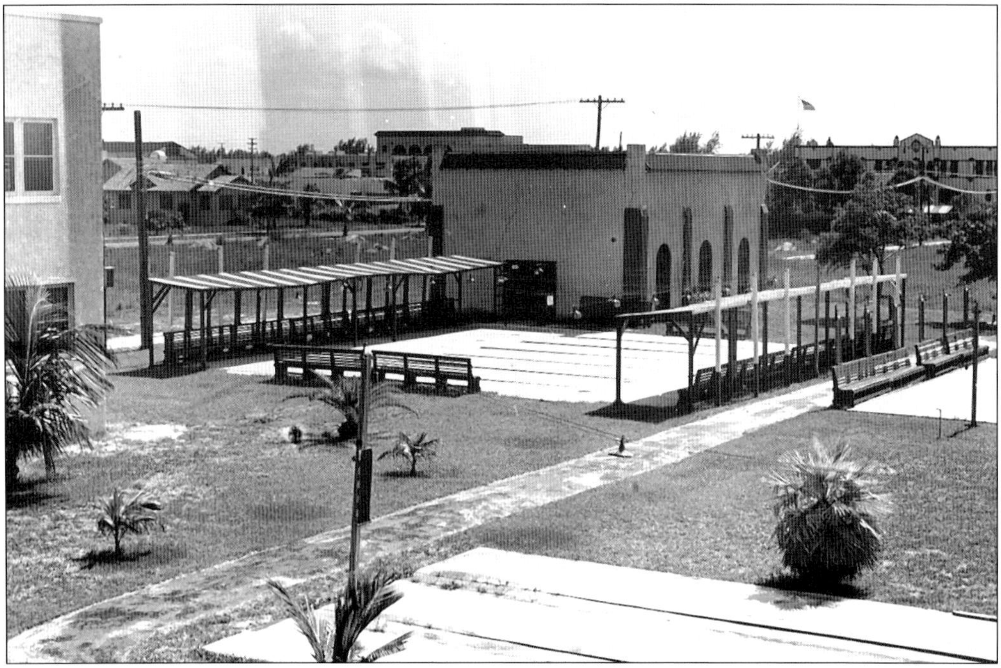

This is a July 1939 view of the shuffleboard courts at the city's Recreation Building at 1845 Polk Street. (Patricia Smith Collection.)

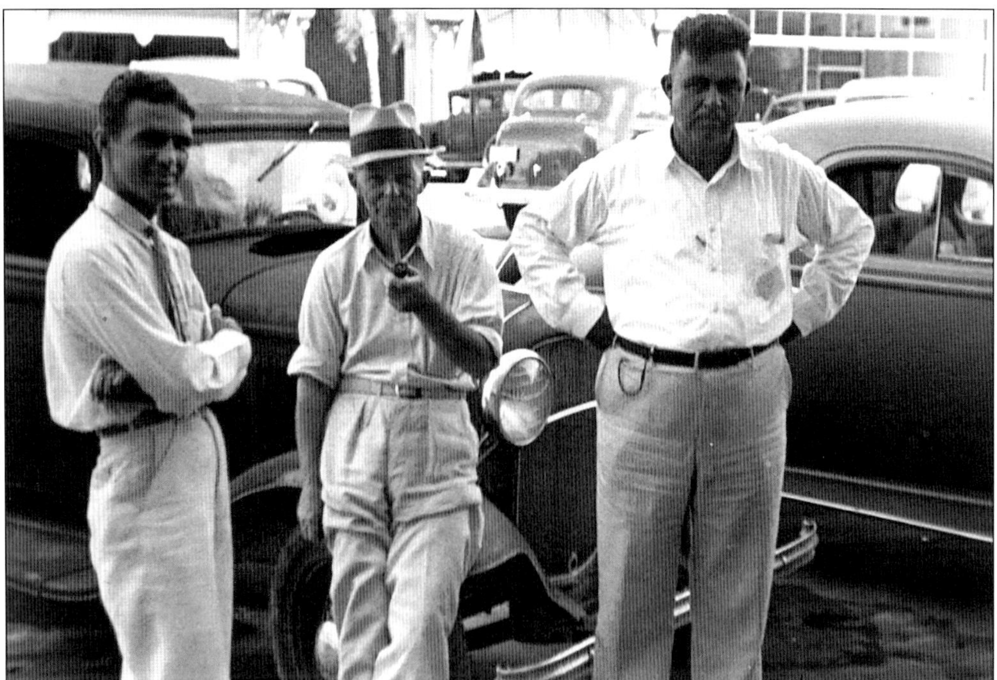

Milt Devoe, George Leaird, and Lester Boggs relax along Hollywood Boulevard. Boggs, on the far right, was elected to the Hollywood City Commission in 1935. He later served as mayor from 1943 to 1947 and from 1949 to 1953. Boggs Field is named in his honor. (Patricia Smith Collection.)

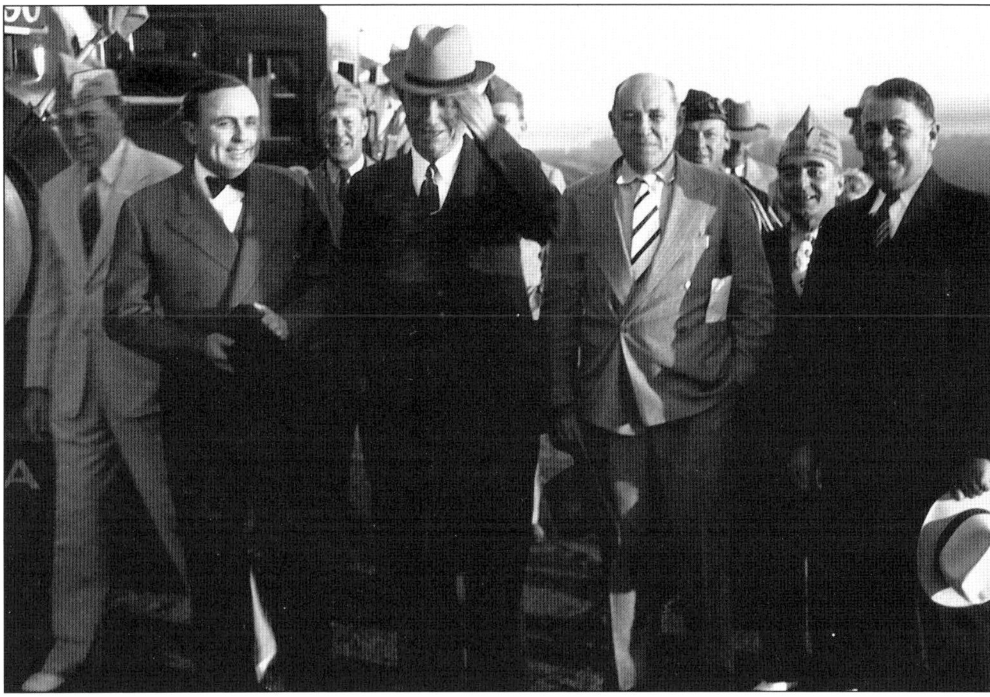

Georgia governor Eurith D. Rivers (second from left in bow tie), Florida governor Fred P. Cone, and Hollywood mayor Ralph B. Springer are photographed with a group of dignitaries at the Seaboard railroad station at 3001 Hollywood Boulevard. (Patricia Smith Collection.)

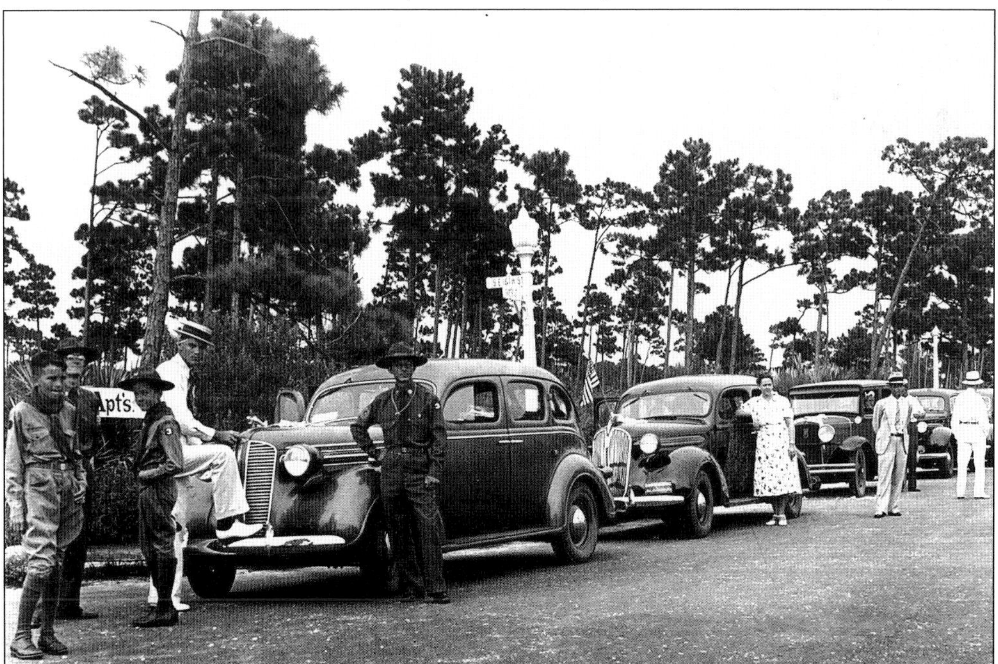

Hollywood residents, including some Boy Scouts, stand alongside their cars during a June 1938 tour, organized by the chamber of commerce, of Lake Okeechobee. (Patricia Smith Collection.)

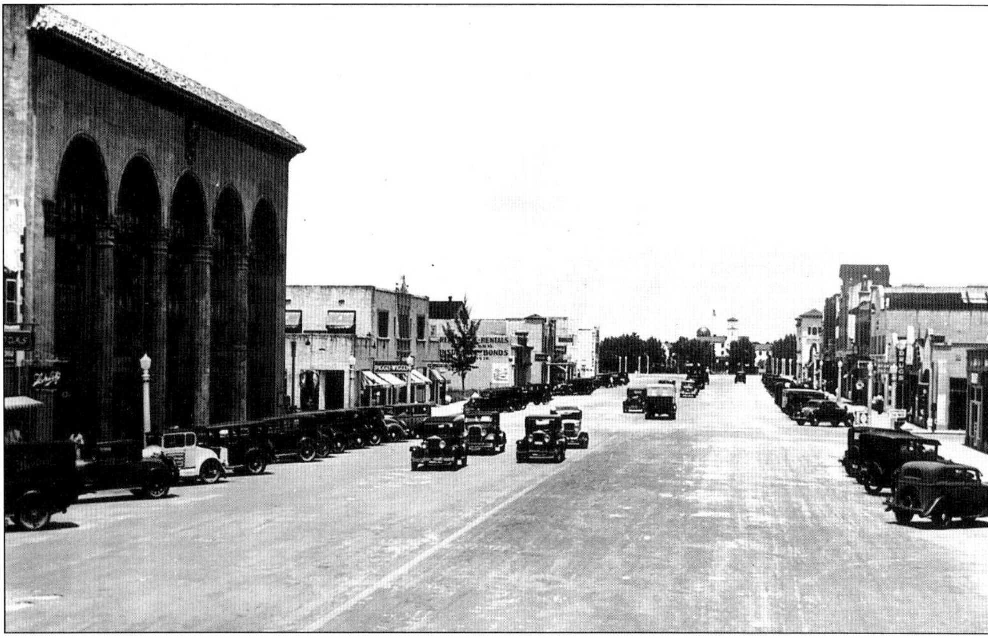

The Hollywood business district appears to be experiencing a relatively slow June 18, 1934. The First National Bank at 2001 Hollywood Boulevard is on the left and in the deep background is the Park View Hotel. (General Collection.)

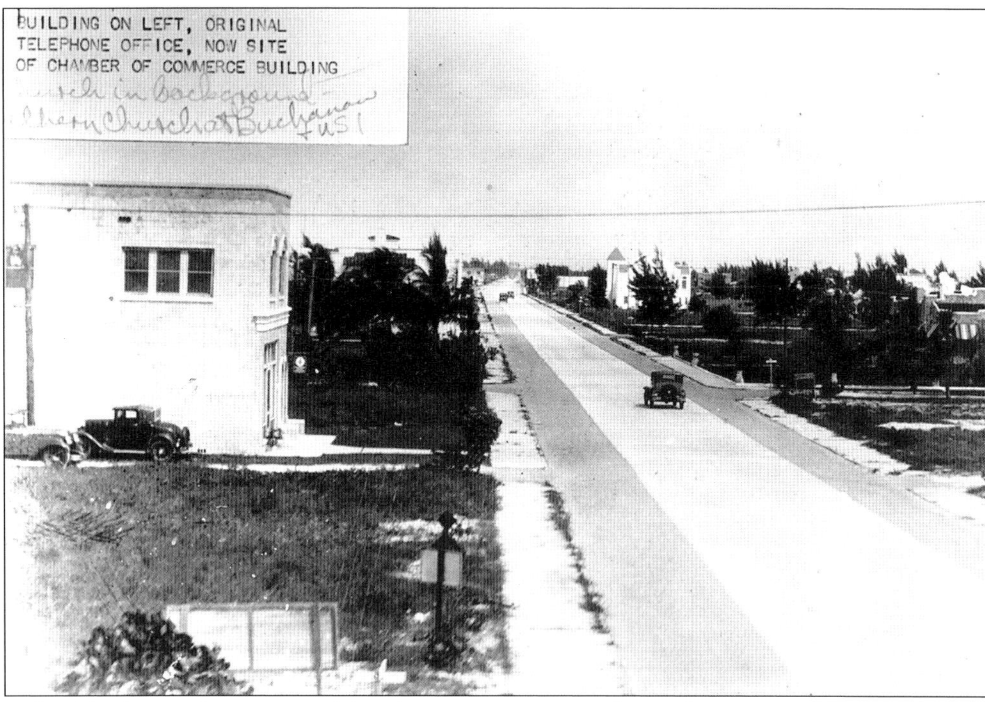

Federal Highway, the main north/south artery in 1930s Hollywood, was not originally a bustling thoroughfare. The building on the left at 312 North Federal Highway, was the telephone company's original office. St. John's Evangelical Lutheran Church at 1742 Buchanan Street can be seen in the center background. (General Collection.)

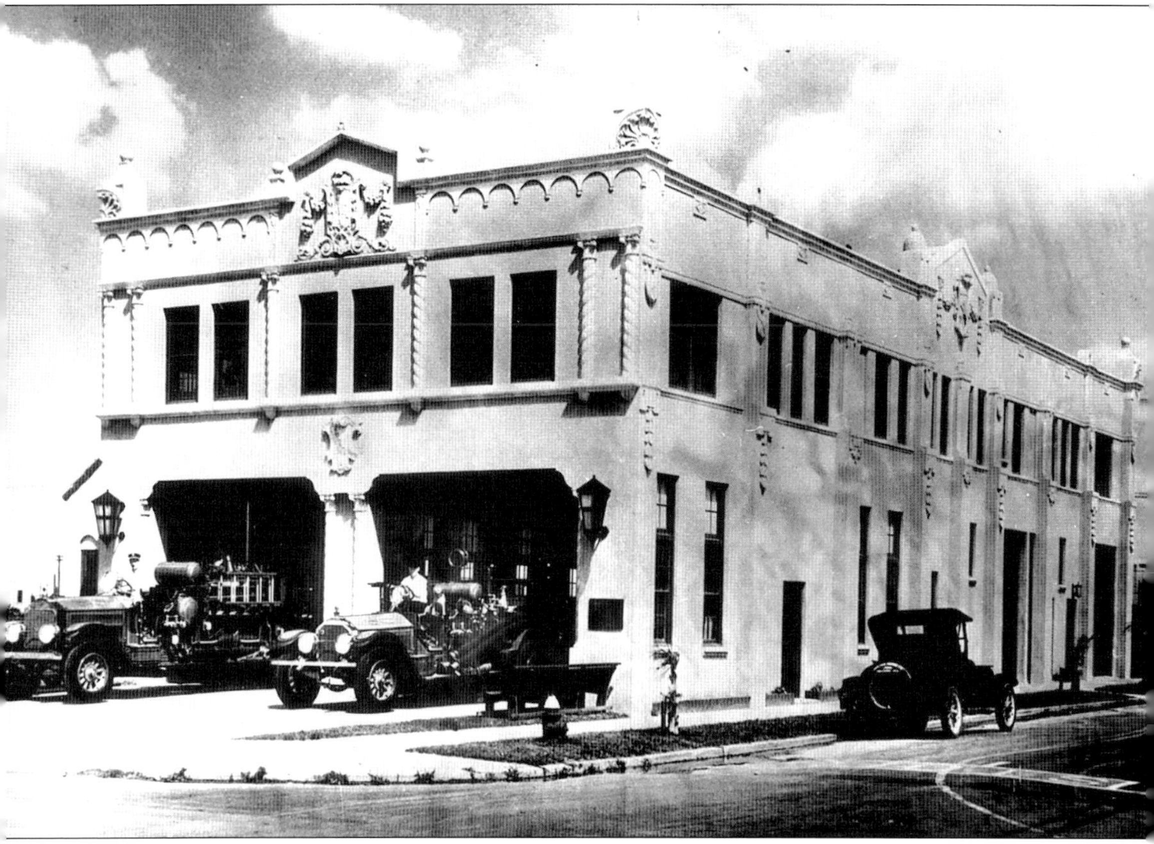

Fire Station Number One, located at 1901 Polk Street, is a greatly expanded facility built to support the growing population of Hollywood. It featured two bays and administrative offices for the fire department. (General Collection.)

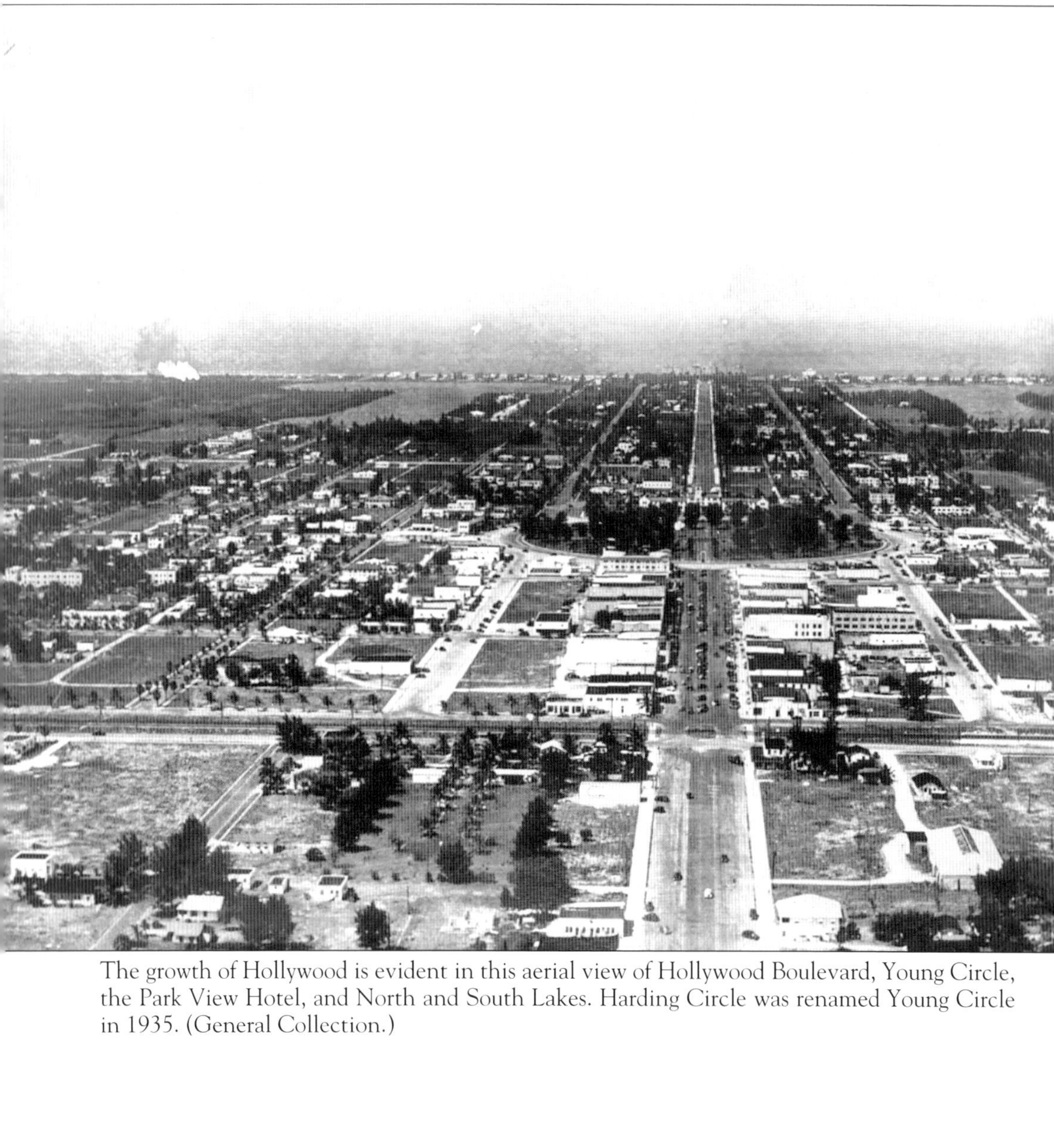

The growth of Hollywood is evident in this aerial view of Hollywood Boulevard, Young Circle, the Park View Hotel, and North and South Lakes. Harding Circle was renamed Young Circle in 1935. (General Collection.)

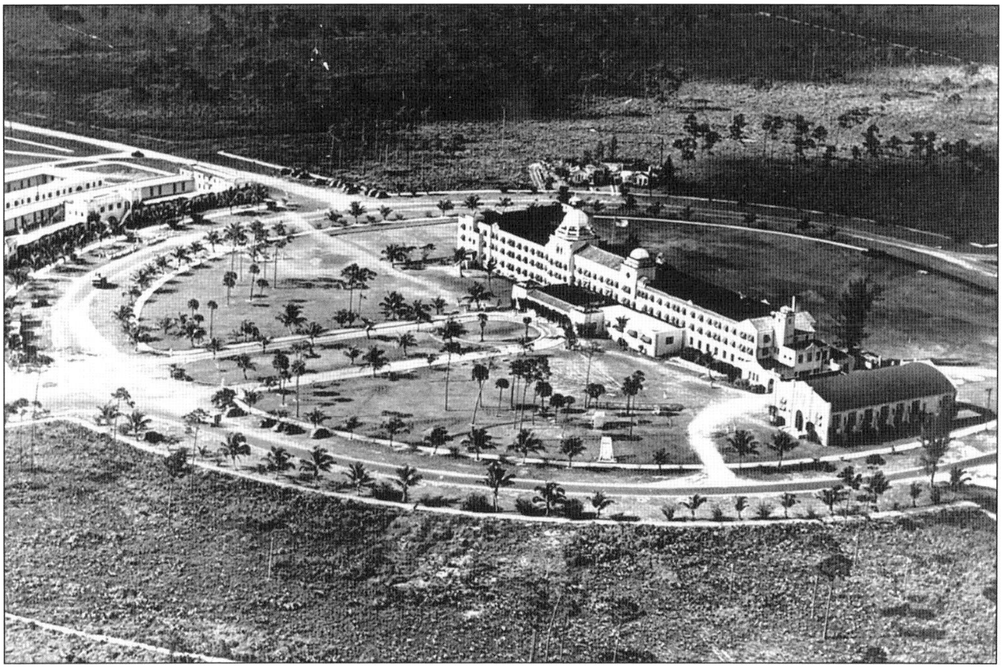

The Riverside Military Academy acquired the Hollywood Hills Inn in the city's westernmost circle in 1932. By the time this 1936 photograph was taken, the school had built Blanton Hall gymnasium and Norton Barracks, to the left of the circle. (General Collection.)

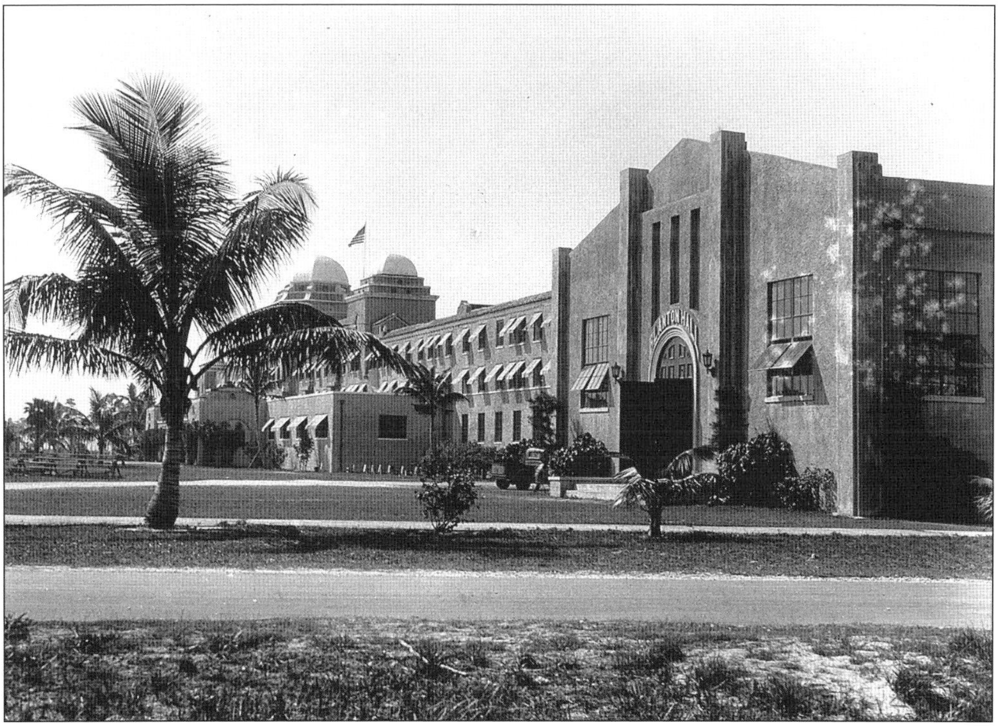

Blanton Hall, Riverside's gymnasium and auditorium, was constructed in 1935 beside the circle's original building, the Hollywood Hills Inn. (Patricia Smith Collection.)

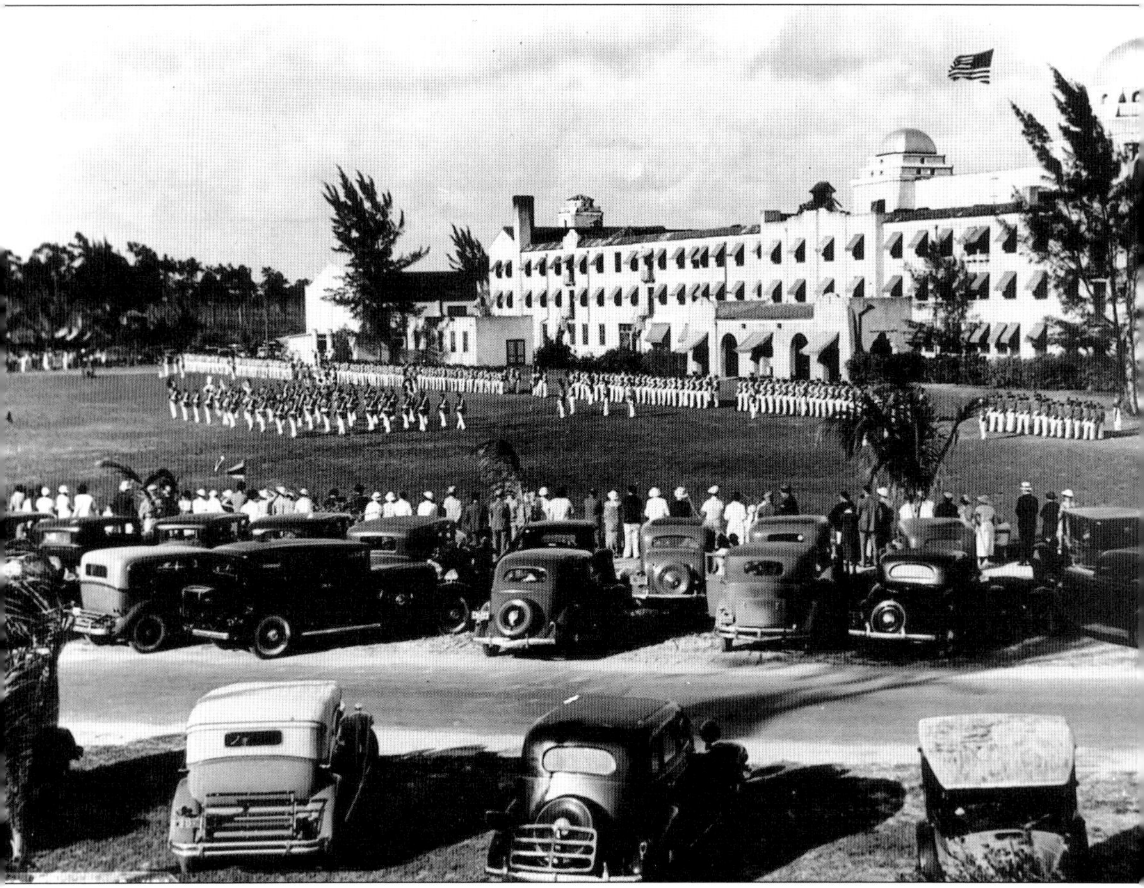

A popular pastime of the late 1930s was the Riverside Military Academy's traditional Sunday afternoon dress parade. Locals gathered for the occasion as cadets performed close order drills and other military maneuvers. (General Collection.)

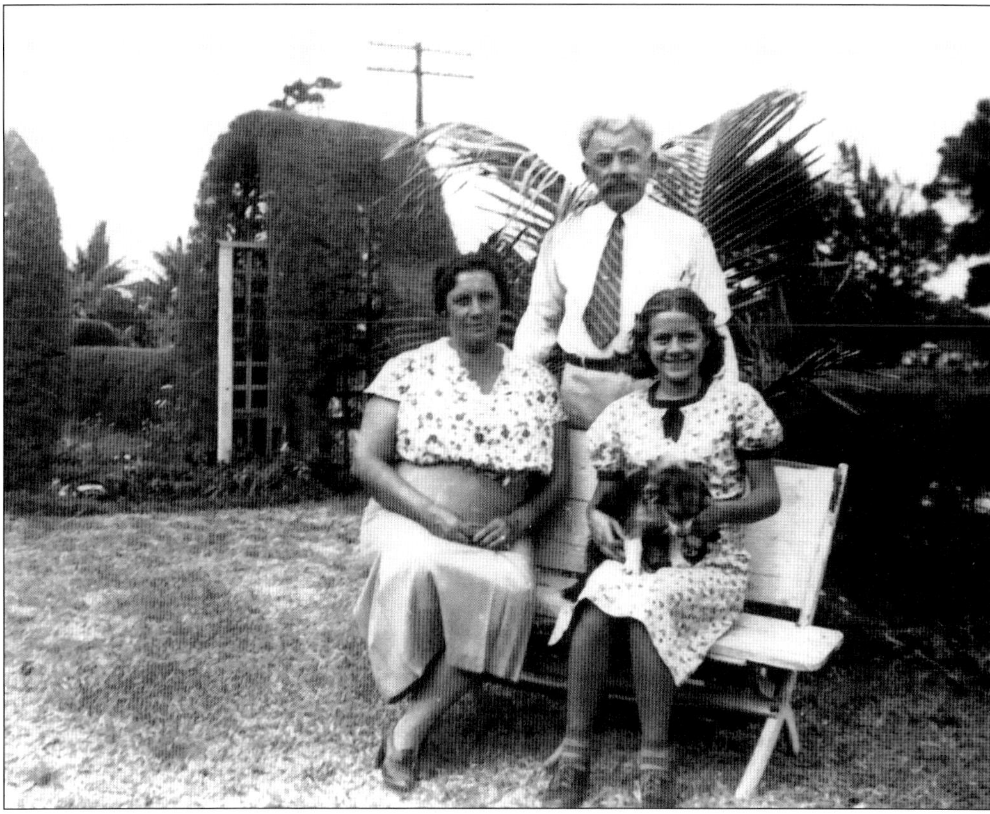

Severina, Ambrose, and Anita Milani pose in the front yard of their home at 826 South Twenty-fourth Avenue. Ambrose Milani is listed in a late 1930s city directory as a gardener by profession. (Maher Collection.)

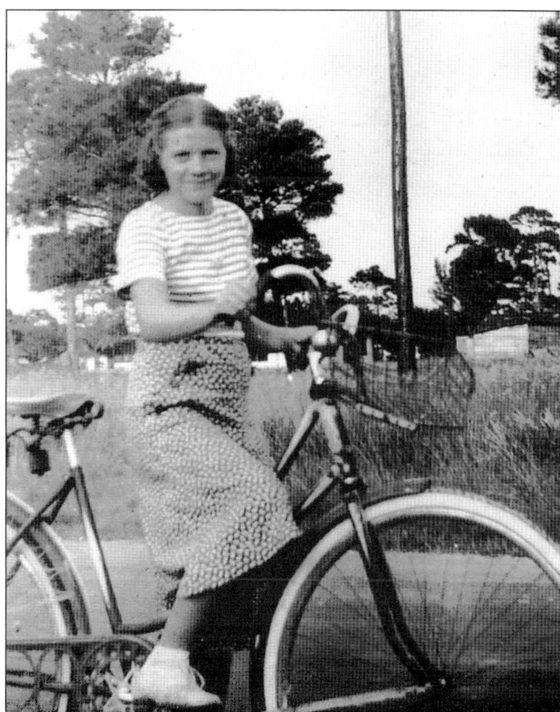

Here, Anita Milani pauses on her bicycle along South Twenty-fourth Avenue. (Maher Collection.)

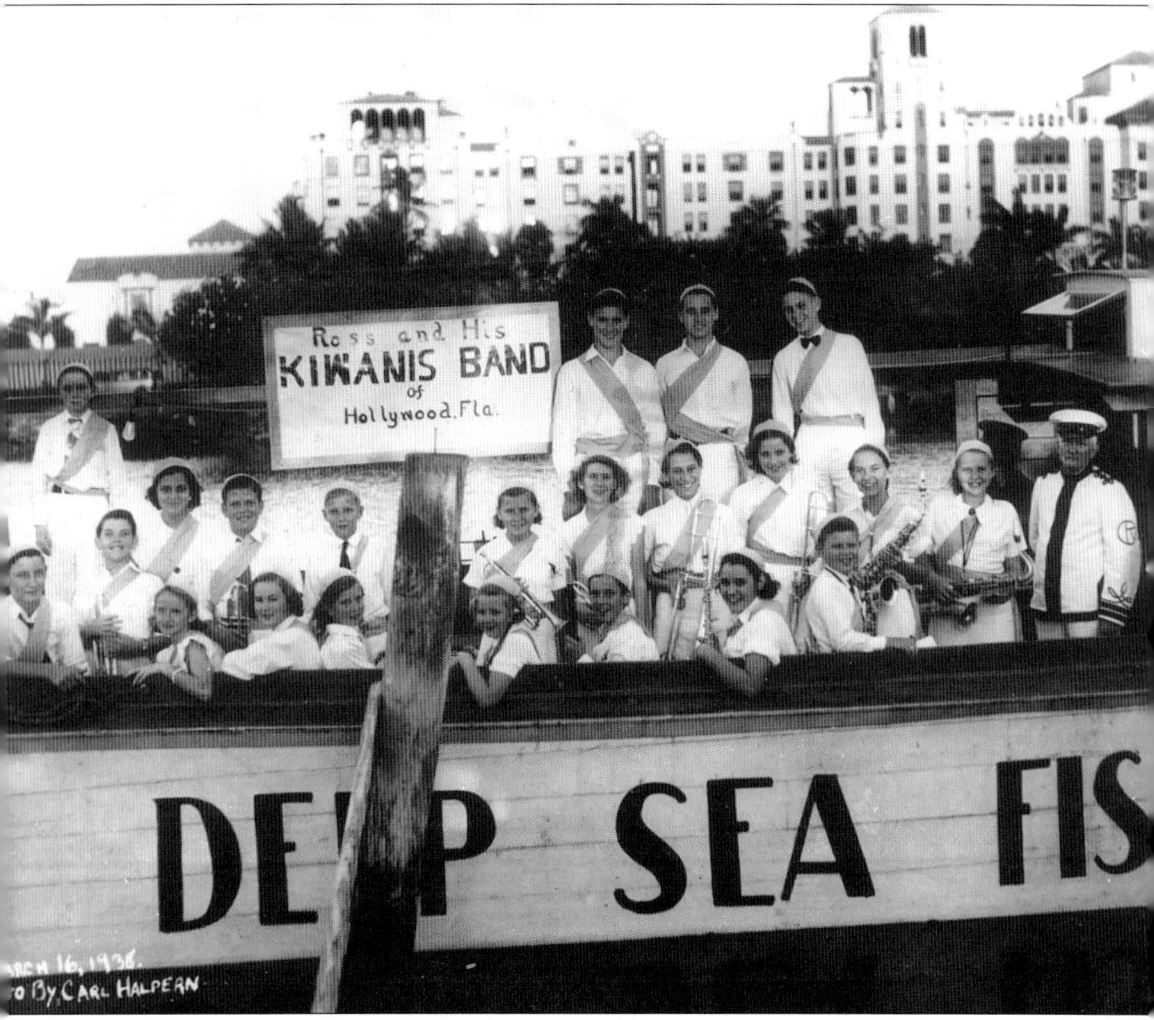

Ross and his Kiwanis band pose aboard a boat moored on the Intracoastal Waterway on March 16, 1938. Pictured from left to right are (front row) J.R. Aspy, Mildred Young, Frances Smith, Katherine Gaines, Bill Bellamy, Elizabeth Hudson, and Lunny Minis; (middle row) Eugene McCombs, Verna Aspy, Jimmie Minis, James ?, Betty Ritter, Pony Overstreet, ? Hudson, Eloise Brooks, Verna Hudson, Helen Whalen, Bandmaster W.H. Ross, and Mrs. Doc Aspy; (back row) Billy Jackson, Frank Verring, Louis Hudson, and Jack Jones. (General Collection.)

Sailfish are the catch of the day aboard the *Arletta* on January 23, 1938. (General Collection.)

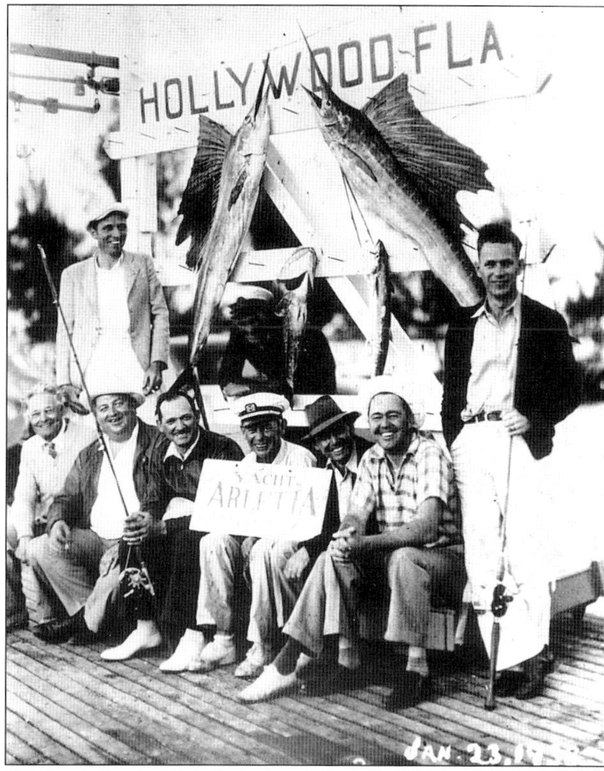

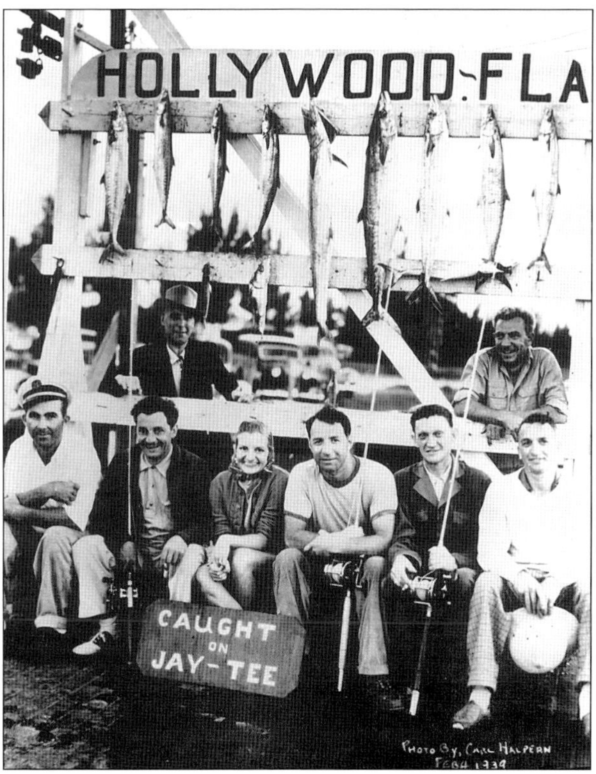

The catch aboard the *Jay-Tee* was not quite as impressive on February 4, 1939. (General Collection.)

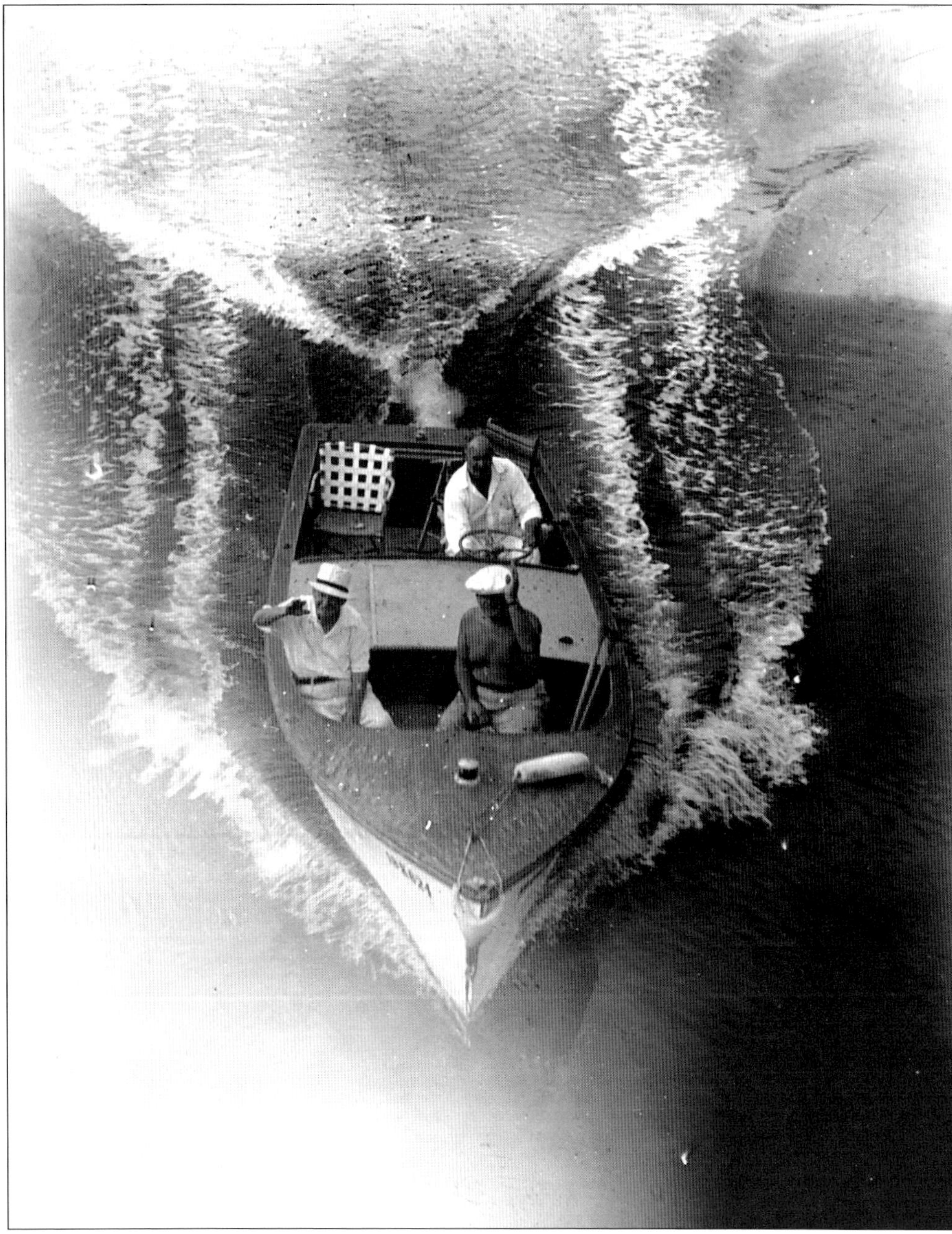

Three men enjoy an outing along the Intracoastal Waterway in this early photo. (Patricia Smith Collection.)

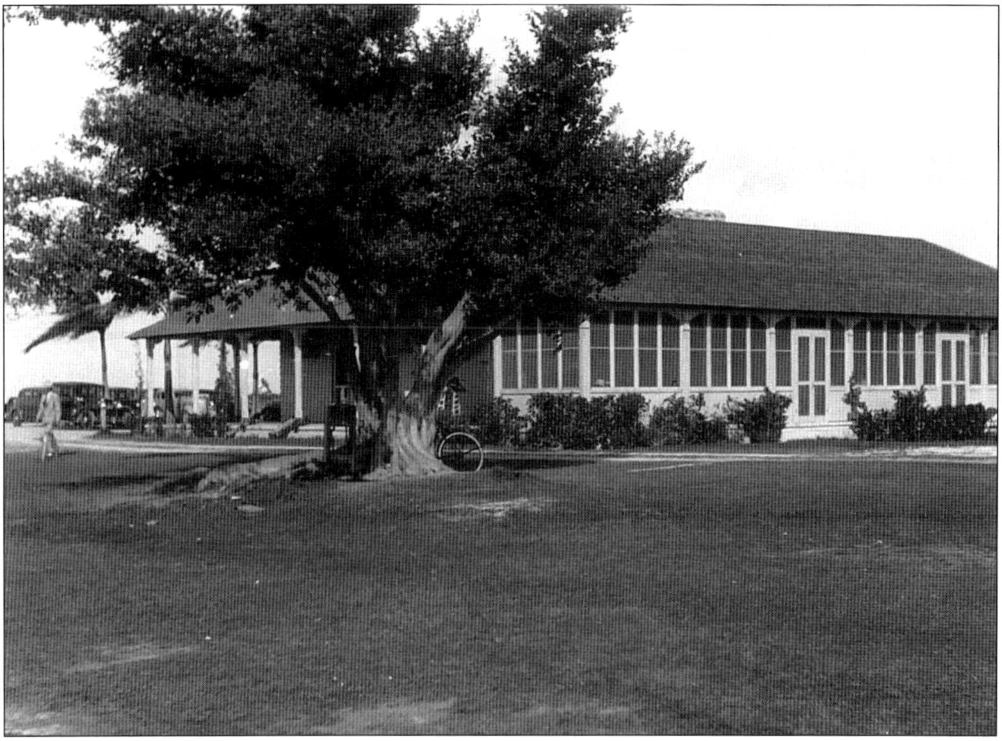

By the mid-1930s, golf had become such a popular pastime in Hollywood that the city purchased land for a municipal golf course in June 1934. Orangebrook Golf and Country Club opened to the public with only seven holes during the 1934–1935 winter season. Nine holes were ready for play by the following summer. (Patricia Smith Collection.)

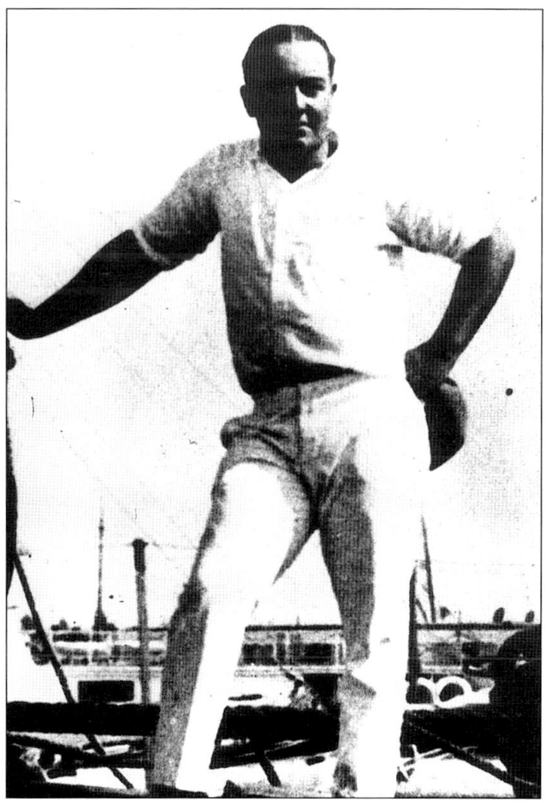

Joseph W. Young Jr., known in the family as "Tonce," strikes a nautical pose aboard his family's boat. Tonce died in Cocoa, Florida on September 13, 1964. (Al Vessella Collection.)

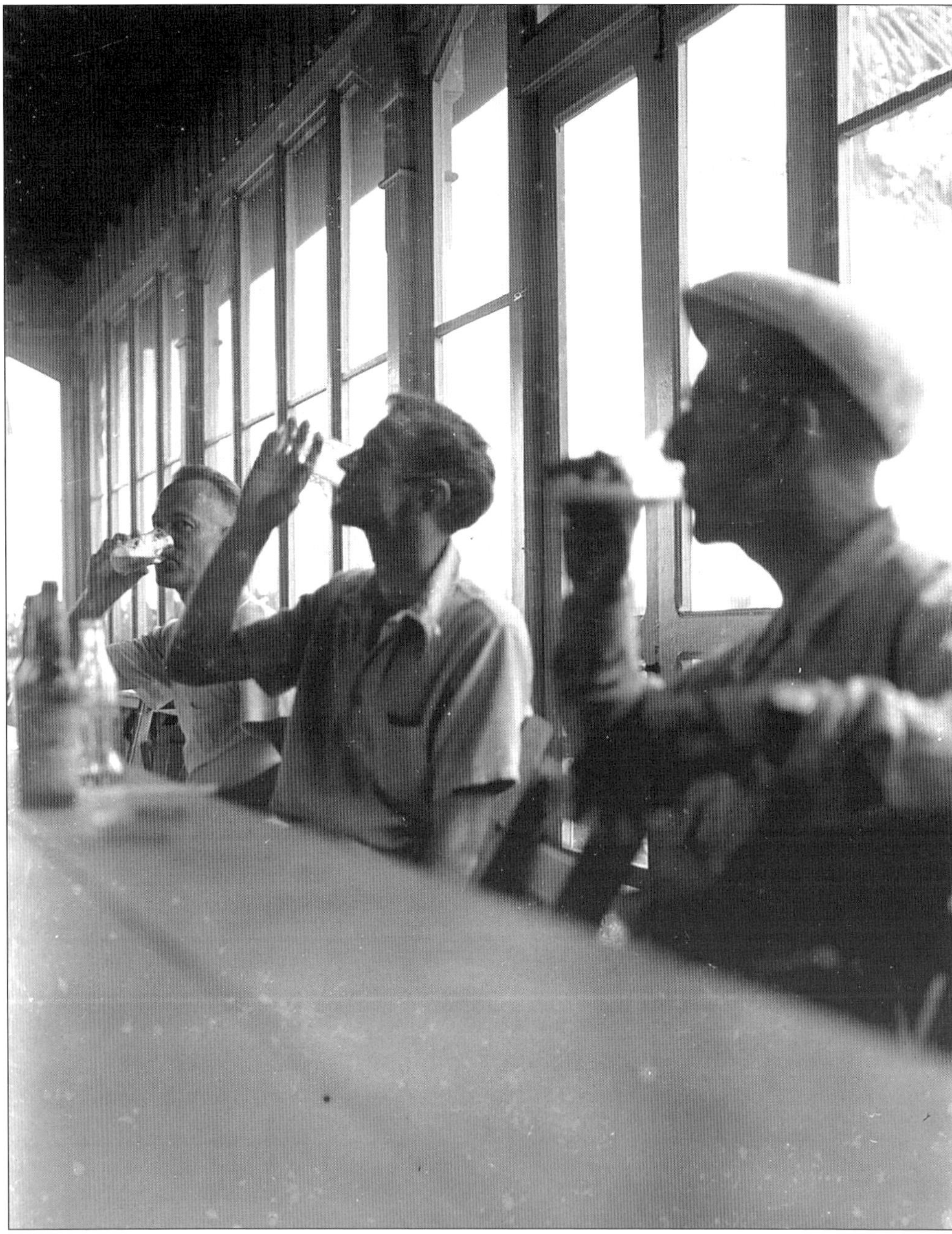

Three duffers enjoy a round at the 19th hole in the Orangebrook Golf and Country Club's clubhouse. (Patricia Smith Collection.)

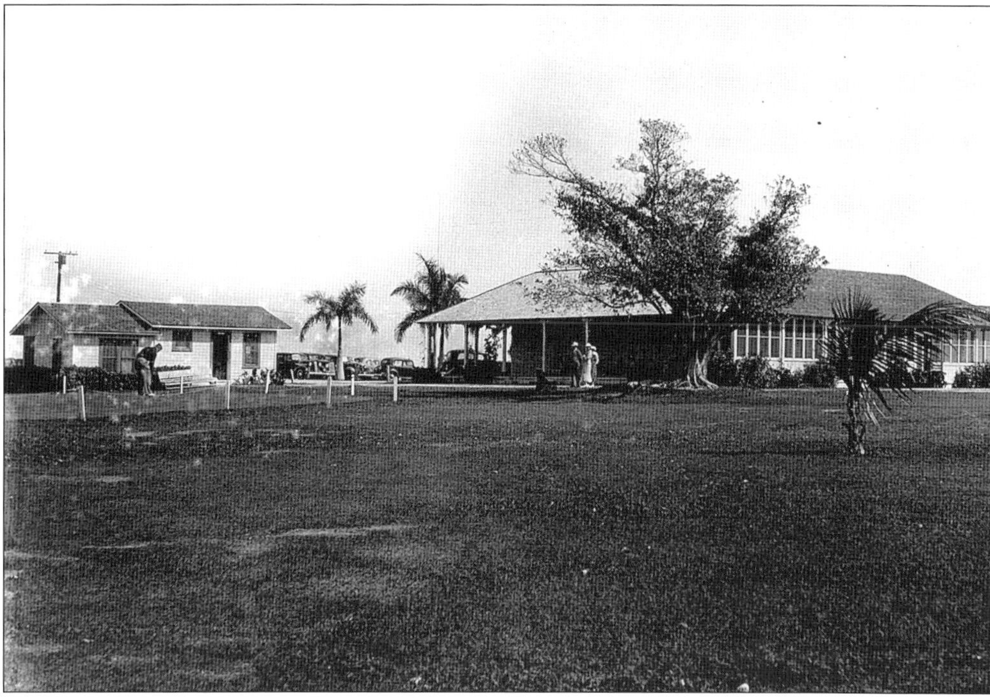

The original Orangebrook Clubhouse, a shed-like structure, was replaced with this more functional clubhouse in 1937. Ralph Young, a friend of the Joseph Young family, designed the course. (Patricia Smith Collection.)

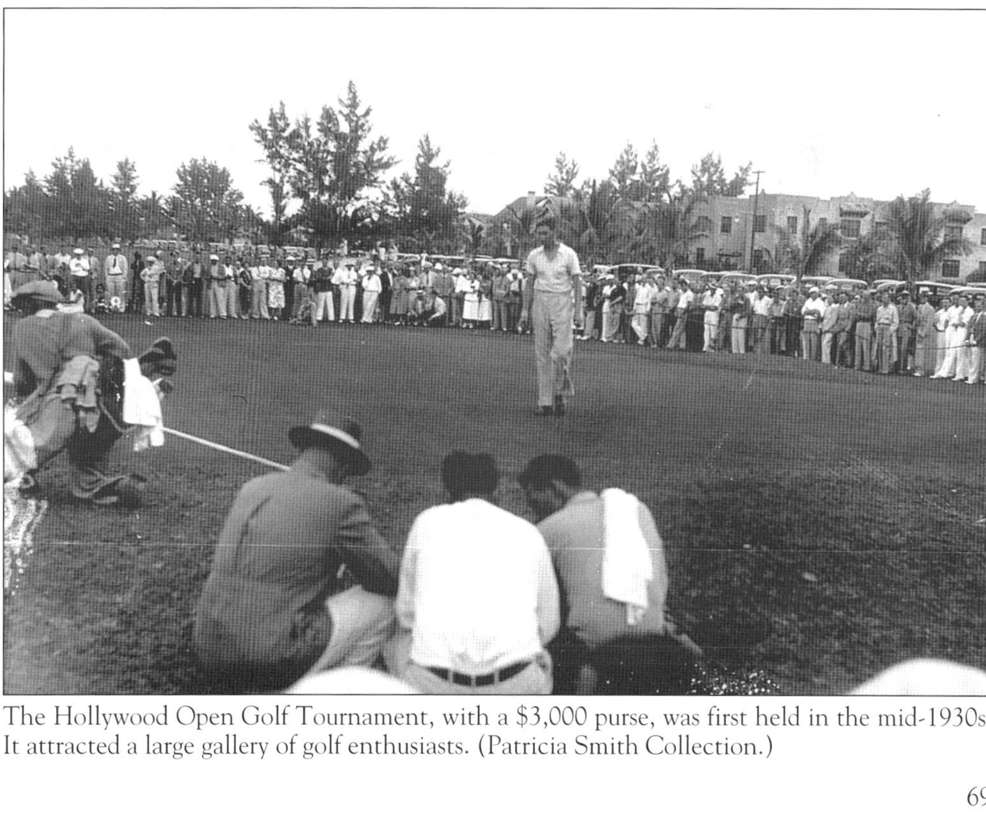

The Hollywood Open Golf Tournament, with a $3,000 purse, was first held in the mid-1930s. It attracted a large gallery of golf enthusiasts. (Patricia Smith Collection.)

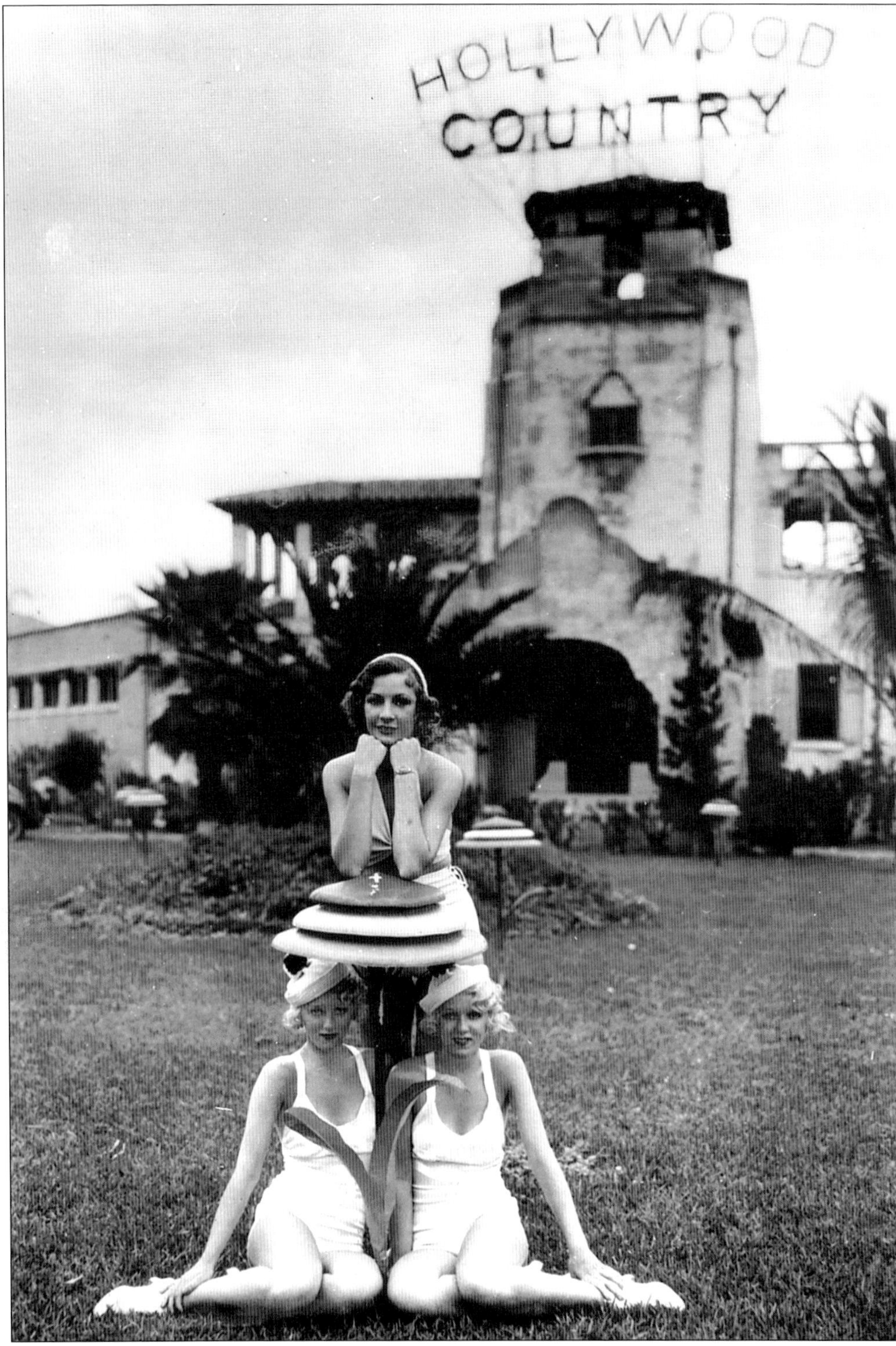

Three entertainers strike a pose beside a light fixture outside the Hollywood Golf and Country Club on February 17, 1935. (General Collection.)

This undated 1930s publicity photo of entertainer Ann Greene was included in a promotional ad for her appearance "opening Saturday night at the Hollywood Yacht Club." (Al Vessella Collection.)

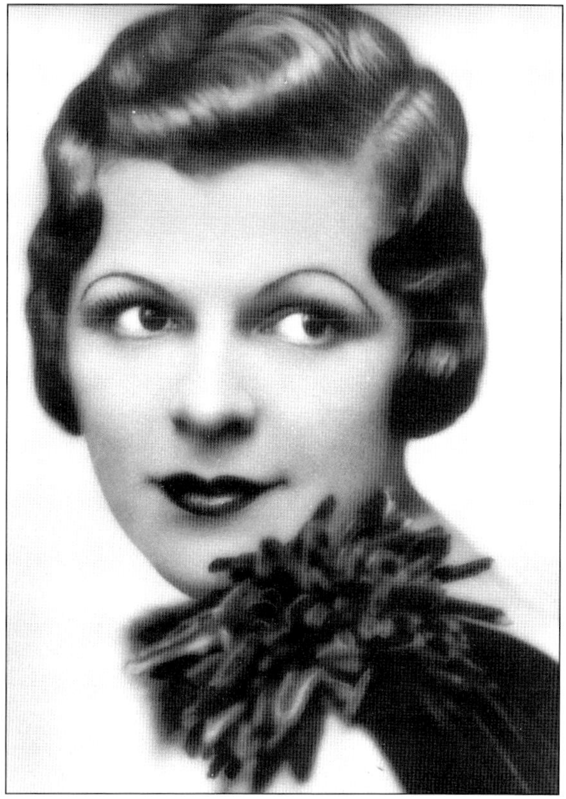

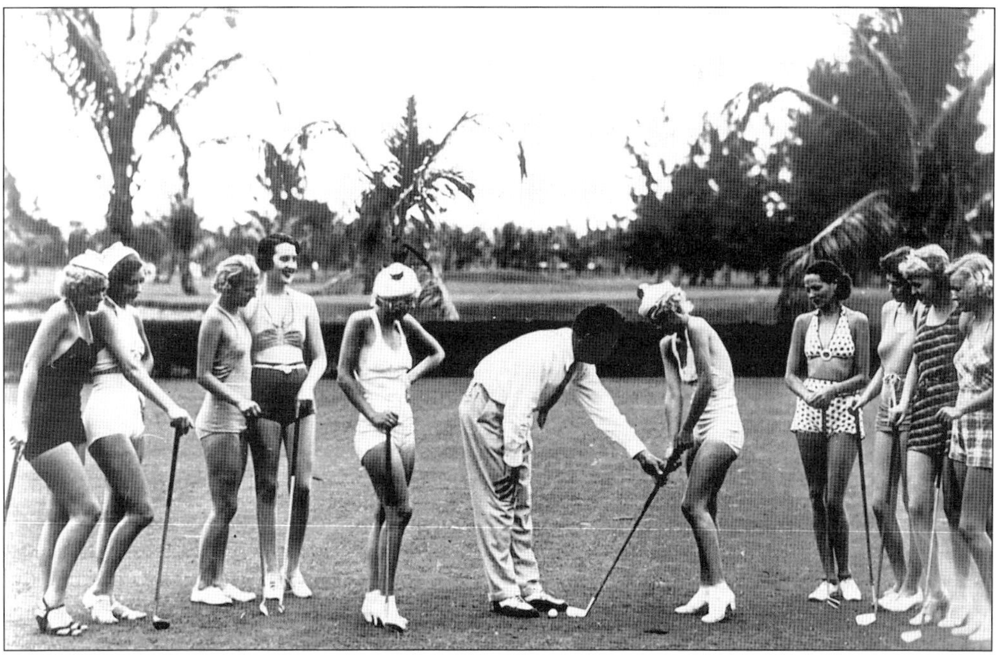

Never too busy to miss a photo opportunity, the Hollywood Golf and Country Club entertainers take some time for golf lessons with an attentive instructor on February 17, 1935. (General Collection.)

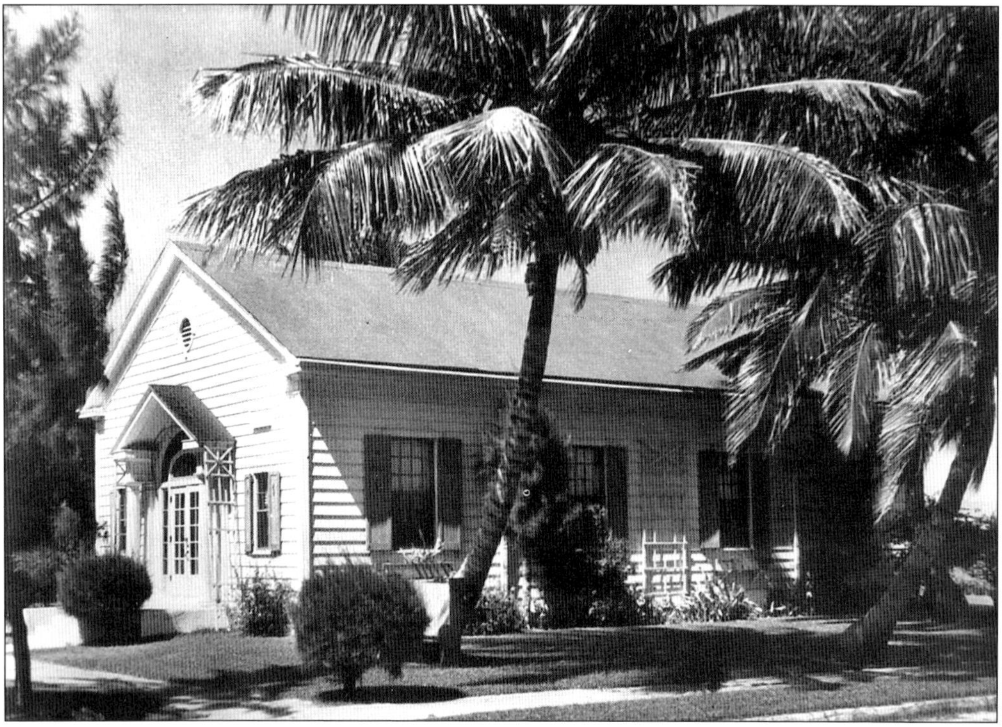

The Hollywood Woman's Club was organized in 1922 and received its charter in 1923. The clubhouse was built in 1925 on a lot at 501 North Fourteenth Avenue that was donated by Joseph Young. (General Collection.)

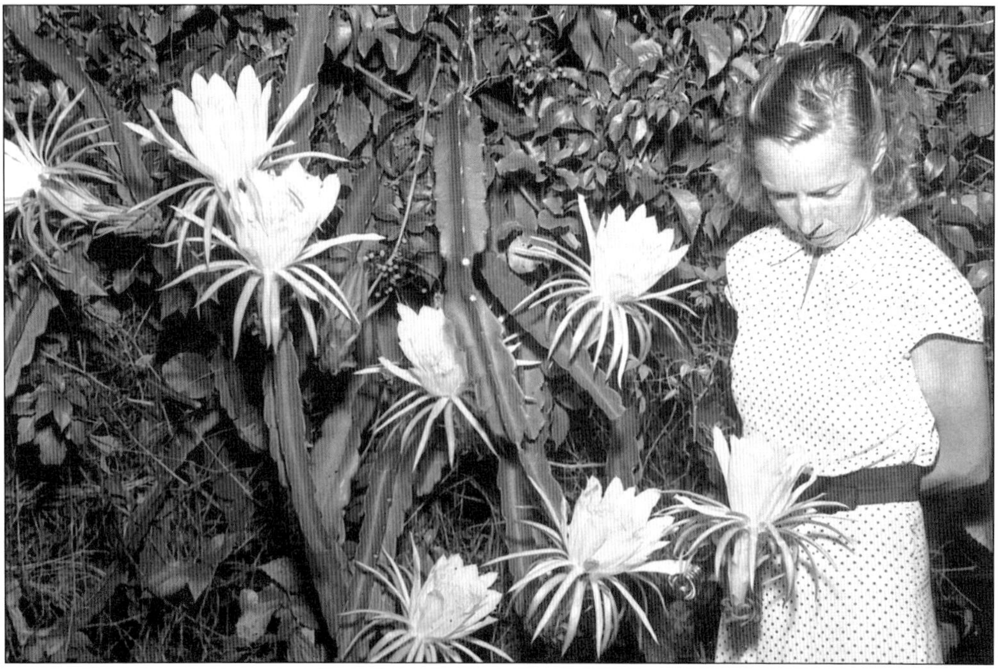

Mrs. Dorothy Martin, a member of the Woman's Club, admires a flowering cactus in 1938. (Patricia Smith Collection.)

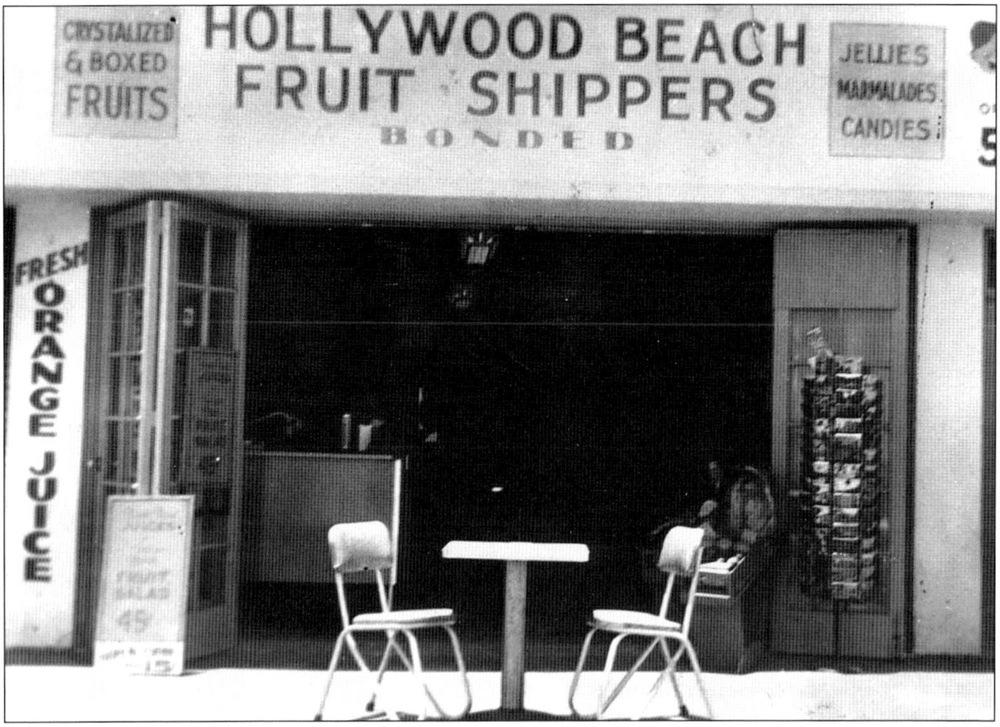

The Broadwalk provided retail opportunities throughout the 1930s. The Hollywood Beach Fruit Shippers store, at 1114 North Broadwalk, provided tropical fruits and juices to beachgoers. (Manesiotis Collection.)

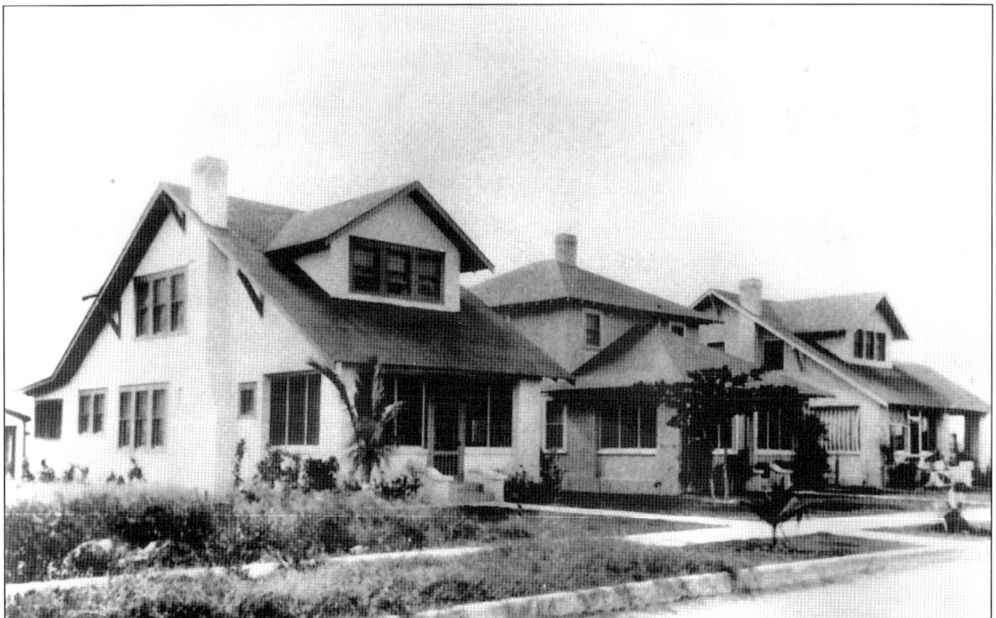

Three houses along an unidentified street in 1930s Hollywood reflect the growing maturity of the community. Landscaping is filling in, reducing the stark appearance of the properties. (Al Vessella Collection.)

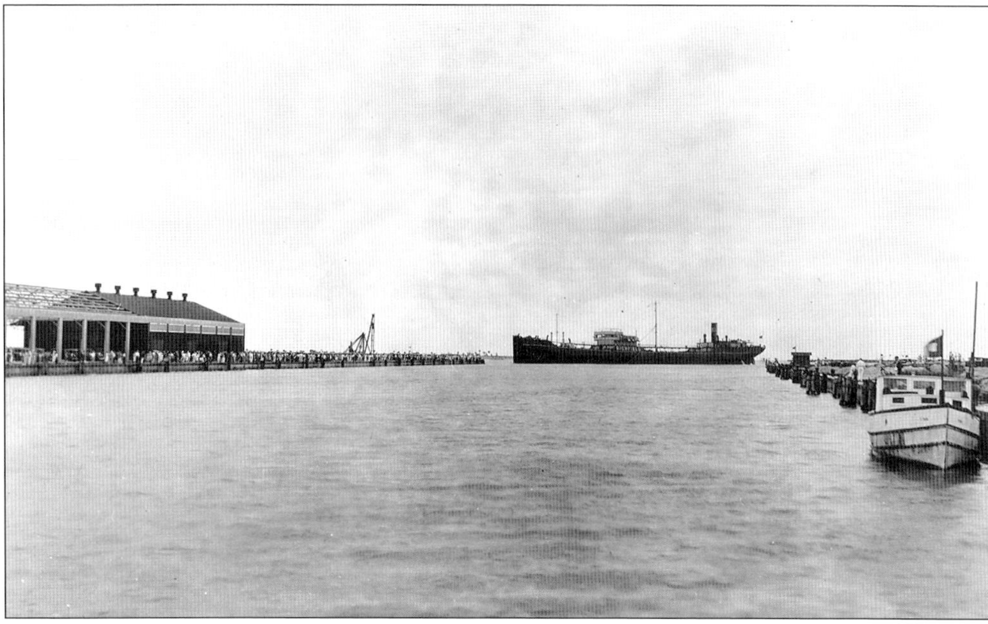

A ship sails into Port Everglades on October 18, 1931 to load and unload cargo. The port, a part of Joseph Young's vision for Hollywood and South Florida, was opened at a grand ceremony on February 22, 1928. Although most of the port lies within the corporate limits of Hollywood, bonds to finance its construction were issued by both Hollywood and Fort Lauderdale. (General Collection.)

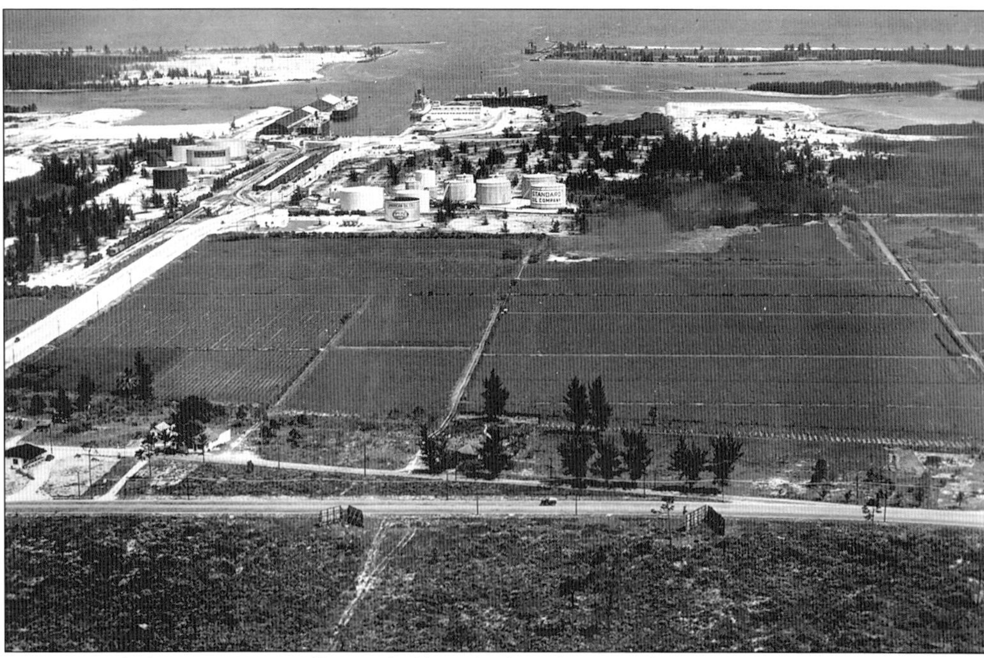

Port Everglades was originally a shallow body of water known as Lake Mabel. Joseph Young bought up the land and surrounding property when he began his initial plans to build the harbor. The lake was separated from the Atlantic Ocean by a narrow strip of land. (General Collection.)

Three

The 1940s

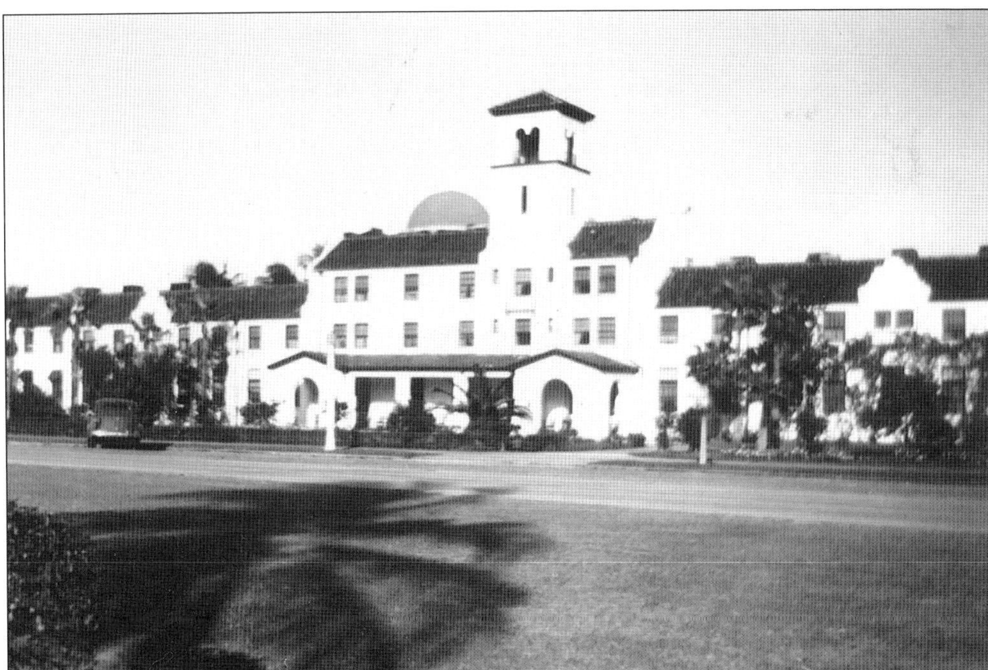

The Park View Hotel, seen here in a 1940s photograph, continued to anchor the eastern portion of Young Circle. It was eventually razed in the early 1960s and was replaced with a grocery store, drug store, and other shops. (General Collection.)

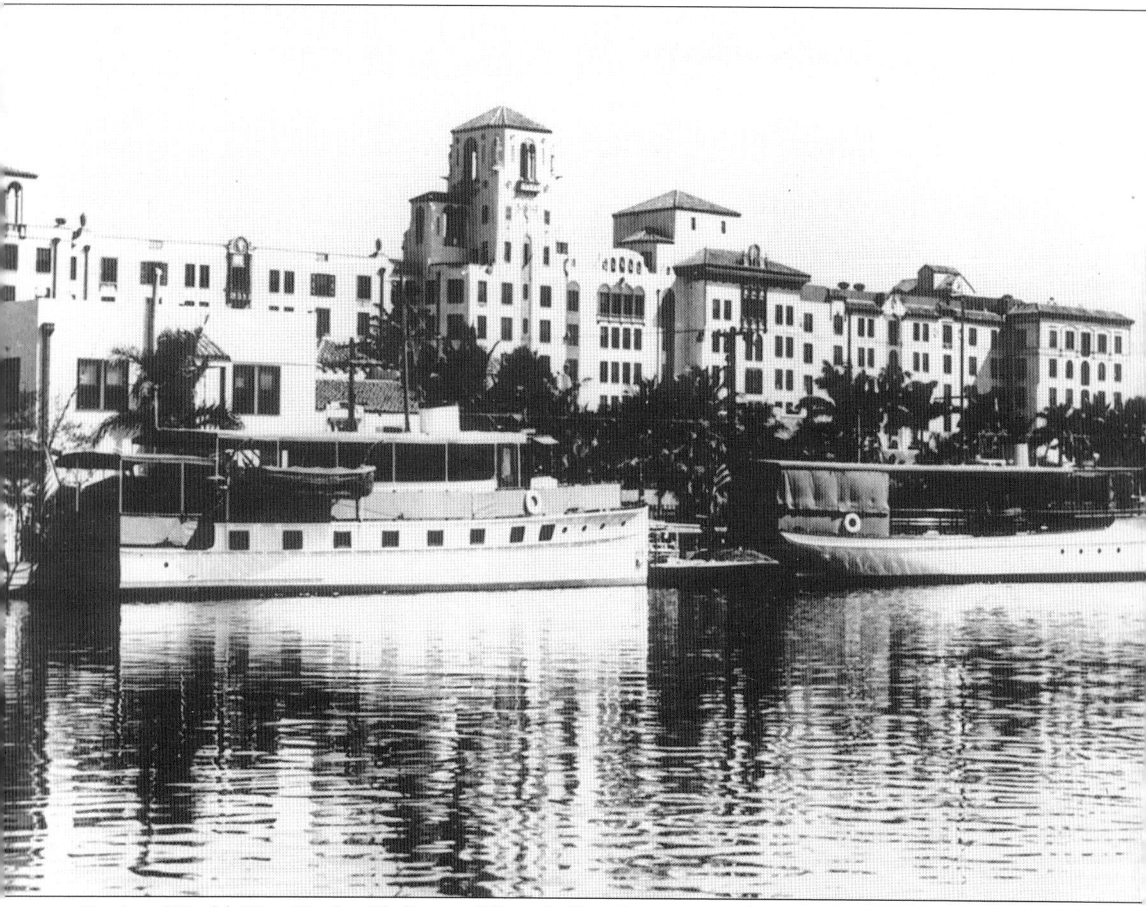

During World War II, the Hollywood Beach Hotel was turned over to the War Department for use as the United States Naval Indoctrination and Training School. The school officially opened on December 16, 1942. The first class of trainees included 1,000 officers with a staff of 50 instructors, drill instructors, medical personnel, and administrative officers. After the first class completed its two-month training, class sizes were increased to 1,500 students. (General Collection.)

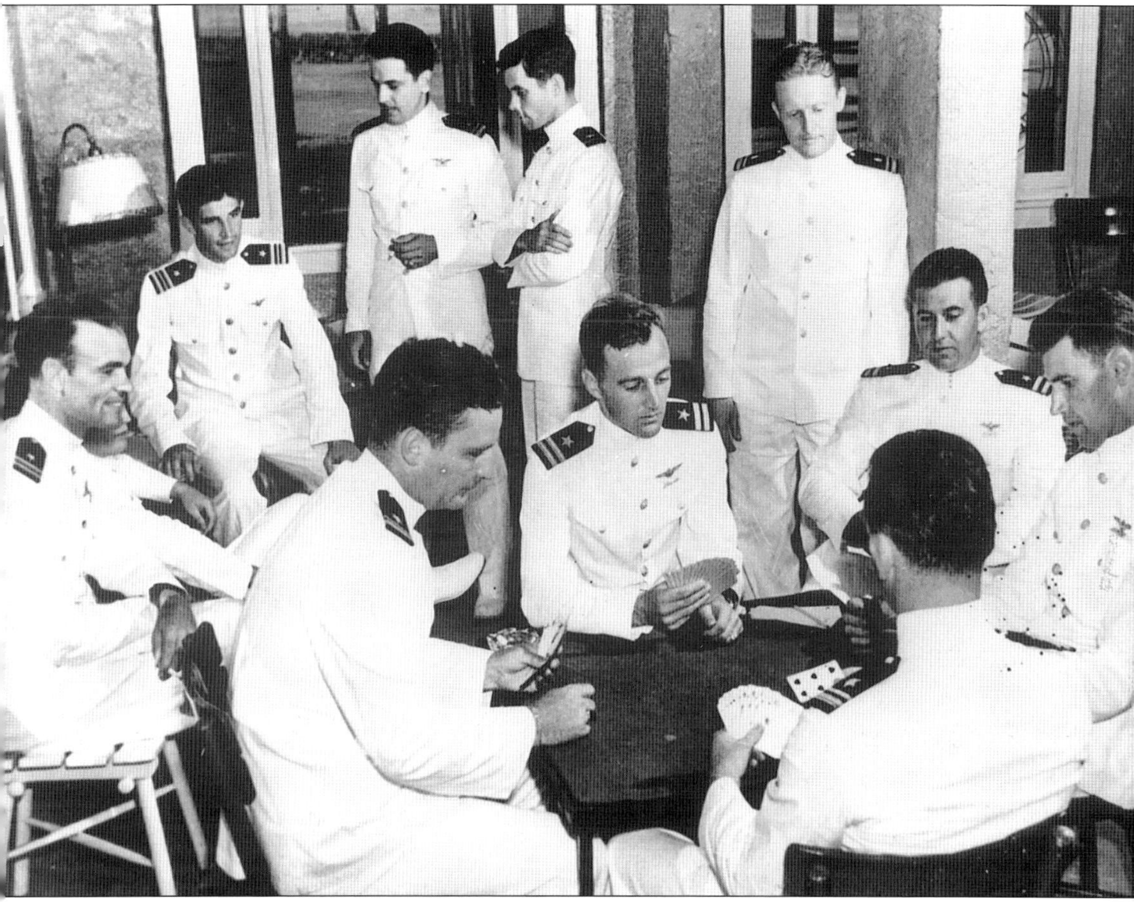

In July 1942, the Hollywood Golf and Country Club was converted into the Servicemen's Country Club, a place where military trainees could relax, socialize, and distance themselves from the rigors of military training. These officers were photographed at the opening of the Servicemen's Country Club. (Al Vessella Collection.)

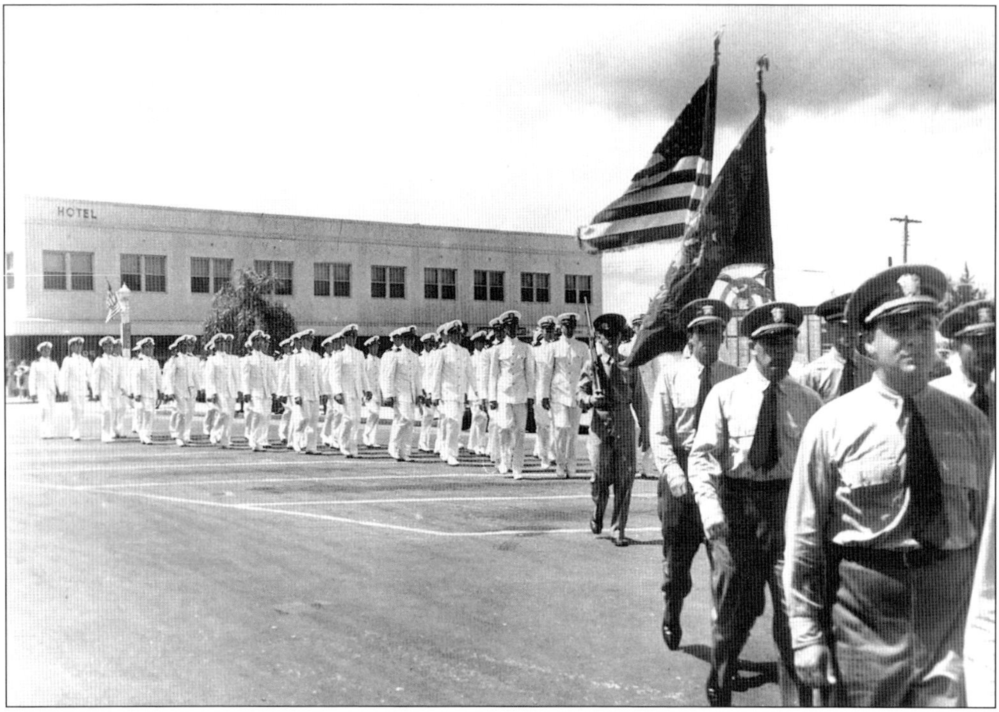

On September 12, 1943, Hollywood hosted a military parade during its third war bond drive. The navy marchers included a marine color guard and units of officers and men from both the Naval Air Gunners School and the Navy's Indoctrination and Training School. (Al Vessella Collection.)

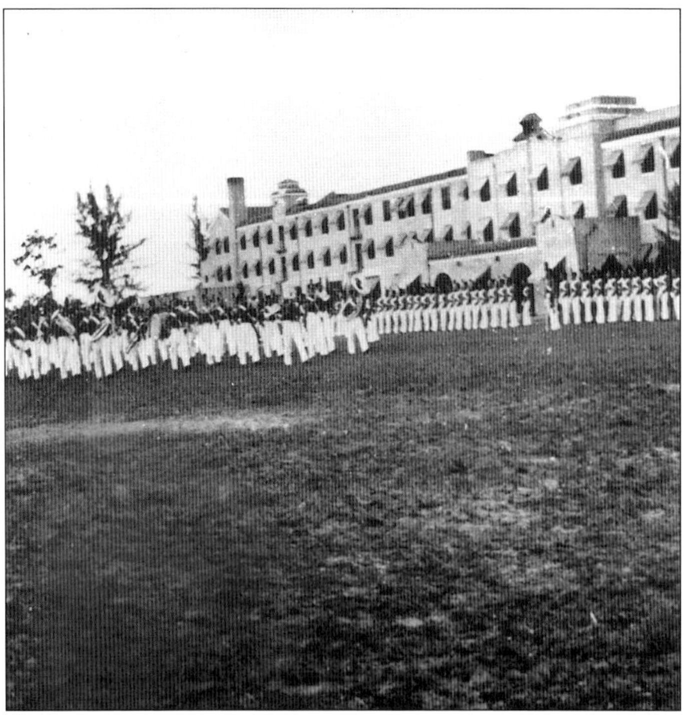

During the early days of World War II, Riverside Military Academy cadets continued their routine drills during the winter session. The academy was soon converted into the Naval Air Gunners School and remained so for the duration of the war. The academy's winter sessions resumed in 1947. (Elsie Johns Collection.)

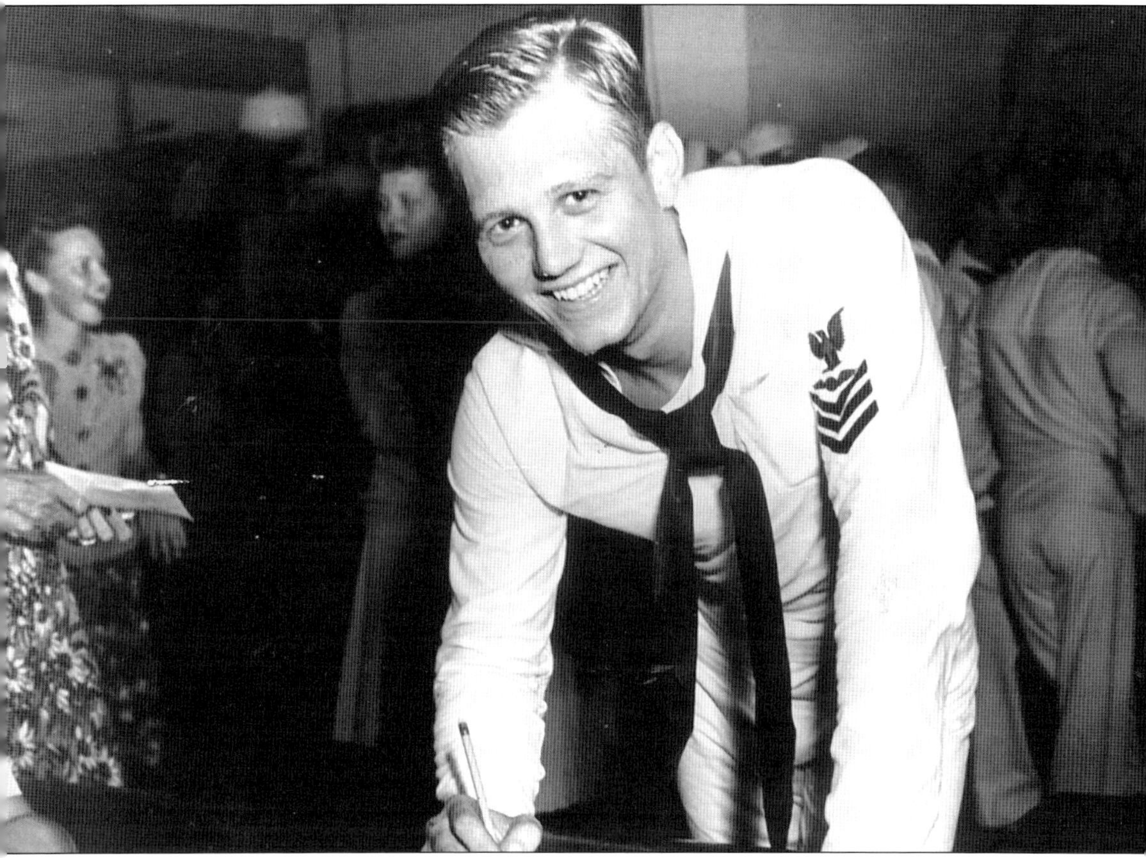

Herbert W. Abrams of Long Island, New York had the honor of being the 100,000th visitor to register at Hollywood's Servicemen's Club. This photograph of Abrams was taken as he signed in on October 1, 1943. He was stationed at the Naval Air Gunners school. (Al Vessella Collection.)

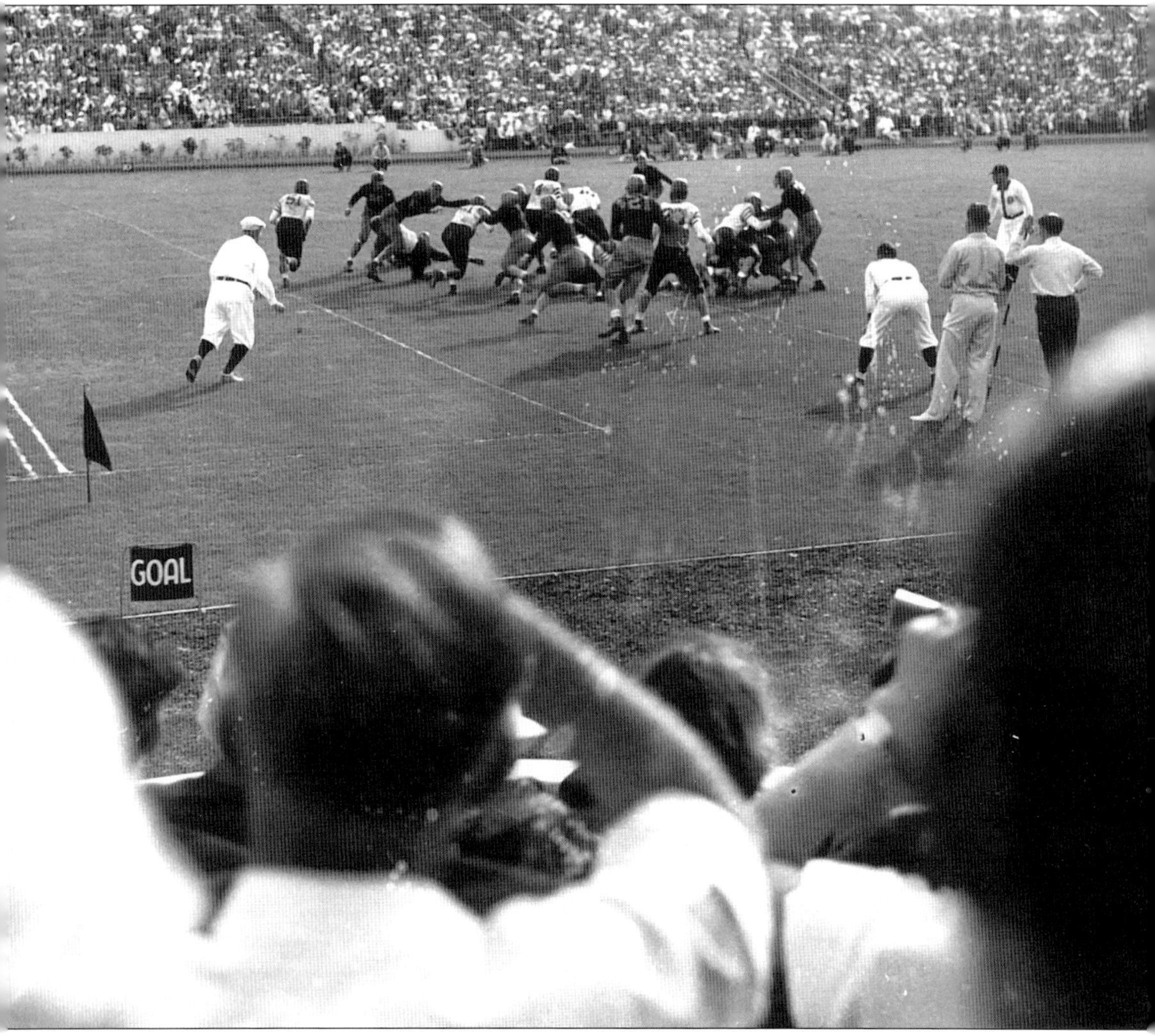

With the sacrifices of war behind them, the people of Hollywood began to enjoy life's little pleasures again. One of those pleasures was high school football. This photograph was taken during a South Broward High School football game. (Patricia Smith Collection.)

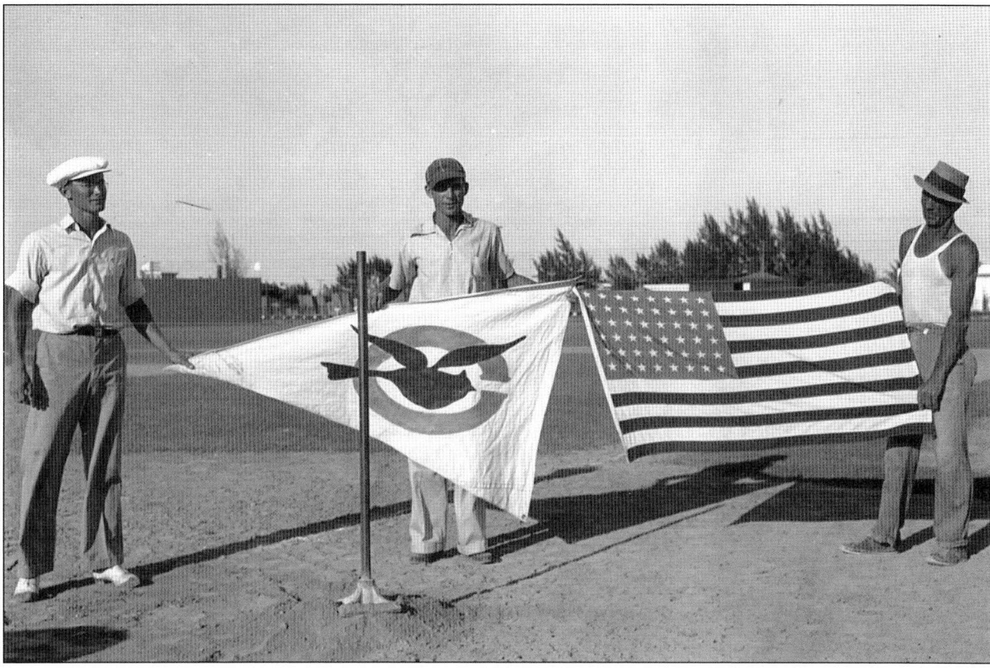

What's more American than baseball? Three men display the pennant of the Columbus Red Birds, a minor league team, along with the American flag—48 stars, of course. (Patricia Smith Collection.)

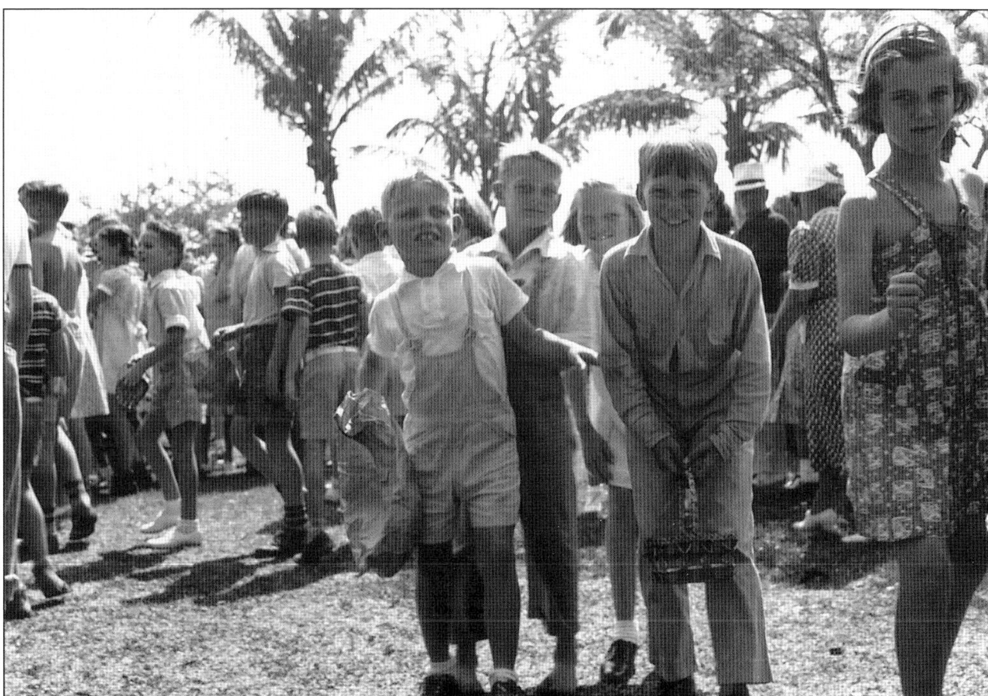

Traditional Easter egg hunts were held for children in Young Circle Park. (Patricia Smith Collection.)

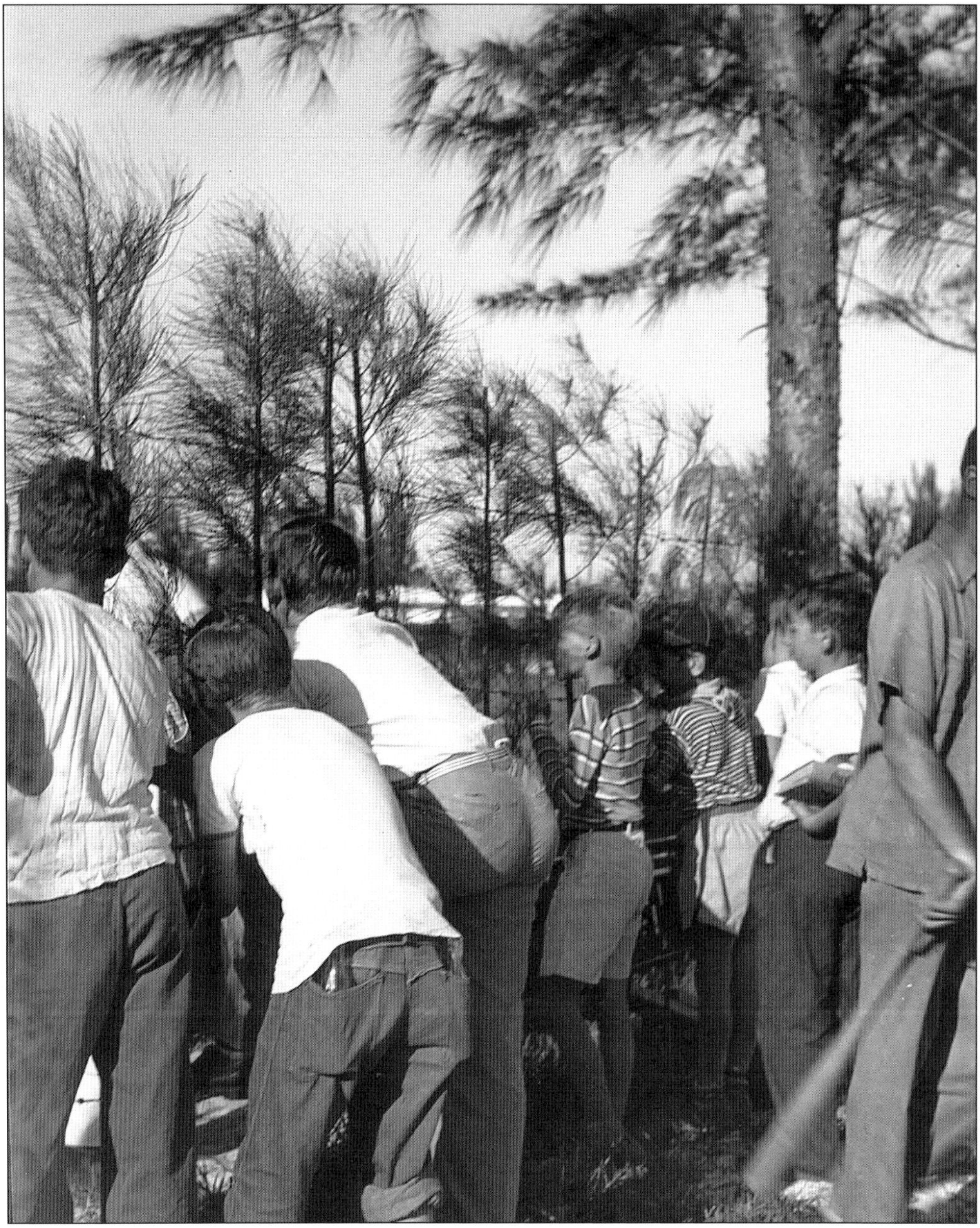

A crowd of boys gathers along the fence to watch a baseball game. Notice the boy with his pants leg rolled up—if he cashed in the deposit for the empty bottles in his back pockets, he might just have enough money for a ticket. (Patricia Smith Collection.)

Costumed people frolic on a car during a late 1940s parade, possibly the Fiesta Tropicale Parade. The Fiesta Tropicale was originally organized in the 1930s but was suspended during the years of World War II. The celebration resumed in 1946. (Manesiotis Collection.)

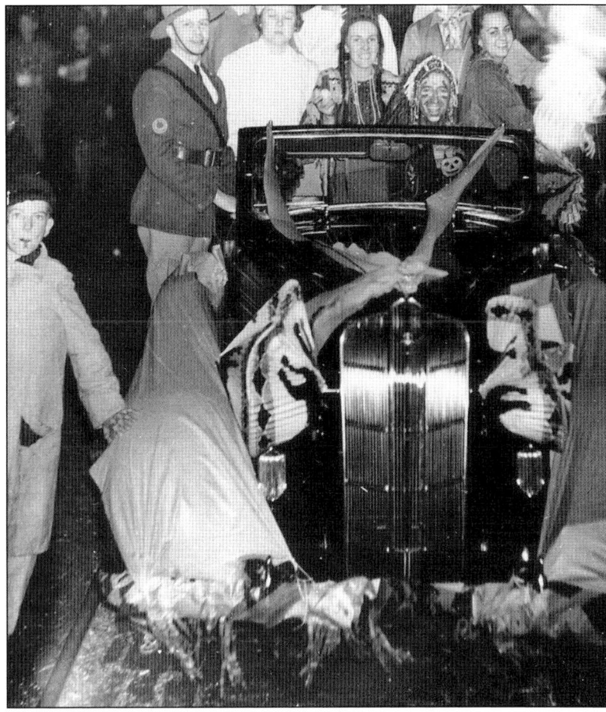

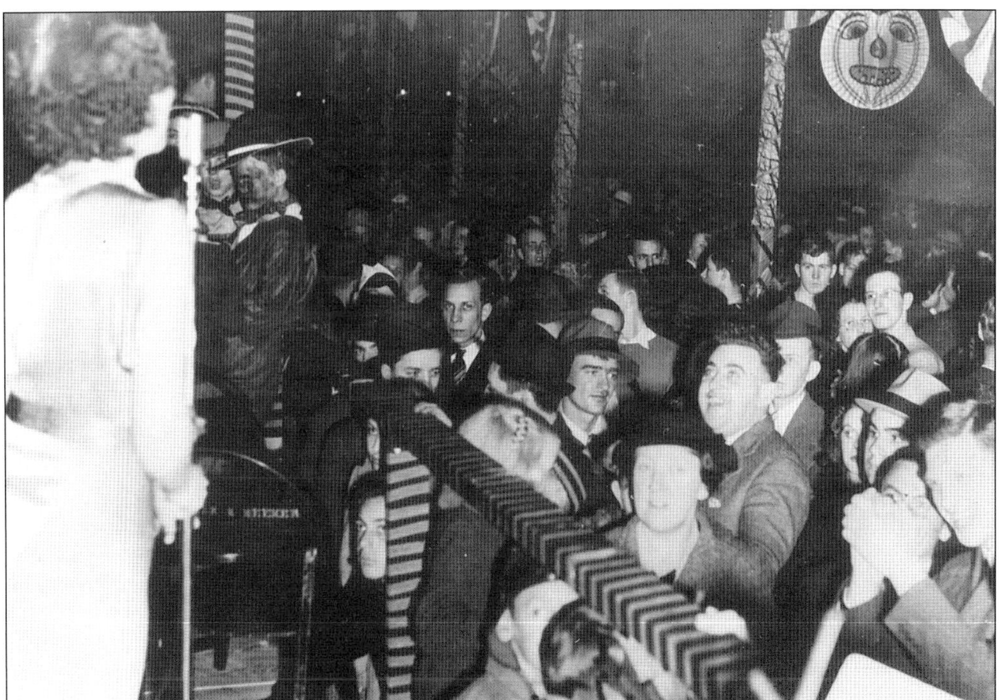

A singer performs for the crowd during a Fiesta Tropicale celebration. The original Fiesta Tropicale had great hopes of being a nationally renowned Spanish-theme festival. It never quite lived up to that lofty goal, and today's modern version is more of a Mardi Gras celebration than a Spanish fiesta. (Manesiotis Collection.)

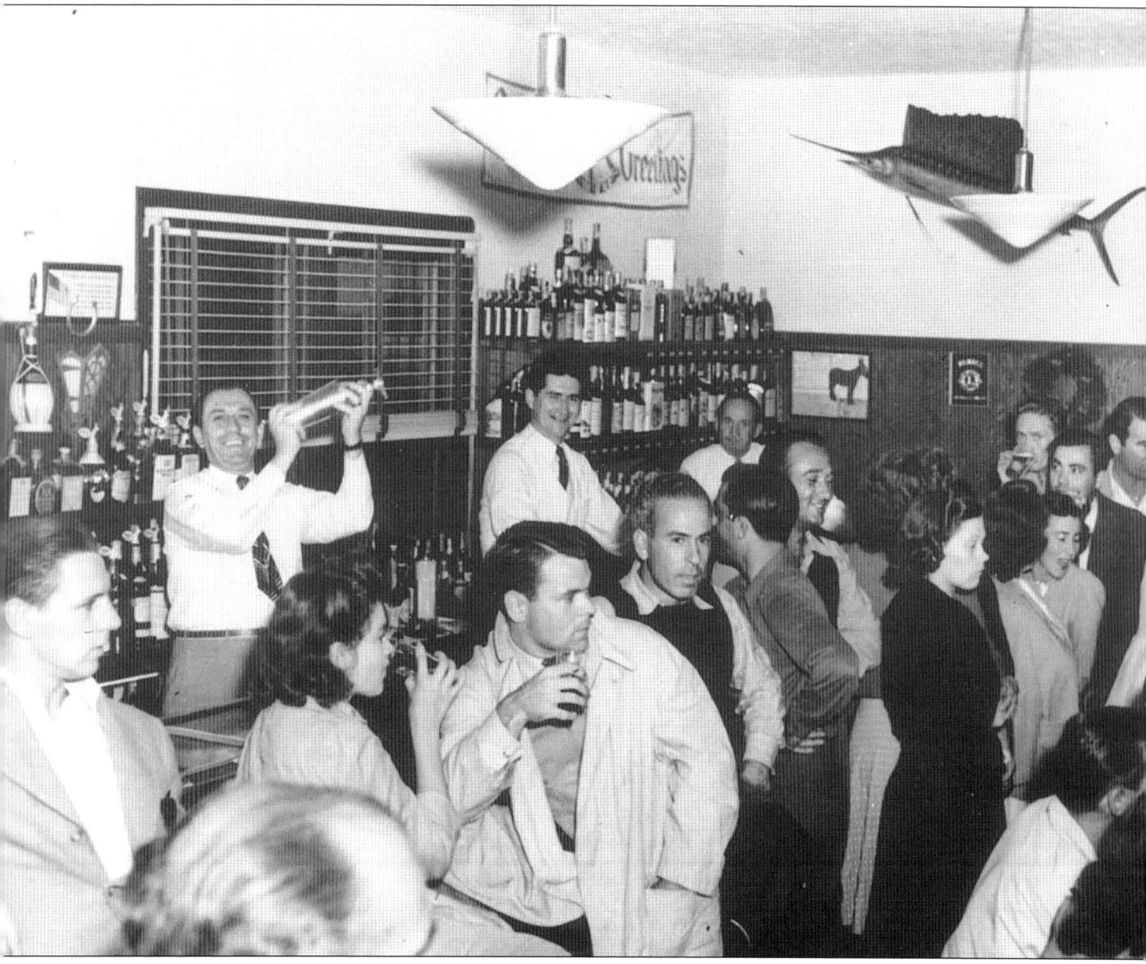

Customers of Chrest's Bar and Grill, one of Hollywood's favorite watering holes, celebrate the last uninhibited holiday season in 1940 before the United States involvement in World War II the following December. Chrest's Bar and Grill was located at 202 North Ocean Drive across from the Hollywood Beach Hotel. The establishment was razed in the early 1960s. (Al Vessella Collection.)

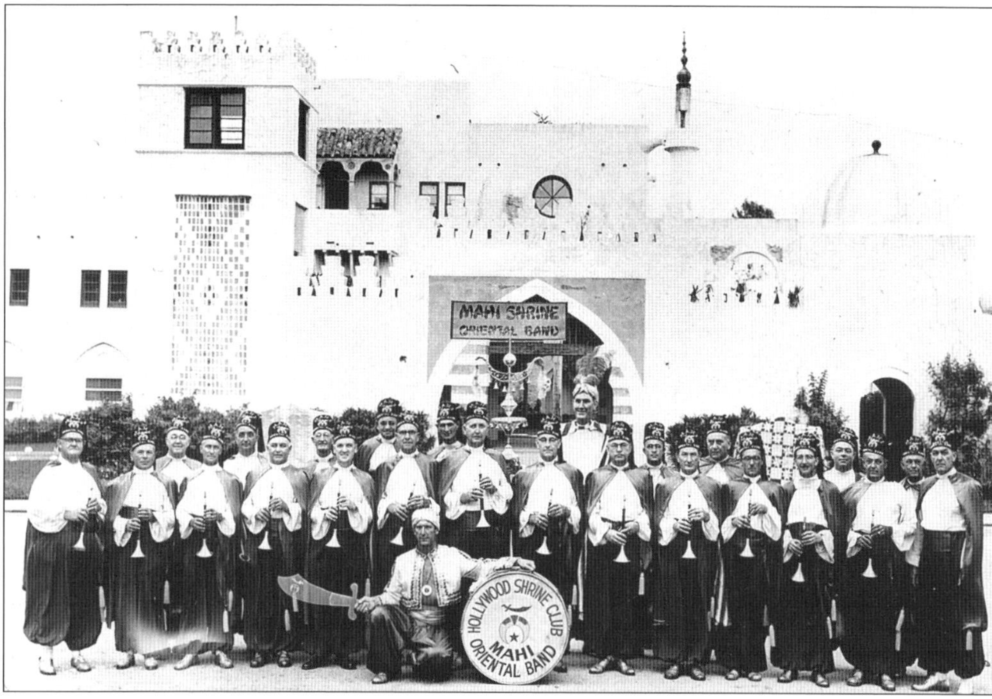

Members of the Hollywood Shrine Club Oriental Band pose in front of the Arabian-style City Hall in Opa-Locka in 1948. The club was affiliated with the Mahi Temple in Miami. (Elsie Johns Collection.)

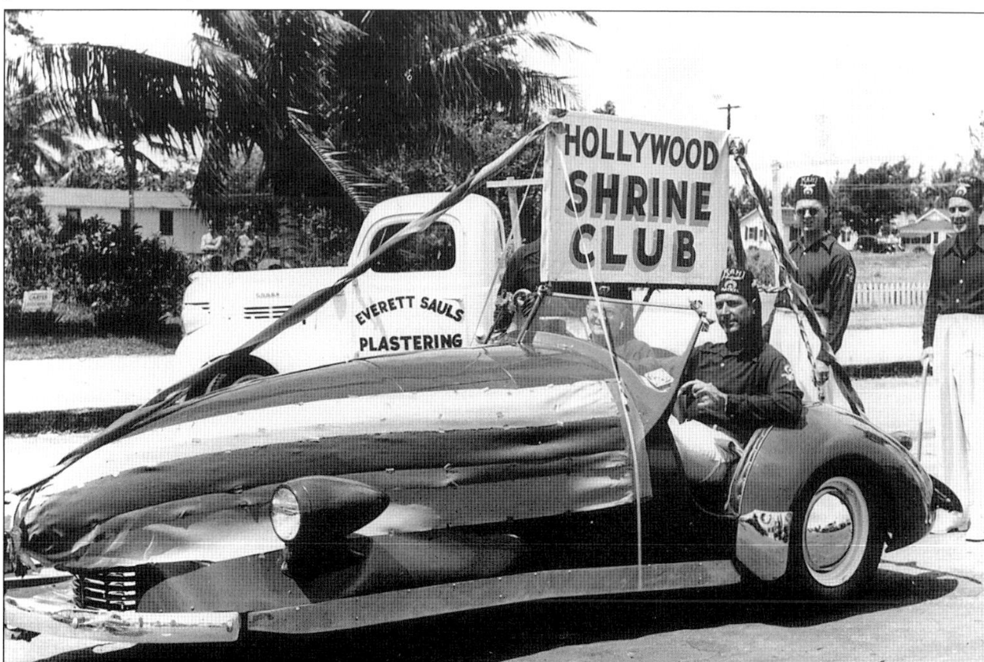

Five members of the Hollywood Shrine Club gear up for a July 4, 1948 event. Everett Sauls, a Hollywood businessman, sits in the driver's seat. (Elsie Johns Collection.)

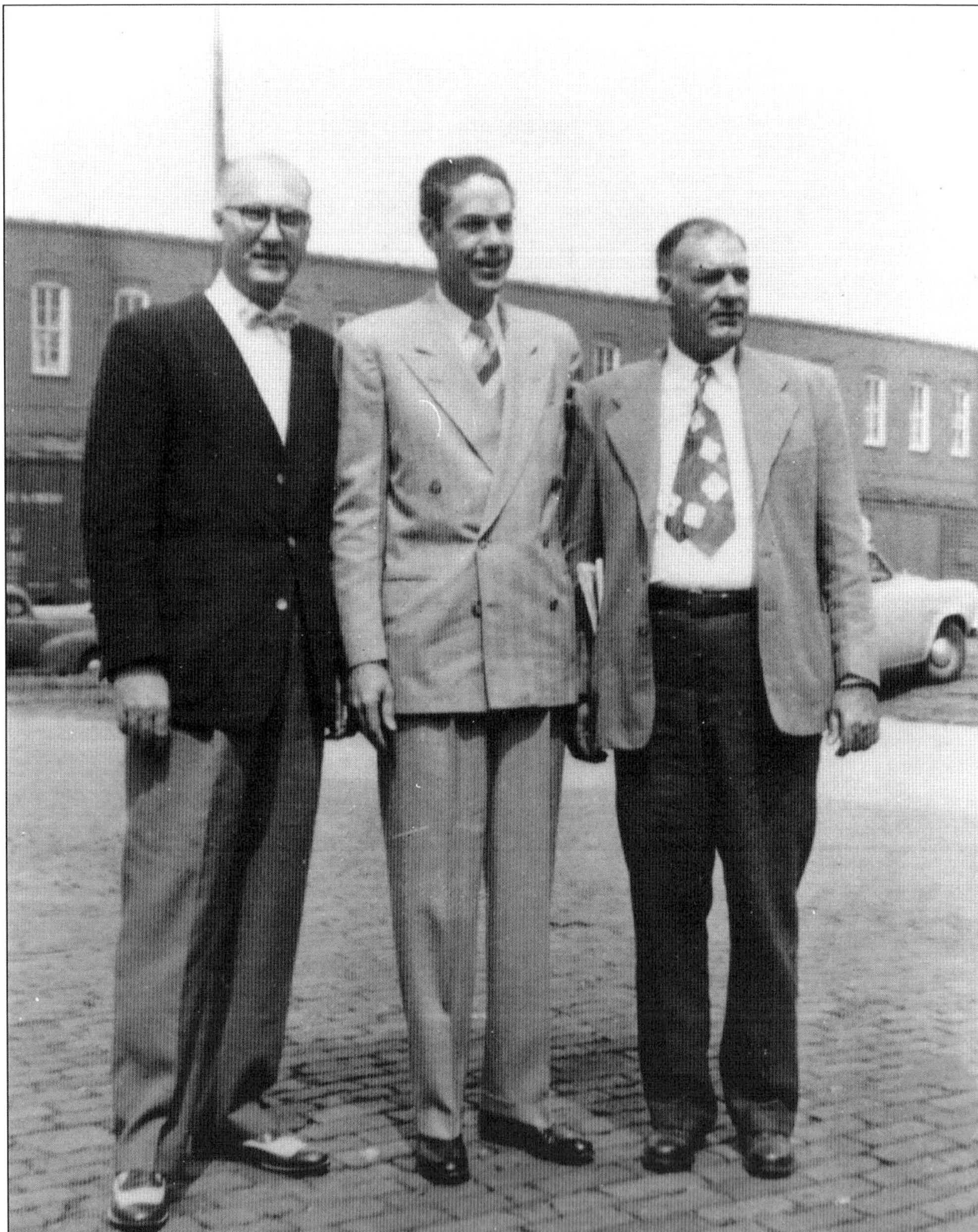

Millard Jones, proprietor of Jones Hollywood Hardware Co., Haydon Burns of Jacksonville, and Holloway Cook are photographed in Hollywood in the late 1940s. Burns was elected mayor of Jacksonville in 1949 and later served as Florida's governor for two years in the mid-1960s. Cook served as chief of the Hollywood Fire Department in the 1950s. (General Collection.)

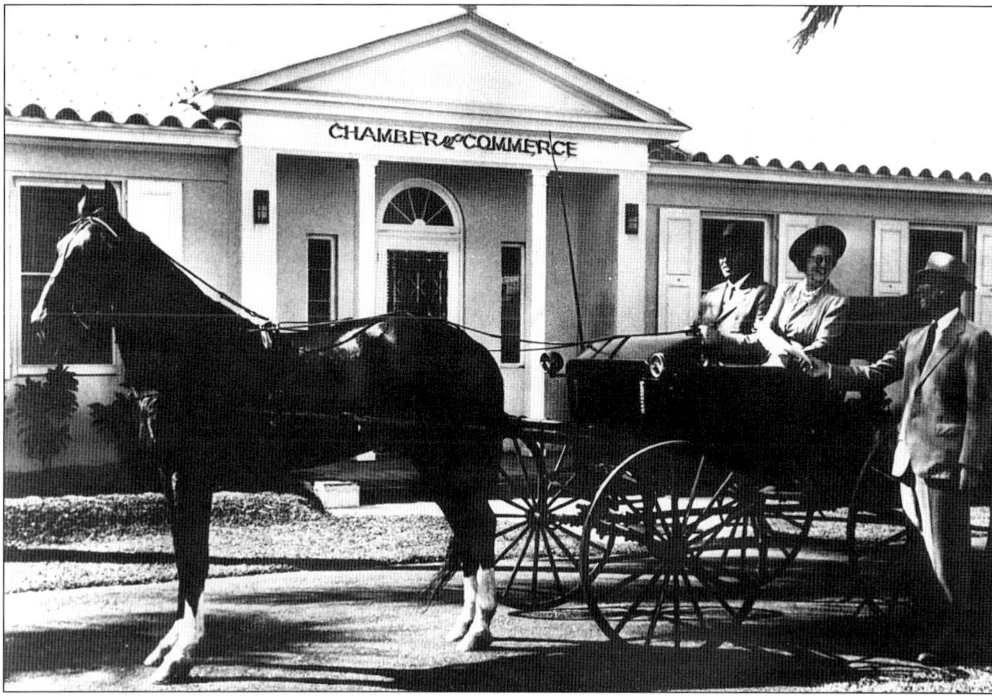

Mrs. and Mrs. Floyd L. Wray were not intimidated by the prospect of rationed fuel and tires. They drove up to the chamber of commerce from their Flamingo Groves home and chatted with City Manager Forrest Blackwell. Mr. Wray was the president of the chamber at the time. (Al Vessella Collection.)

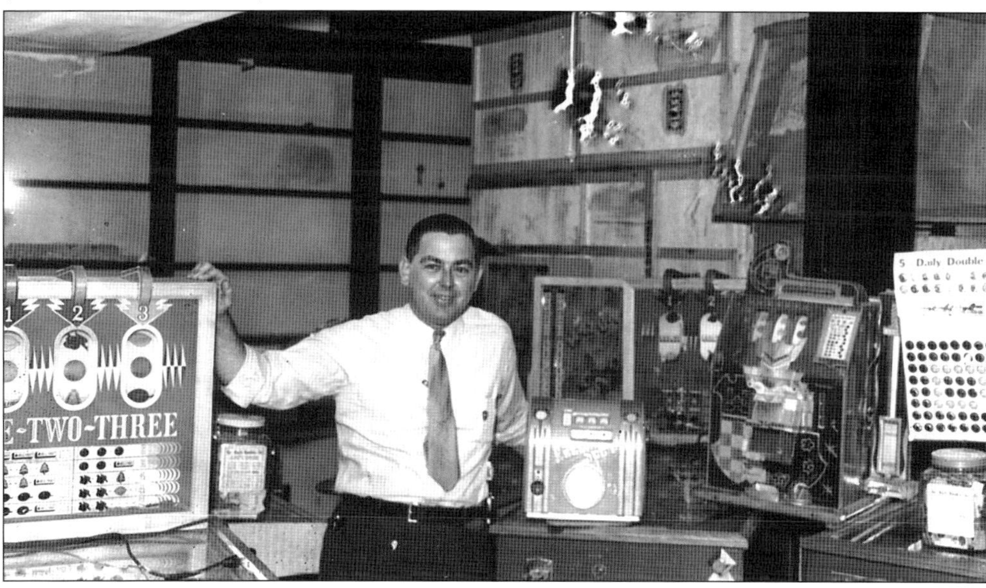

Gambling had been an accepted, if illegal, pastime in South Florida from its earliest days as a resort area. At the December 16, 1947 Hollywood City Commission meeting, an angry citizen rose to denounce gambling in the city, forcing the commission to vote to insure that all gambling operations in the city be put out of business. Slot machines, poker games, and punchboards were all closed down and equipment confiscated. (Patricia Smith Collection.)

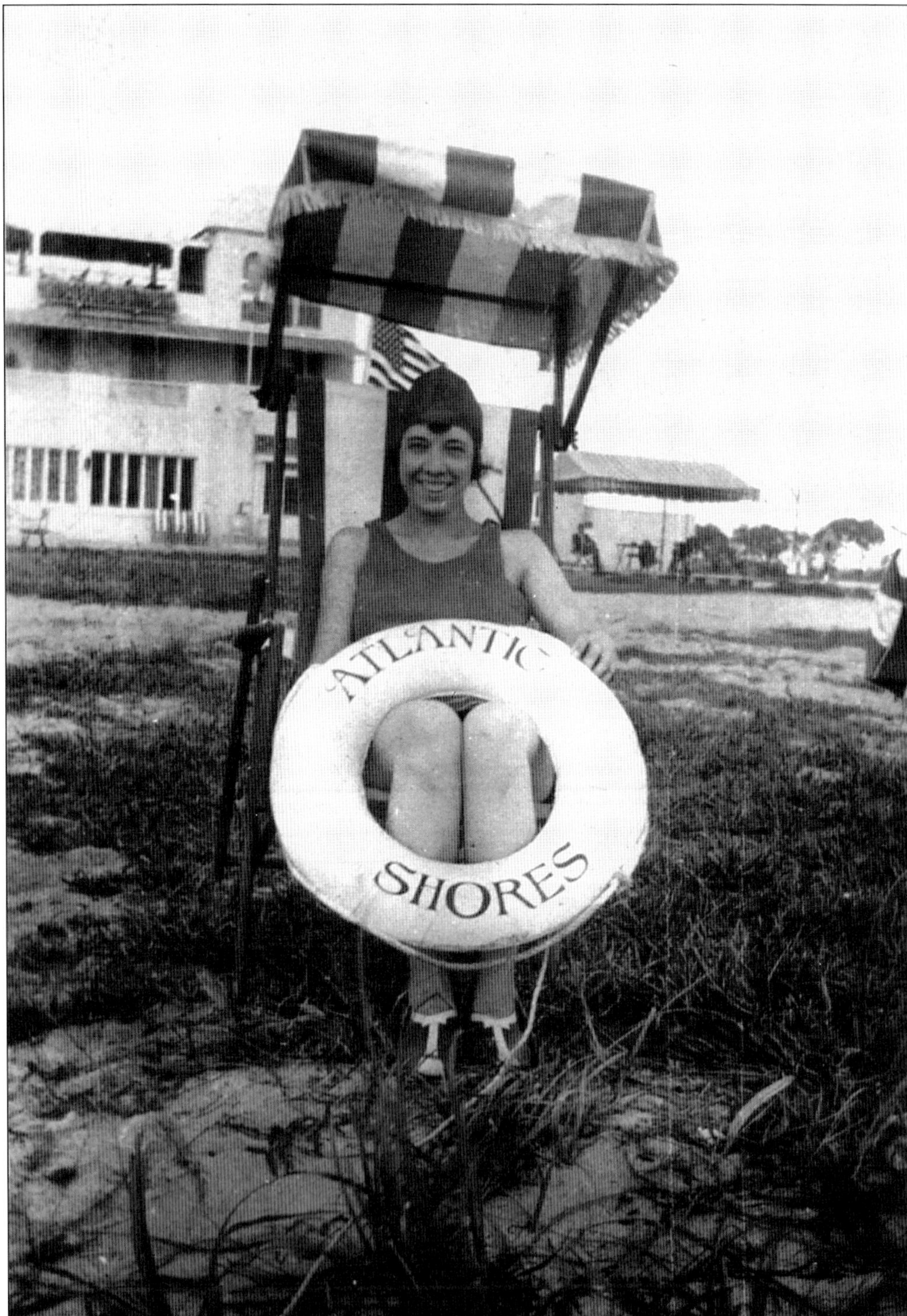

A young woman seated in a beach chair holds a life preserver from the Atlantic Shores Apartments, possibly for an advertising or publicity shot. The Atlantic Shores Apartments were located at 1500 South Ocean Drive. (General Collection.)

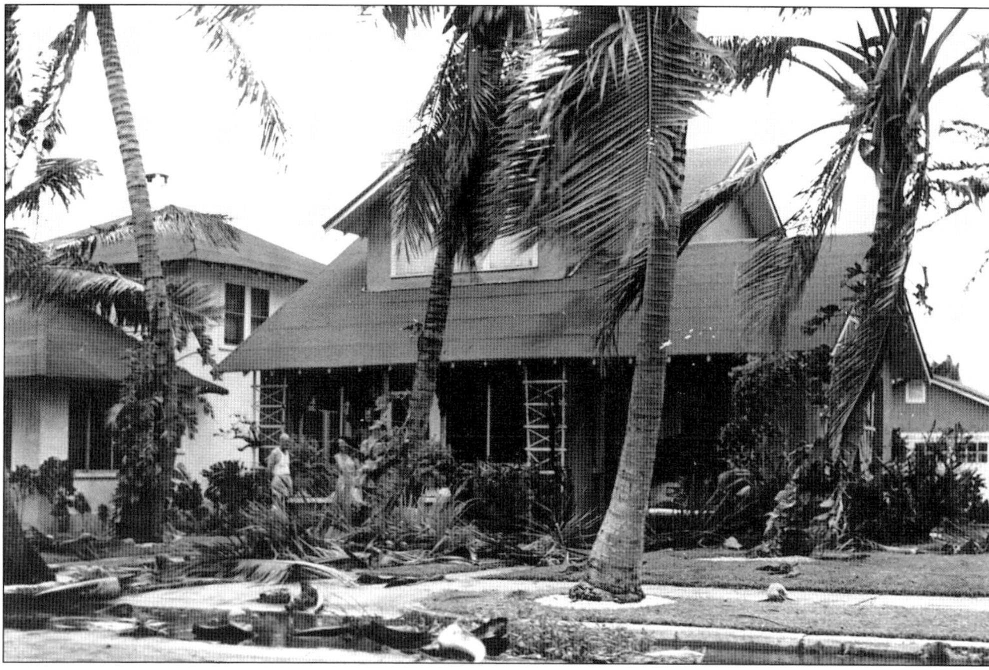

Two hurricanes in 1947, one on September 17 and the other on October 11, hit Hollywood. The first caused major damage on the beach, but resulted in no deaths. The Edwin H. Whitson home at 1624 Monroe Street suffered typical "in-town" damage. (Whitson Collection.)

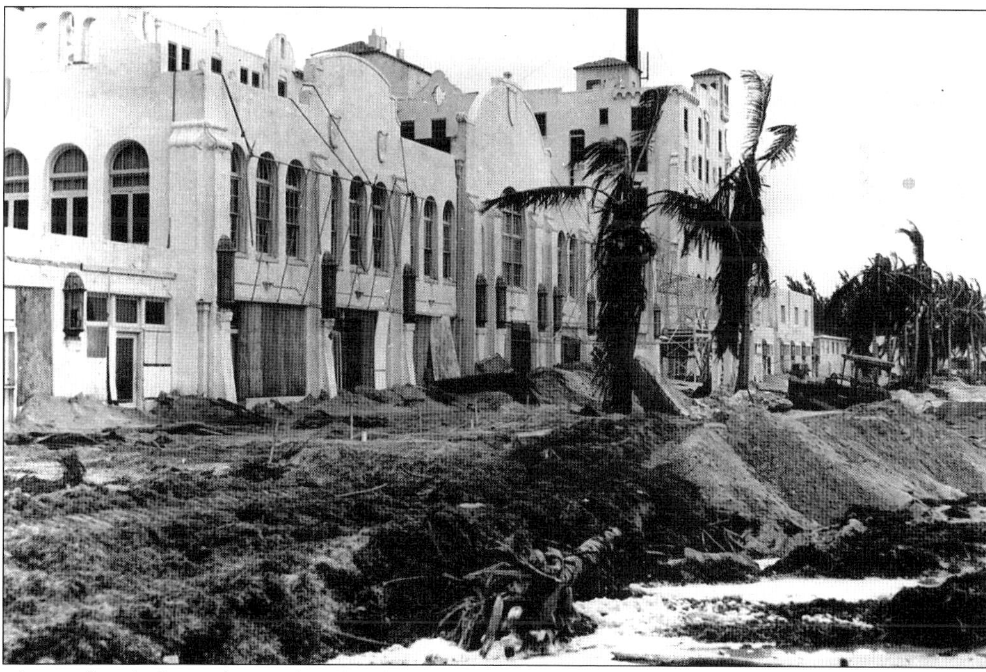

The Hollywood Beach Hotel suffered some damage during the September storm. A note on the back of the original photograph reads, "Notice how the waves have cut the beach back many feet. It will take much work and money if tourists will have any comfortable place to sit this winter." (Whitson Collection.)

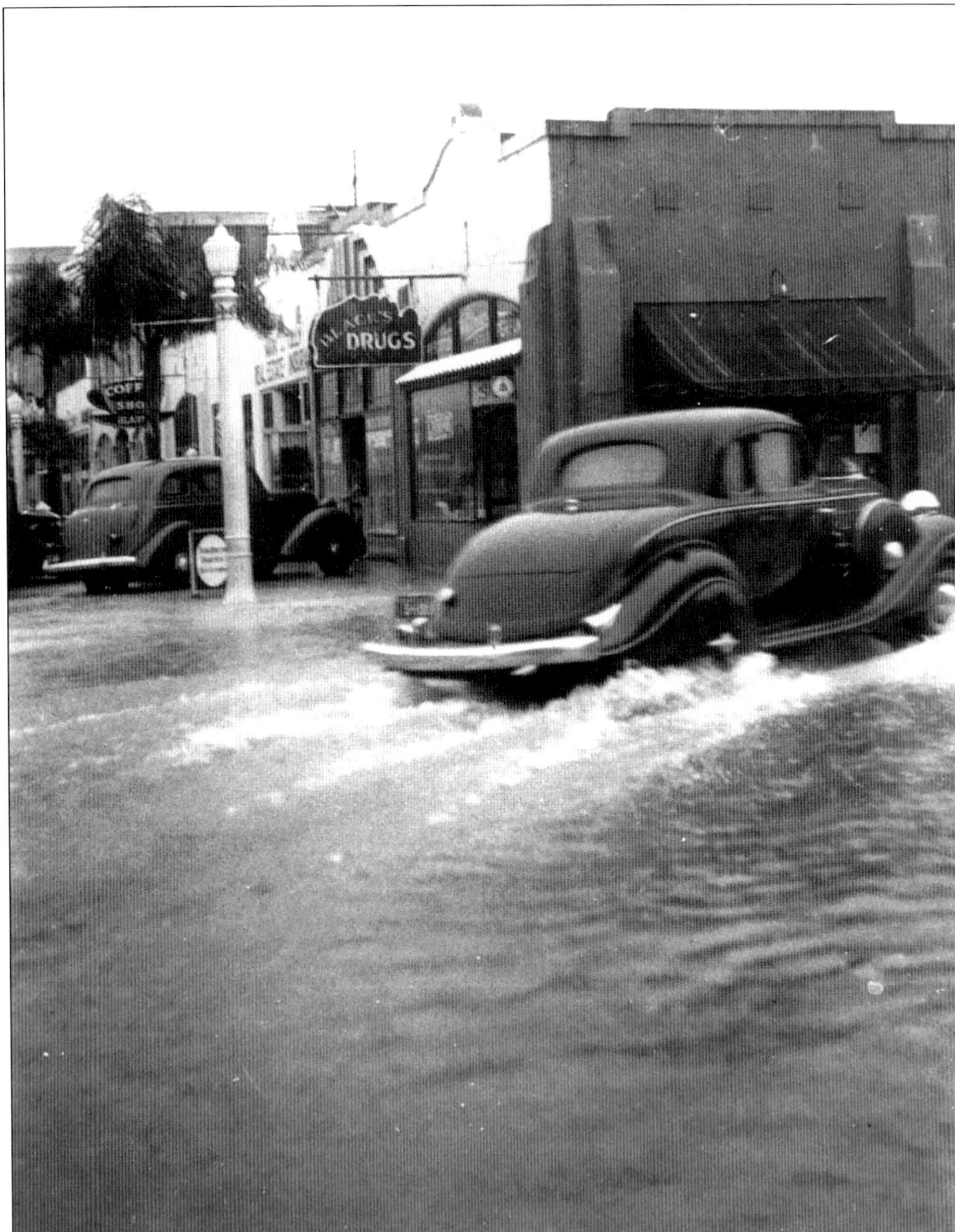

The October storm, while actually less severe than the earlier storm, caused more damage because of its "wet" nature. Torrential rains inundated the area causing massive flooding throughout South Florida. Pembroke Road, Taft Street, Johnson Street, and Hollywood Boulevard, seen here, were nearly impassable. (Patricia Smith Collection.)

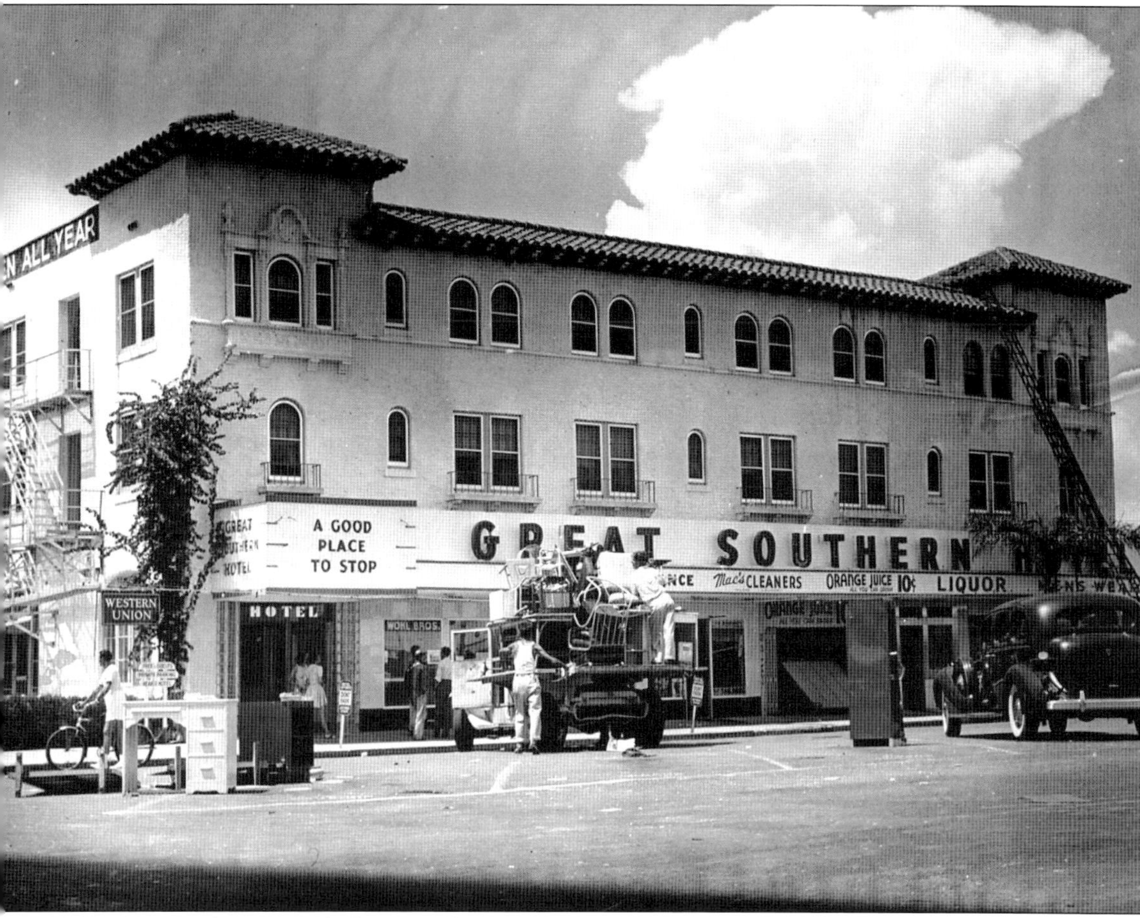

The Great Southern Hotel, the second hotel built by Joseph Young, was completed in the fall of 1924. It continued to be a dominant part of Hollywood Boulevard throughout the 1940s. The hotel had 100 rooms and was built at a cost of $500,000. (General Collection.)

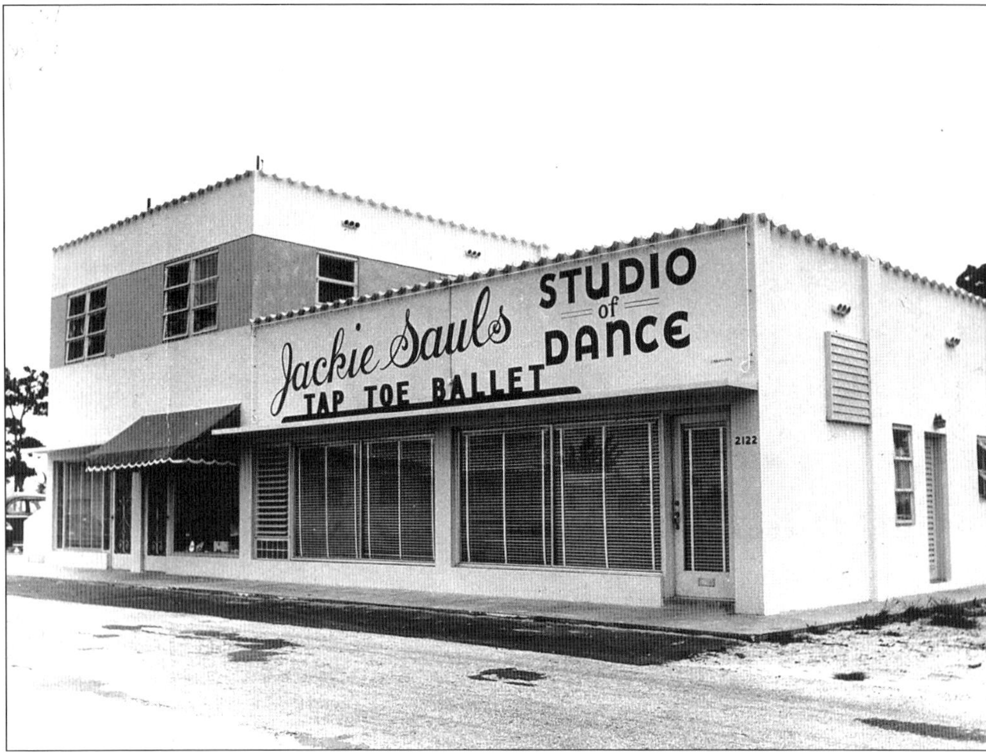

The Jackie Sauls Studio of Dance, 2122 Washington Street, offered dance classes for children and adults. This photograph was taken around 1948. (Elsie Johns Collection.)

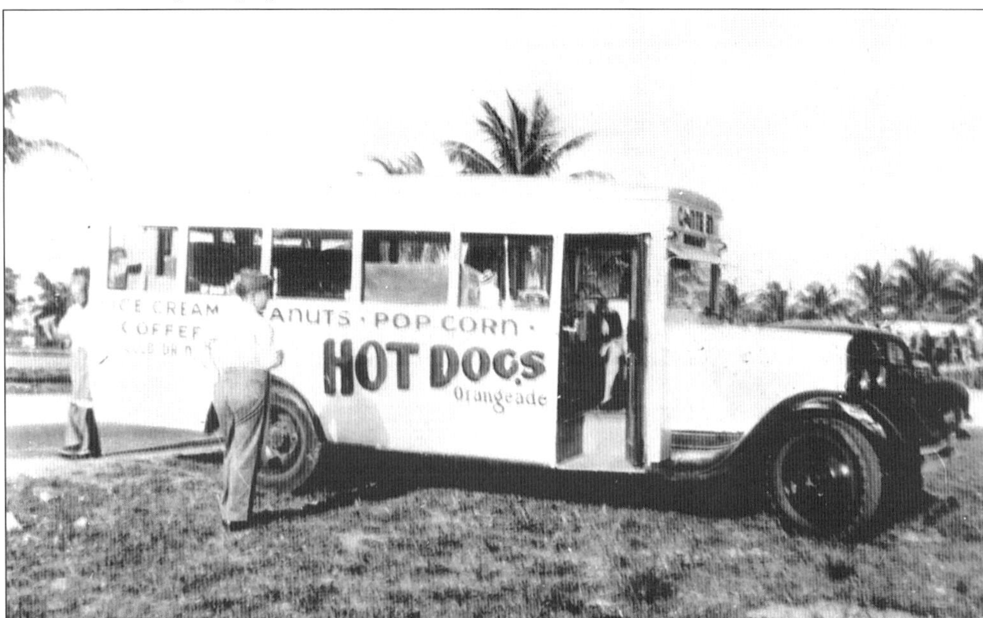

Midge's Canteen, a mobile restaurant serving hot dogs, peanuts, popcorn, and cold drinks to workers in need of a quick lunch, was photographed on December 11, 1946. Millage D. Parr was the proprietor of Midge's Canteen. (General Collection.)

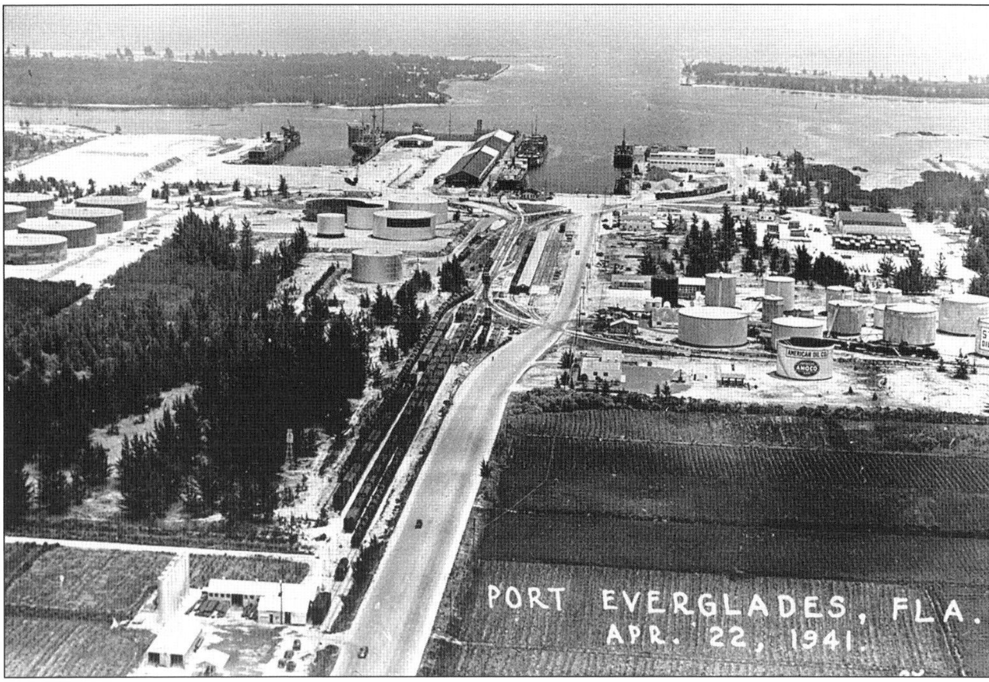

This April 22, 1941 aerial view of Port Everglades shows the channel to the Atlantic. The area in the left background is Fort Lauderdale's Point of Americas and the right background is the area of Hollywood that is now a part of John U. Lloyd State Park. (General Collection.)

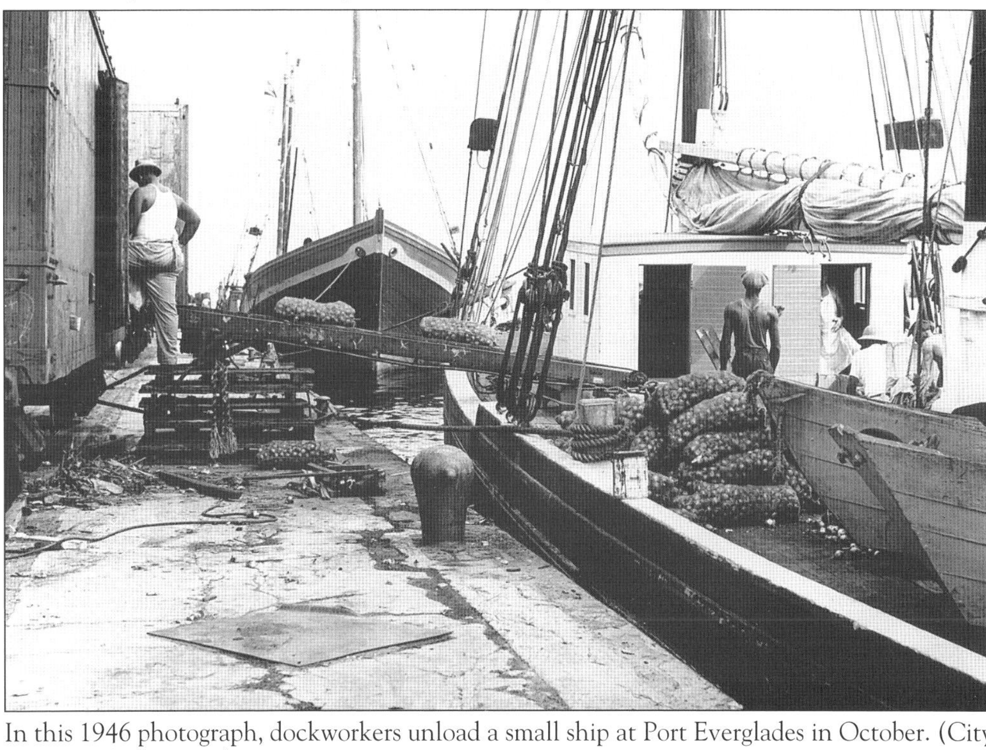

In this 1946 photograph, dockworkers unload a small ship at Port Everglades in October. (City Manager Collection.)

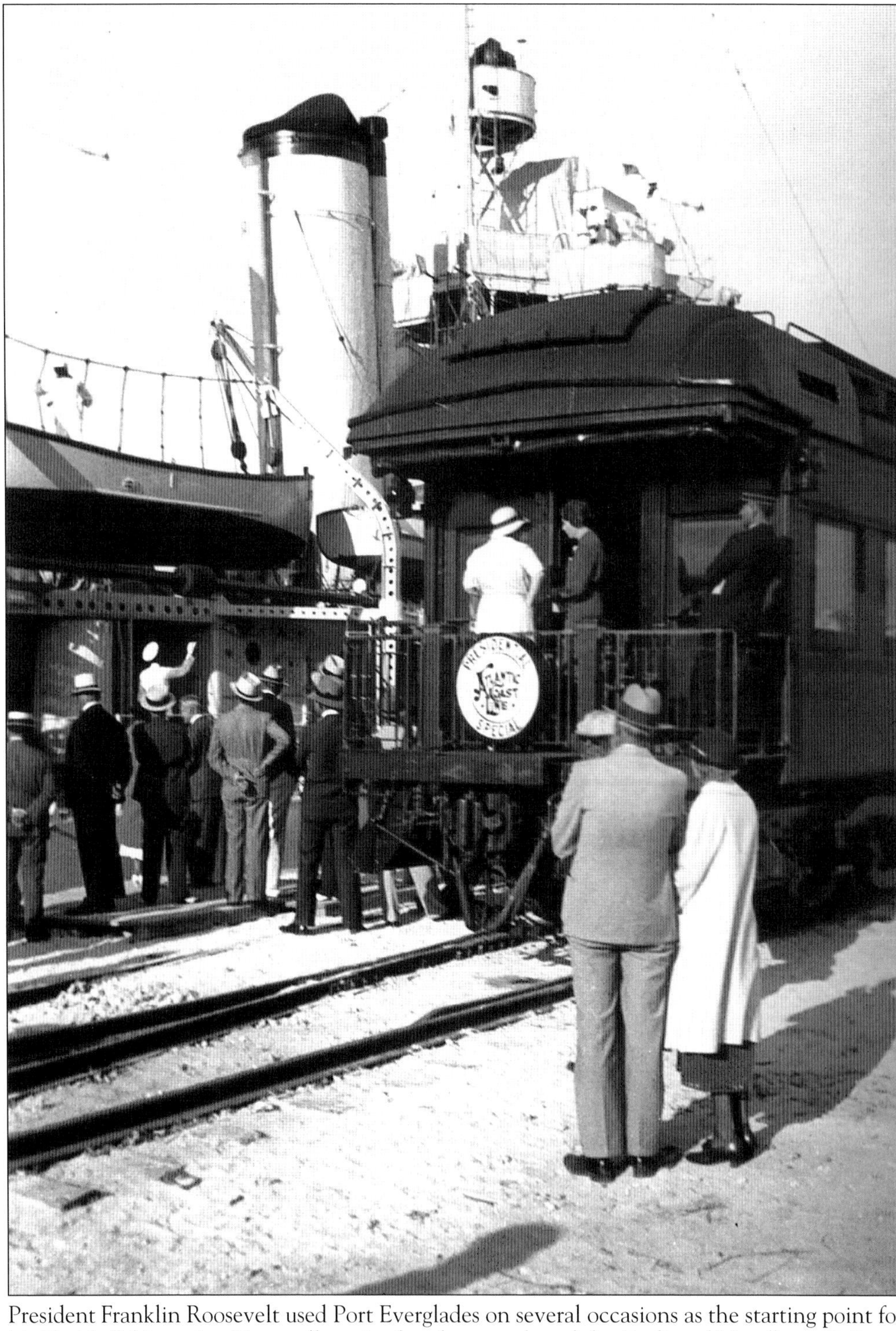

President Franklin Roosevelt used Port Everglades on several occasions as the starting point for his Florida fishing trips. He usually arrived at the port aboard the *Ferdinand Magellan*, a Pullman railroad car custom-built for the President. It was presented to Roosevelt on December 18, 1942, and he used it until his death in 1945. (Patricia Smith Collection.)

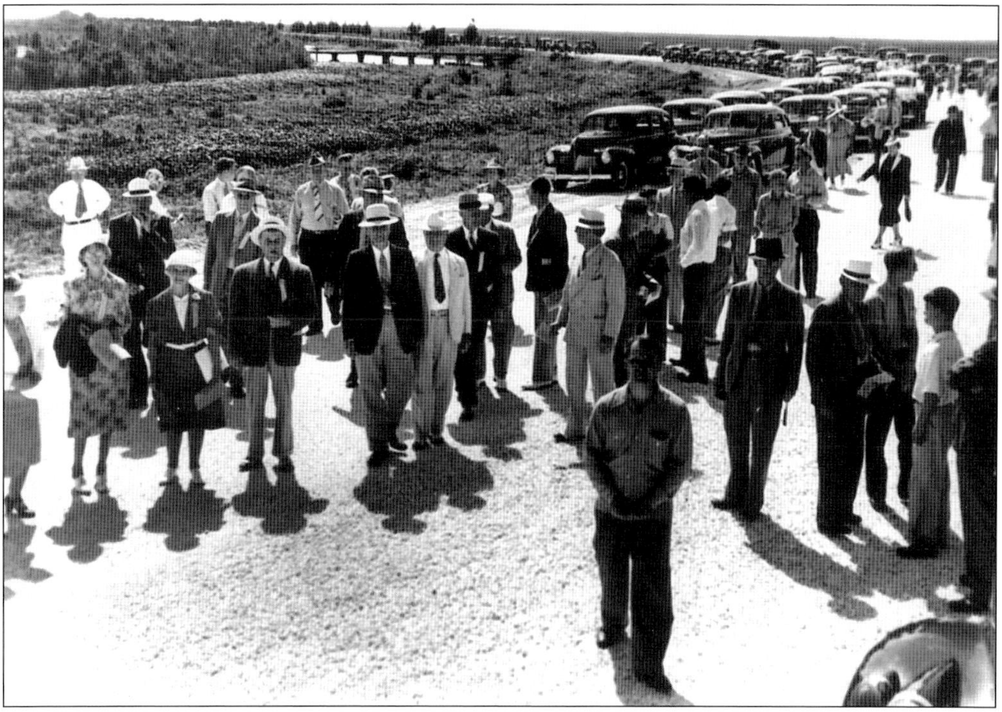

By the 1940s, automobile traffic was increasing at a rapid pace. New roads were needed to accommodate travelers arriving in Hollywood by car. In April 1941, Road 26 (later State Road 84), connecting southern Broward County to Lake Okeechobee, was inaugurated. Hollywood civic leaders led a caravan to the dedication ceremony. (Al Vessella Collection.)

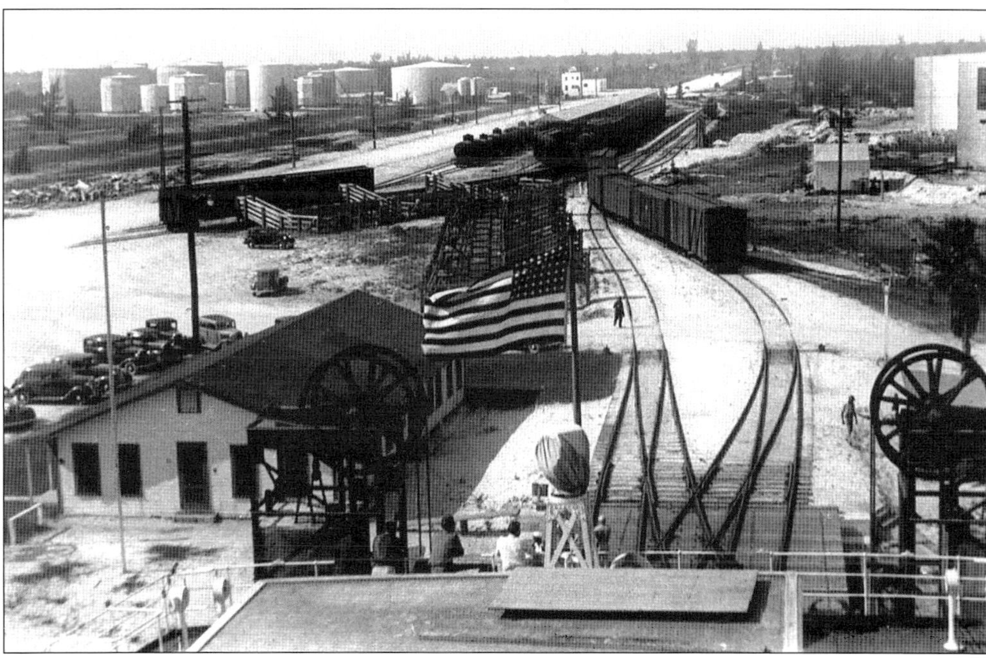

This 1940s view of Port Everglades was taken from the deck of a ferry as railroad cars were eased into position. (Patricia Smith Collection.)

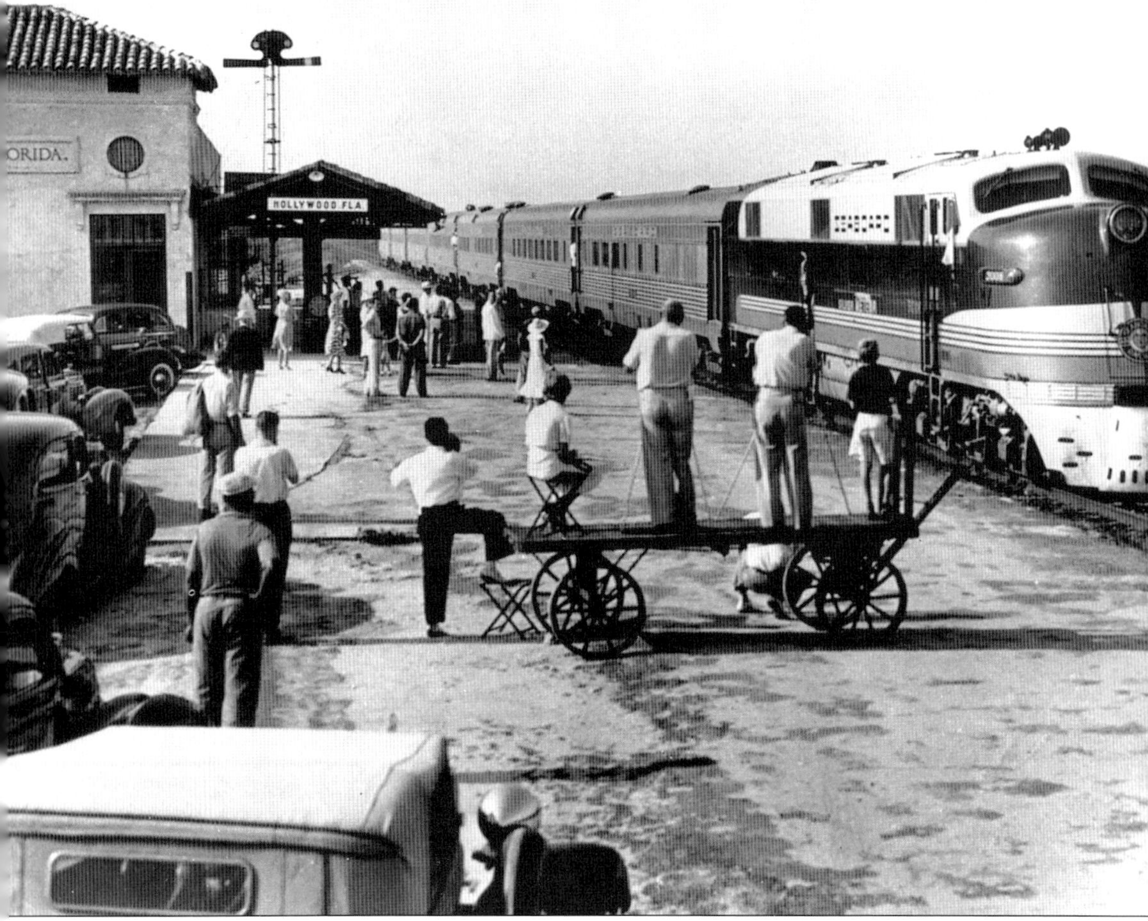

The Seaboard Airline's first diesel locomotive to stop in Hollywood pulled into the station at 3001 Hollywood Boulevard in the 1940s. It was an important enough event to draw a small crowd and several photographers to record the occasion. (General Collection.)

Four

THE 1950s

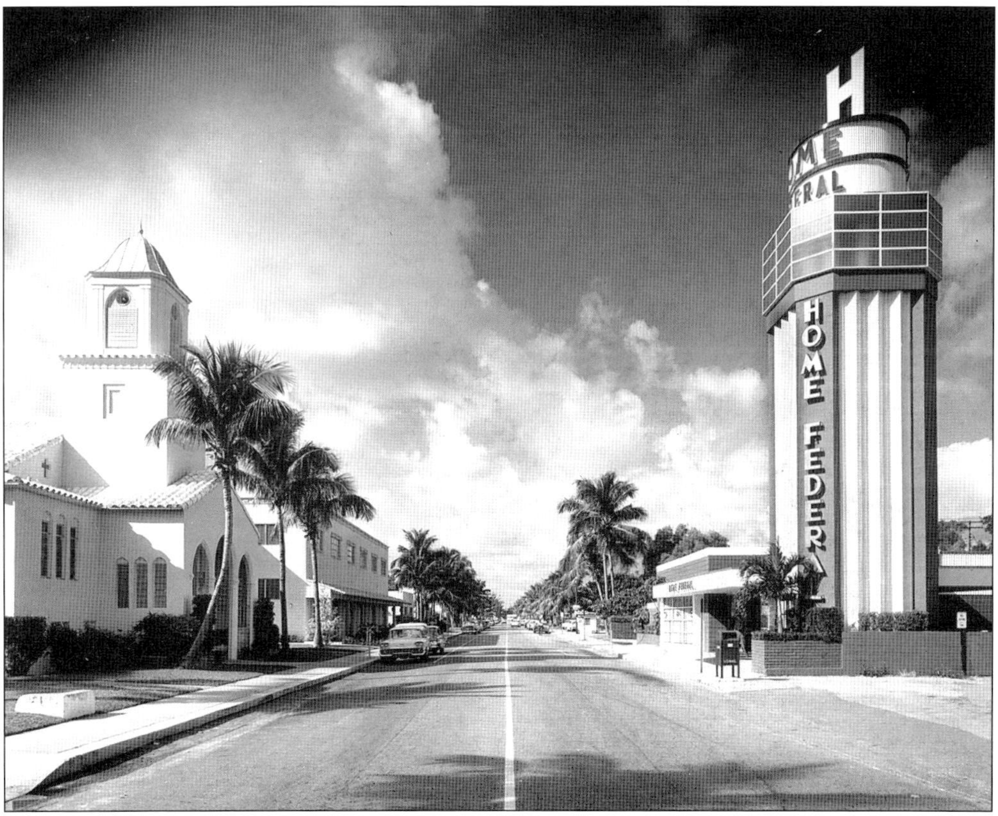

The distinctive tower of the Home Federal Savings and Loan building rises above the spire of the Temple Methodist Church (now First United Methodist) at 1819 Van Buren Street. This photograph was taken in 1958. (General Collection.)

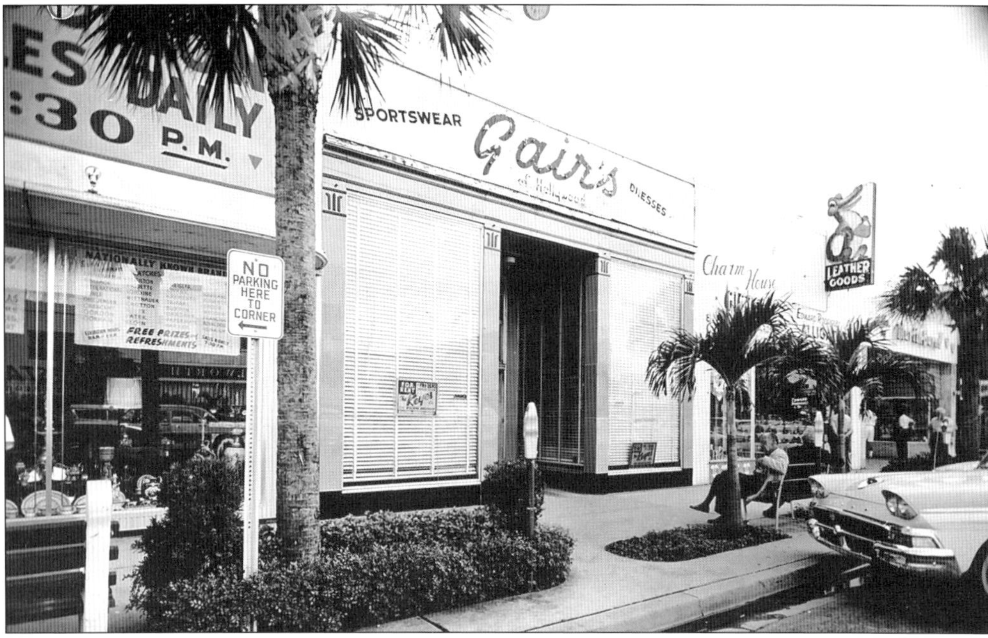

Businesses in 1950s Hollywood still favored downtown over the less-traveled areas. This view includes Gair's of Hollywood at 1902 Hollywood Boulevard (available for rent through Keyes Realty), Charm House Gifts at 1904, Leather Goods at 1904 1/2, and Martin-Burns at 1906 Hollywood Boulevard. Benches were provided along the boulevard for weary shoppers. (General Collection.)

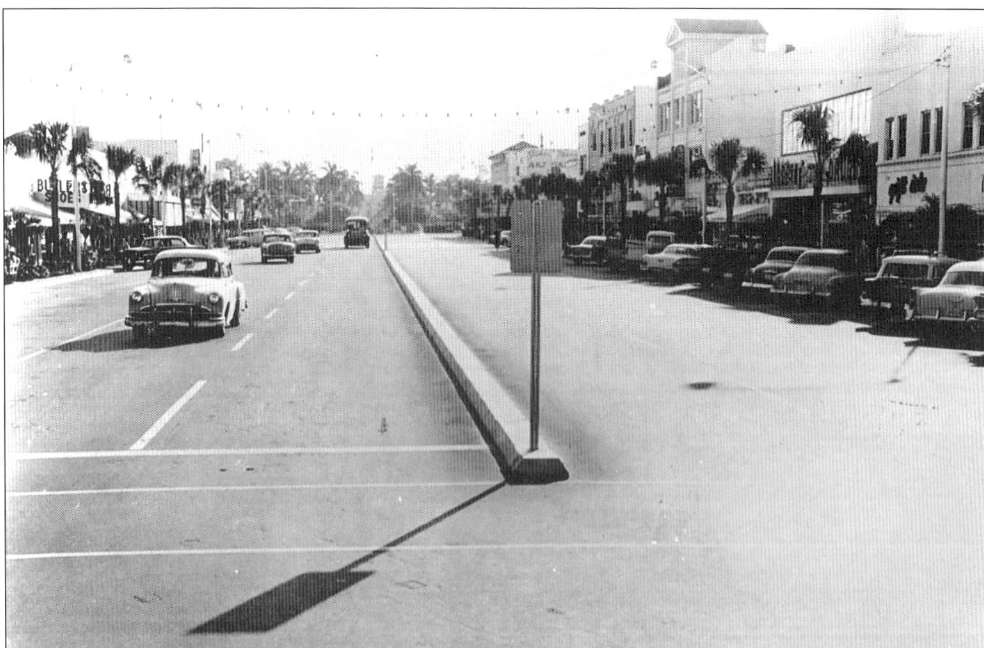

This 1959 image looks east down Hollywood Boulevard in relatively light traffic. The businesses pictured include Town and Resort at 1938 Hollywood Boulevard, the Gift Isle at 1936, and the Liggett Drug Store at 1932 Hollywood Boulevard. (General Collection.)

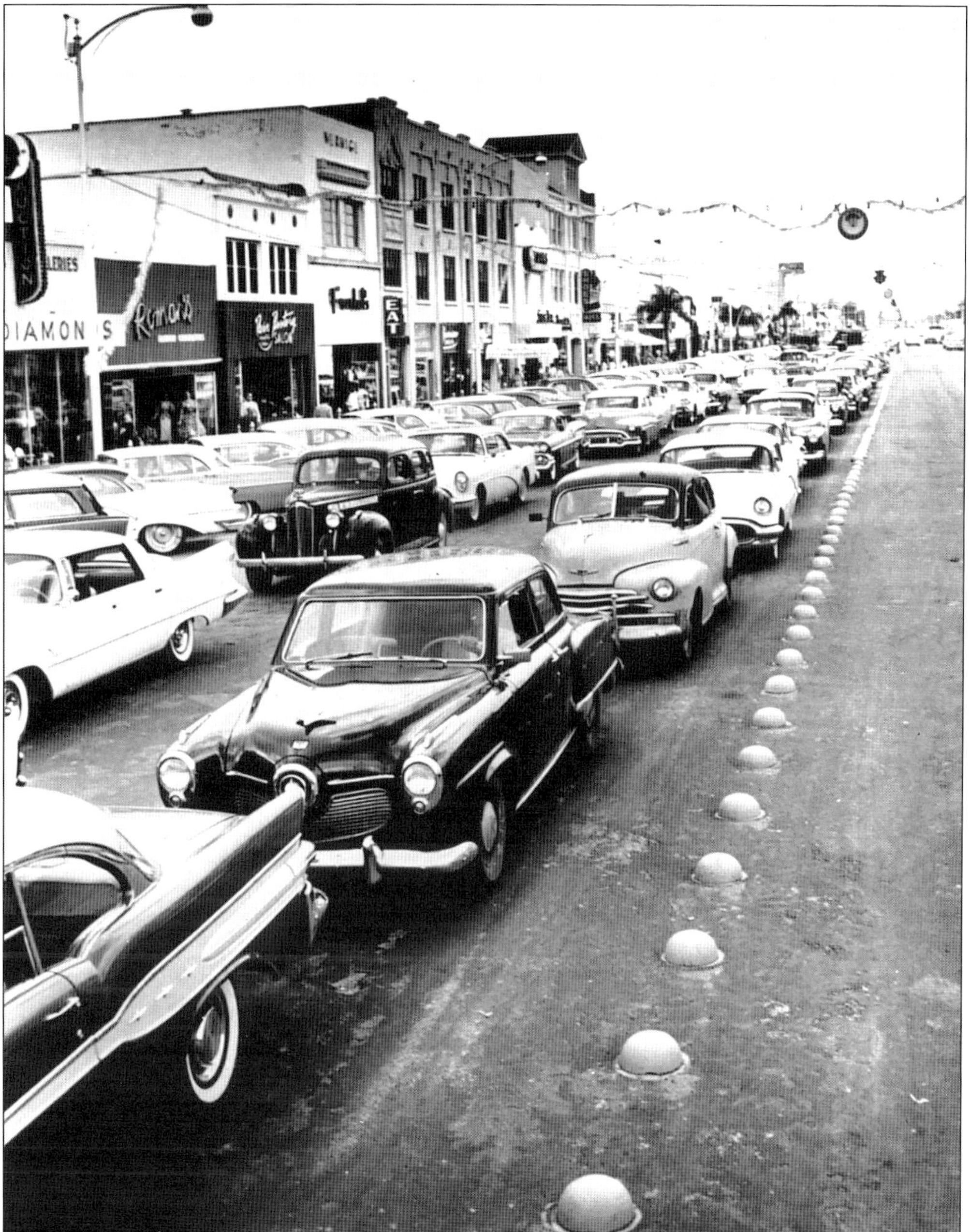

On January 6, 1958, at the time this photograph was taken, Hollywood Boulevard was still decked out in its holiday finery. In-season eastbound traffic was heavy passing the Half Moon Art Gallery at 1908 Hollywood Boulevard, Roman's at 1910, the Rose Bootery at 1912, and Frankel's at 1914 Hollywood Boulevard. (General Collection.)

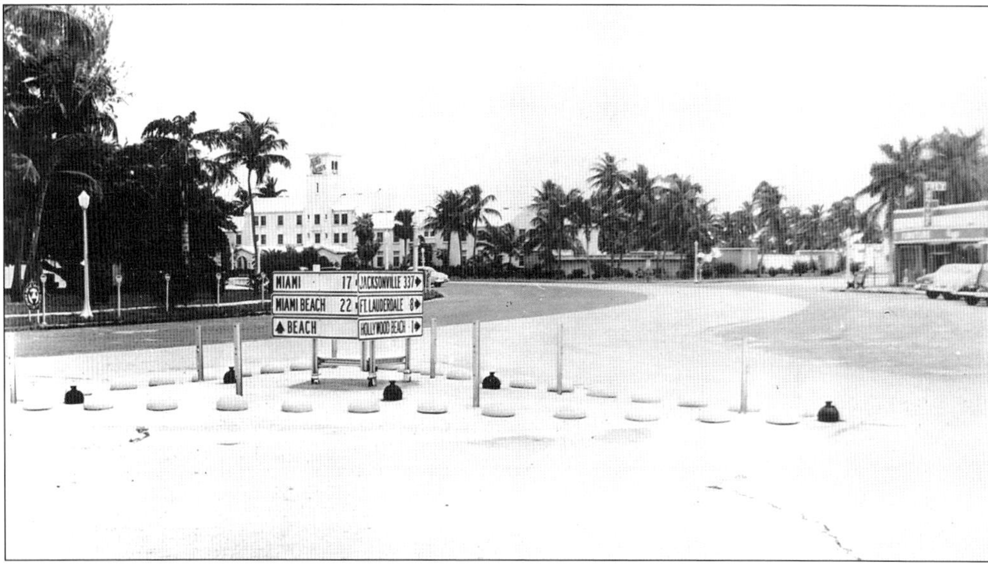

This view is the 1953 version of traffic on Young Circle where northbound Federal Highway intersects the circle. The Park View Hotel is in the background. (General Collection.)

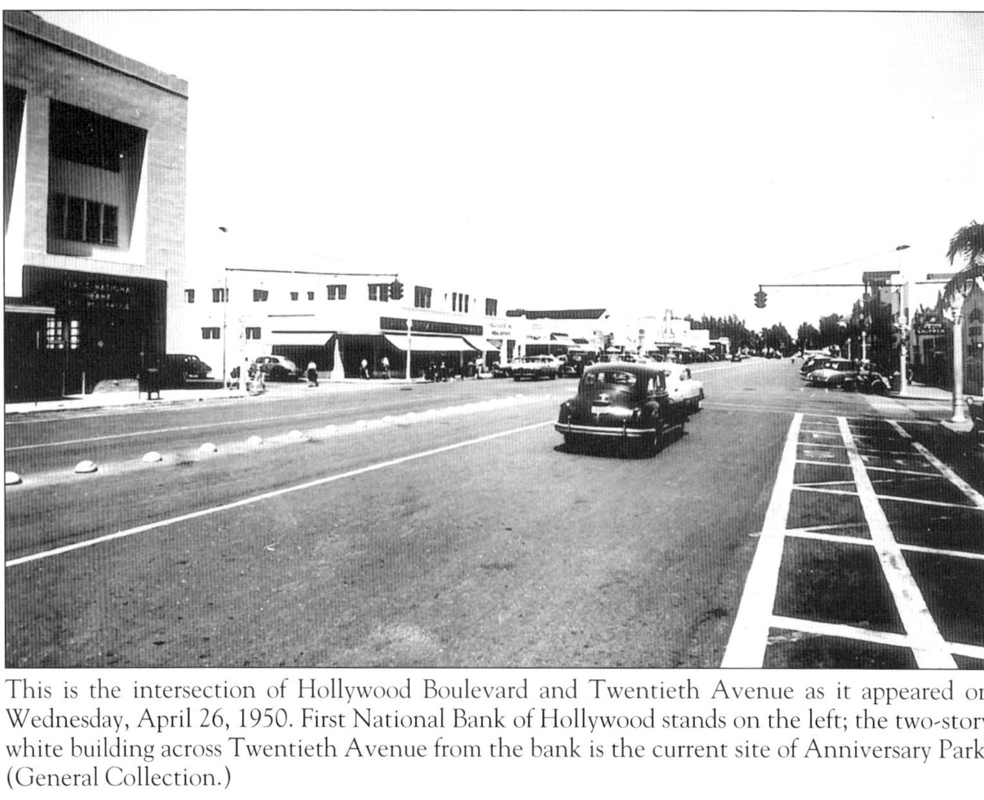

This is the intersection of Hollywood Boulevard and Twentieth Avenue as it appeared on Wednesday, April 26, 1950. First National Bank of Hollywood stands on the left; the two-story white building across Twentieth Avenue from the bank is the current site of Anniversary Park. (General Collection.)

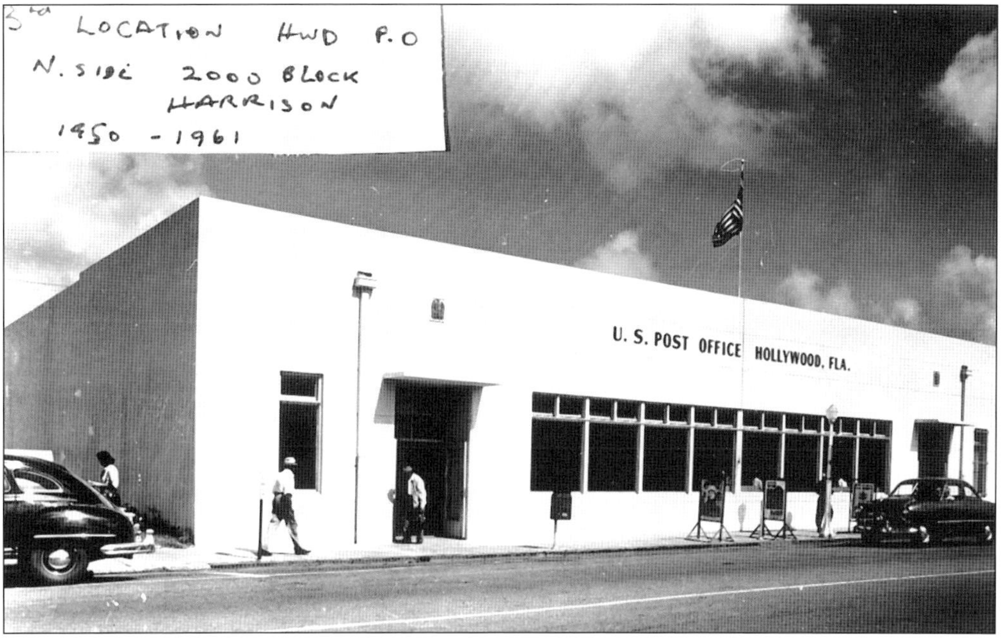

During the 1950s, Hollywood's U.S. Post Office occupied the third of its four locations. The first post office was destroyed by the 1926 hurricane; the second location was in the First National Bank building on Hollywood Boulevard. This building served as the post office at 2029 Harrison Street from 1950 to 1961. (General Collection.)

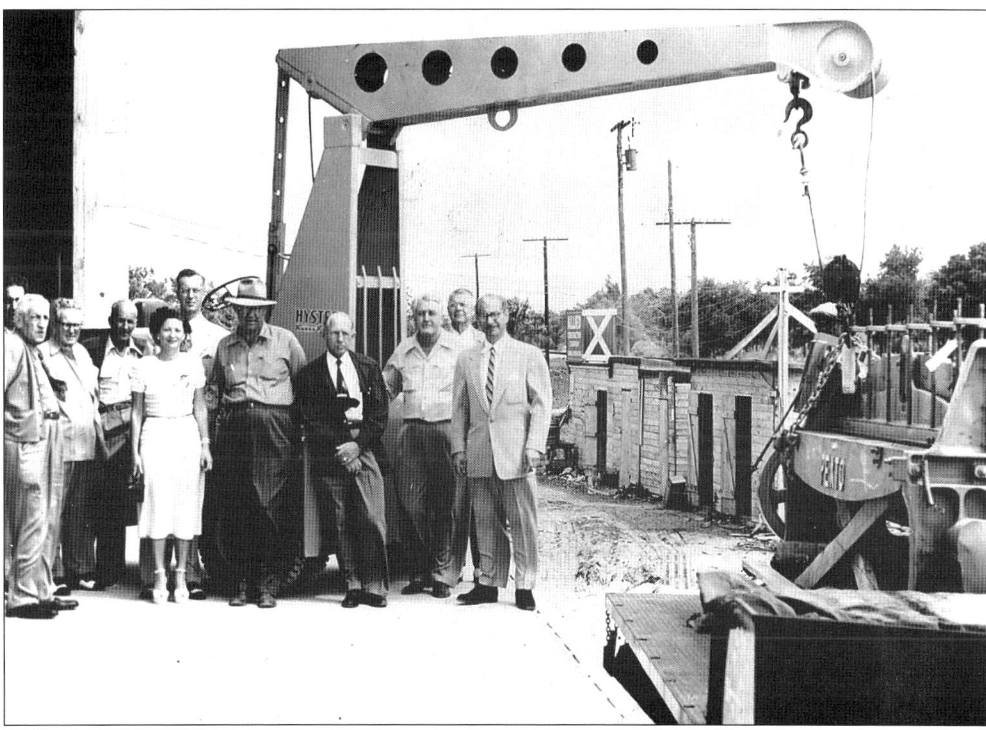

Employees of the Heinicke electronics plant pose on their loading dock along the Florida East Coast railroad tracks and Harding Street on March 29, 1951. (General Collection.)

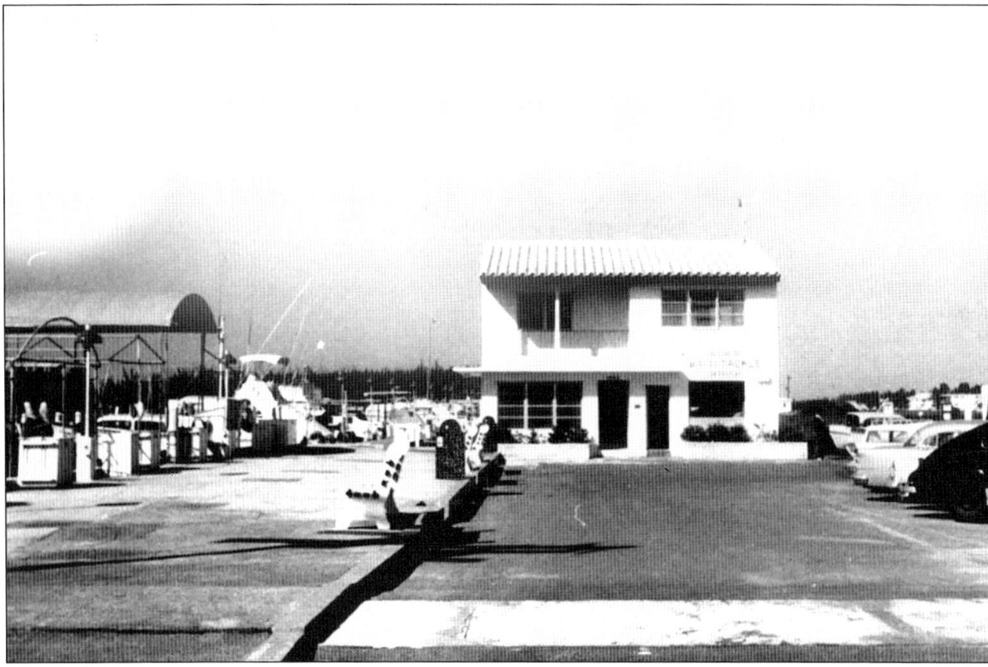

Bob's Bait and Tackle Shop operated out of the Hollywood Marina at 700 Polk Street. (General Collection.)

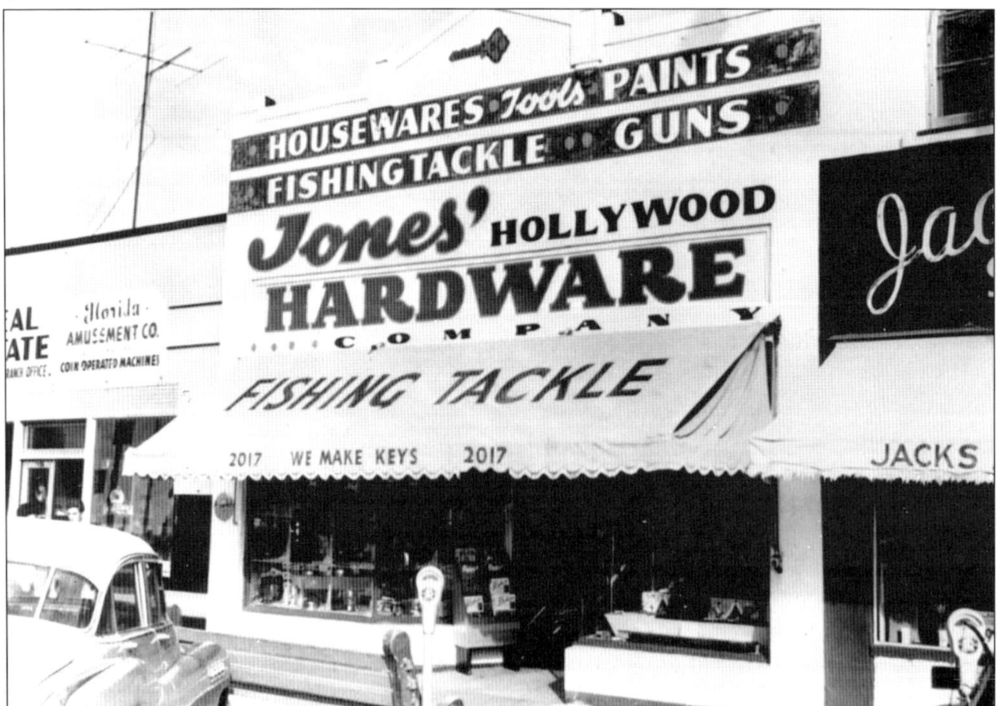

Jones's Hollywood Hardware Company at 2017 Hollywood Boulevard was one of the favorite destinations for the do-it-yourselfer before the days of huge home repair centers. (General Collection.)

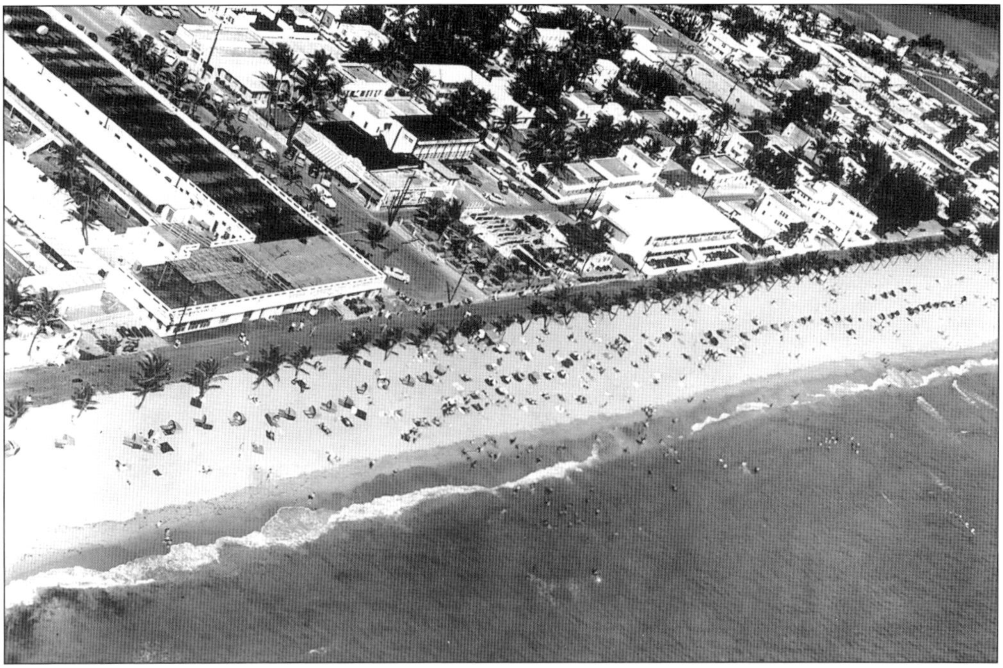

Johnson Street and the Broadwalk, shown here in 1953, was the home of Murray's Sundry Store and the Beach Delicatessen and Grocery. By the early 1950s, construction had claimed most of the available beach lots. (General Collection.)

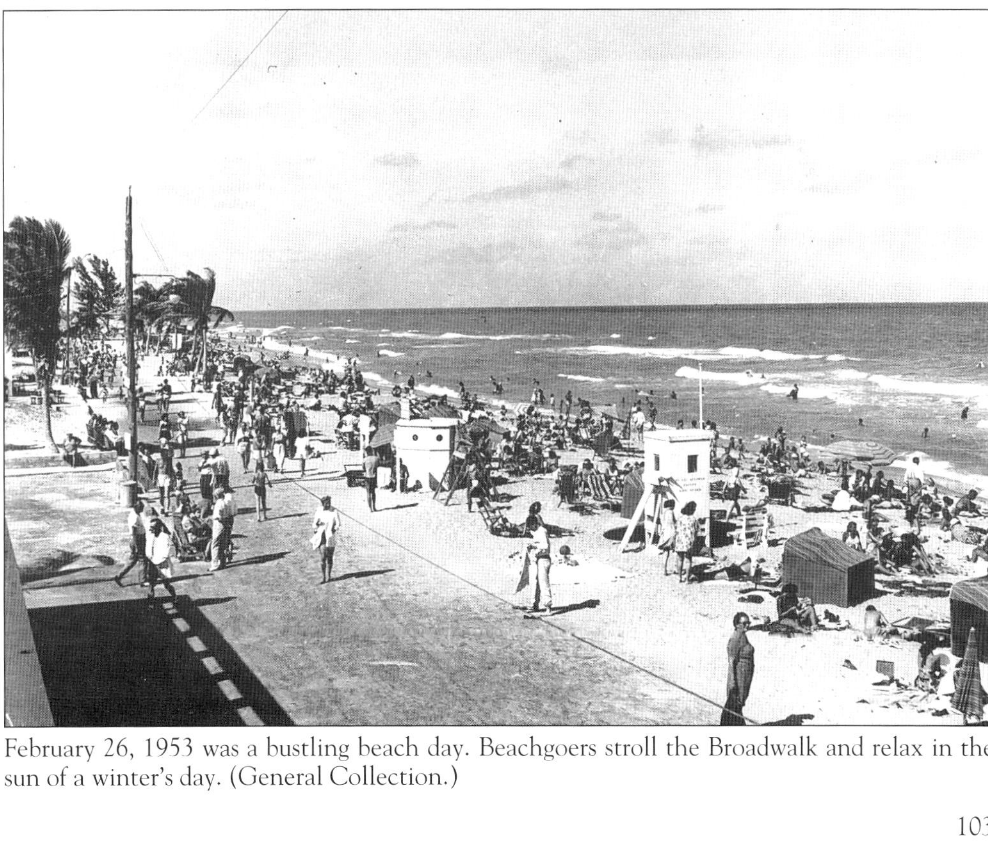

February 26, 1953 was a bustling beach day. Beachgoers stroll the Broadwalk and relax in the sun of a winter's day. (General Collection.)

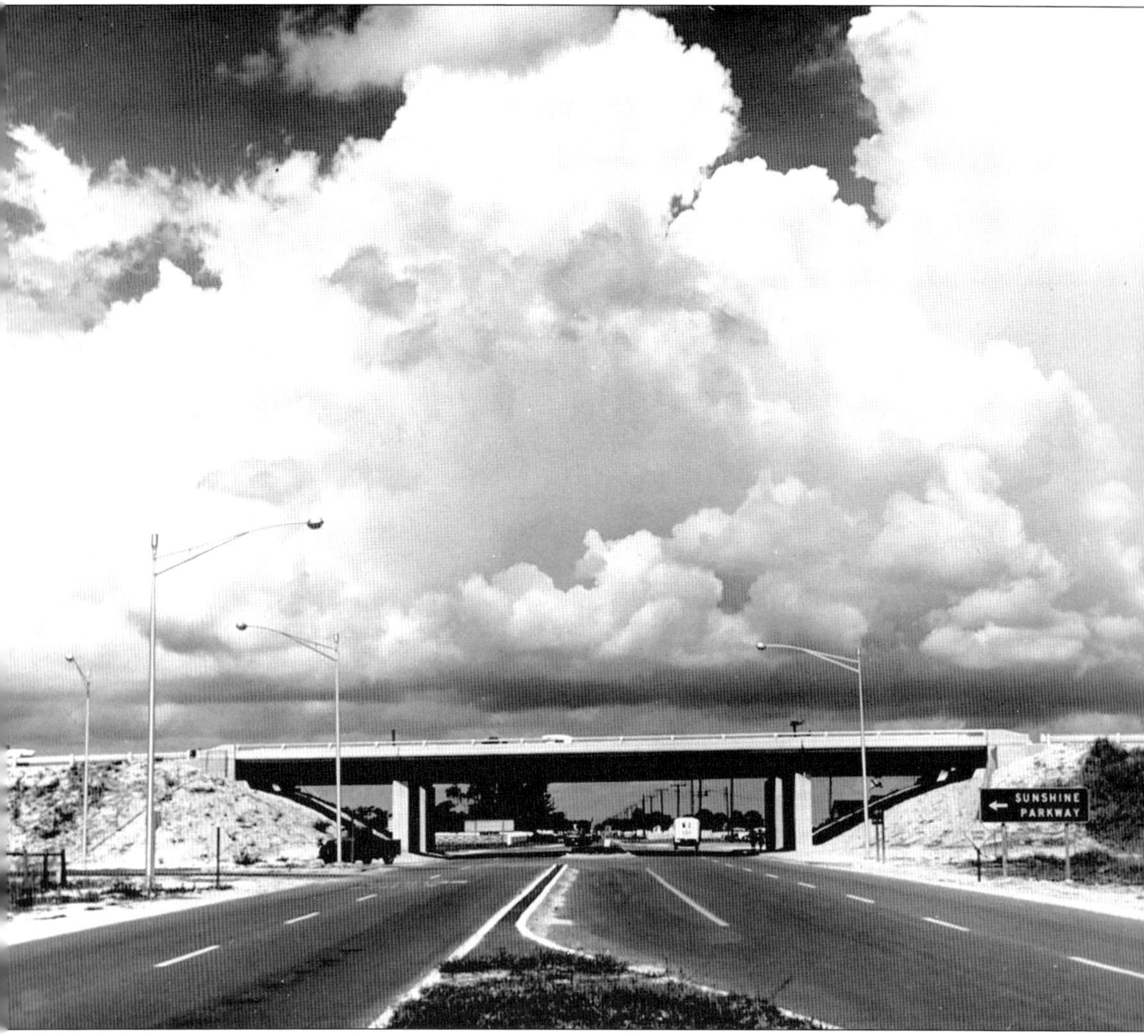

West Hollywood, not yet a part of the City of Hollywood, remained relatively undeveloped in the 1950s. This is the intersection of Hollywood Boulevard and the Florida Turnpike on June 27, 1957. (General Collection.)

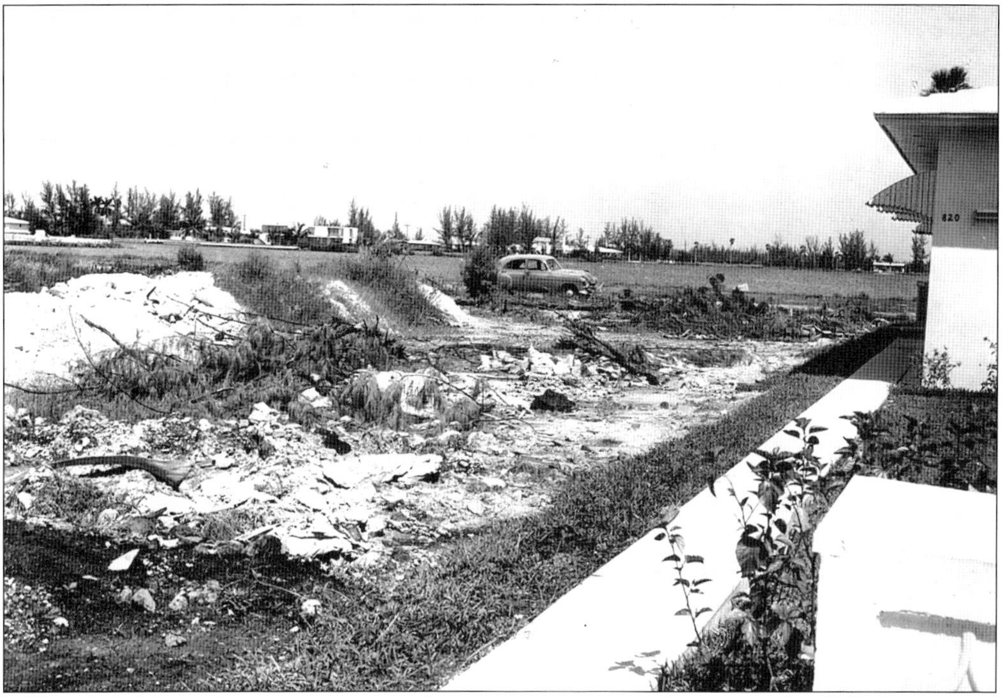

West Hollywood was primarily a bedroom community for Hollywood in the 1950s. Residential building, as seen here in the 1956 photograph, was the primary construction of the decade. (General Collection.)

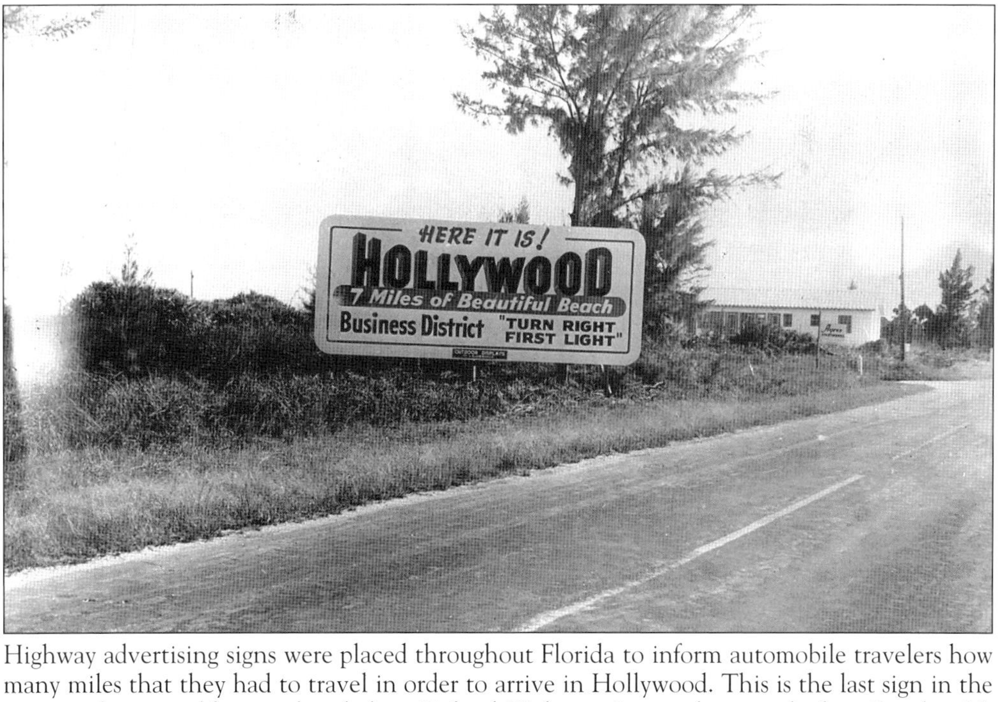

Highway advertising signs were placed throughout Florida to inform automobile travelers how many miles that they had to travel in order to arrive in Hollywood. This is the last sign in the series and presumably was placed along Federal Highway. It was photographed on October 15, 1951. (General Collection.)

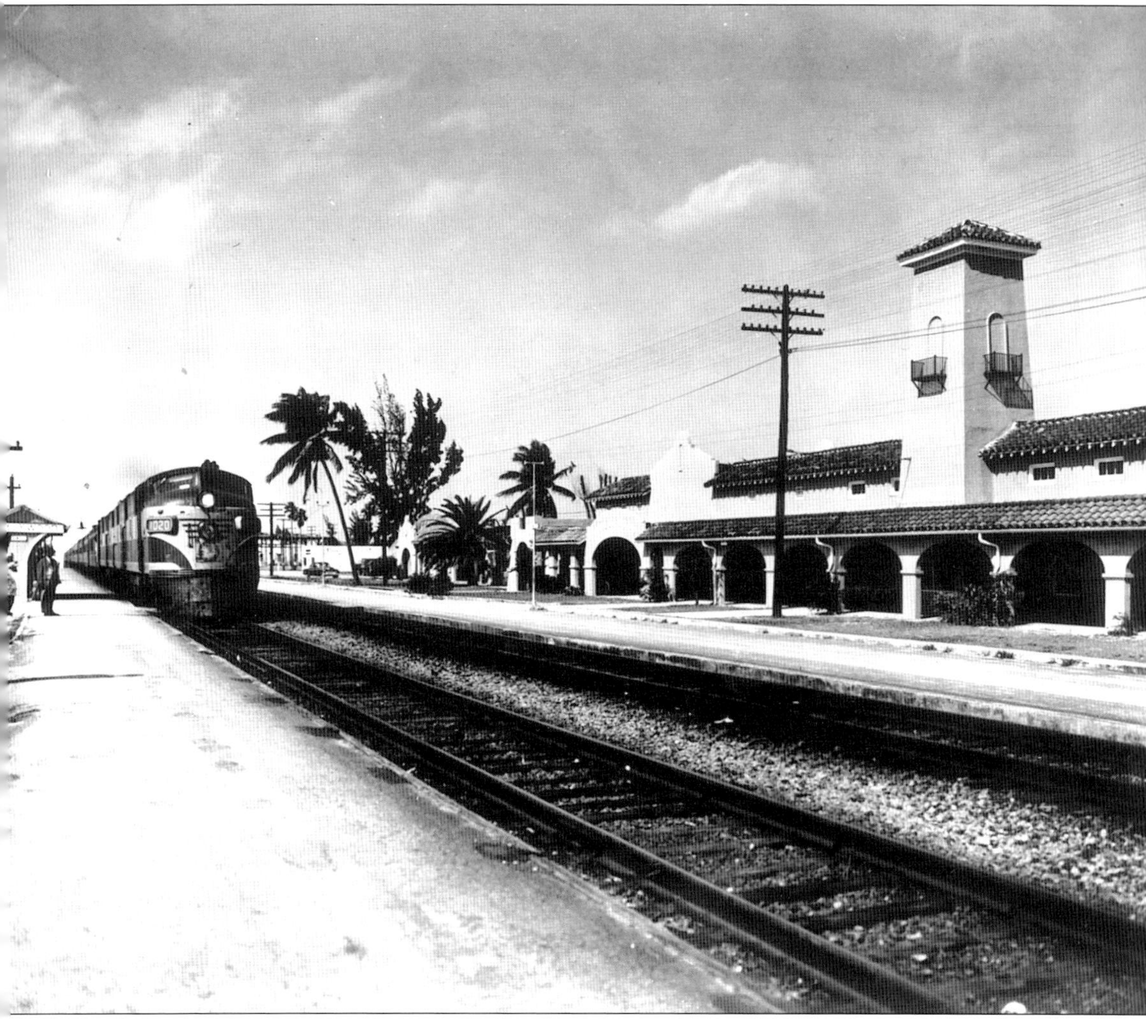

A passenger train approaches the Florida East Coast railroad station at 420 North Twenty-first Avenue. The station was torn down in 1967 and is now the site of the city-owned shuffleboard courts. (General Collection.)

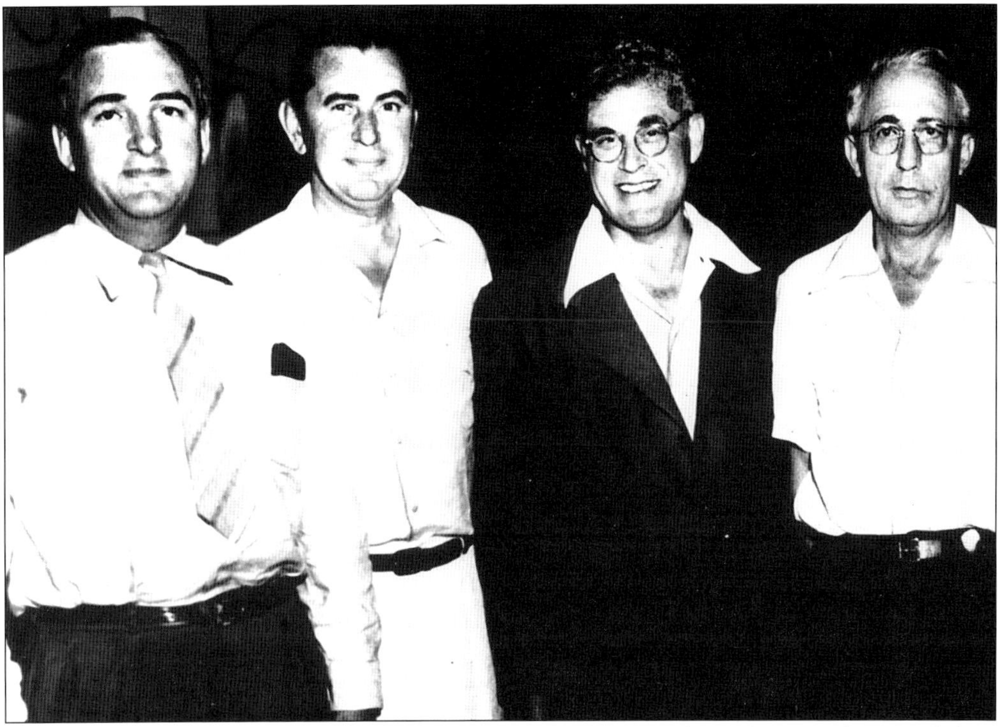

Several officers of the Hollywood Chamber of Commerce pose for a photograph. From left to right, they are C.H. Landfield Jr., E. Rex Judy, Nelson Elsasser, and Fred E. Willis. Landefeld was an attorney, Judy was affiliated with Hollywood Motors, and Willis operated an insurance agency. (Al Vessella Collection.)

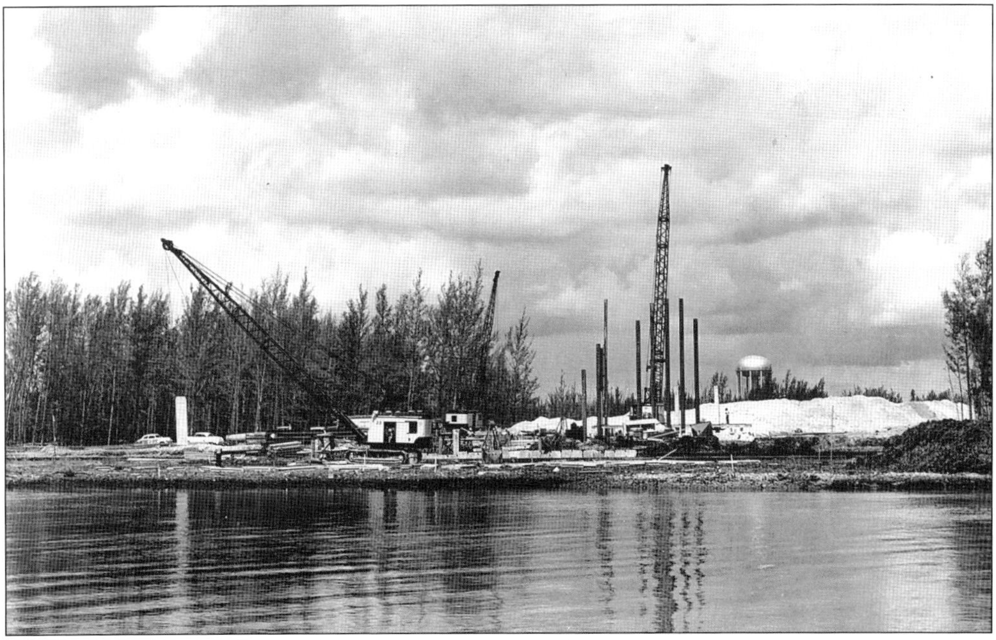

This image is presumed to be the construction of the Sheridan Street Bridge at the Intracoastal Waterway. (General Collection.)

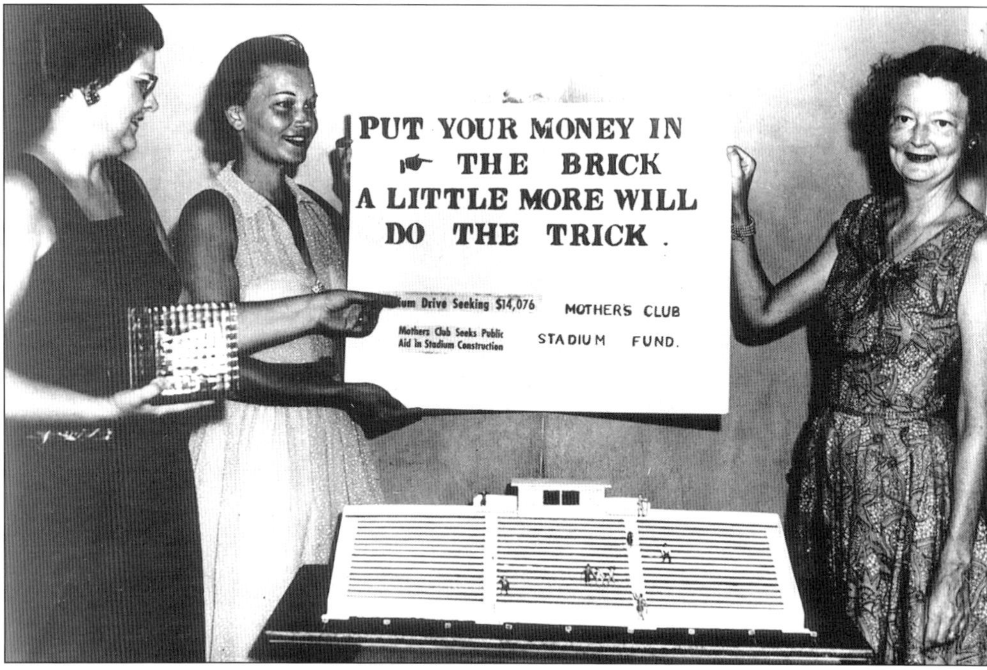

The Mother's Club Stadium Fund Campaign was launched in 1952 to assist in the construction of a stadium. (Al Vessella Collection.)

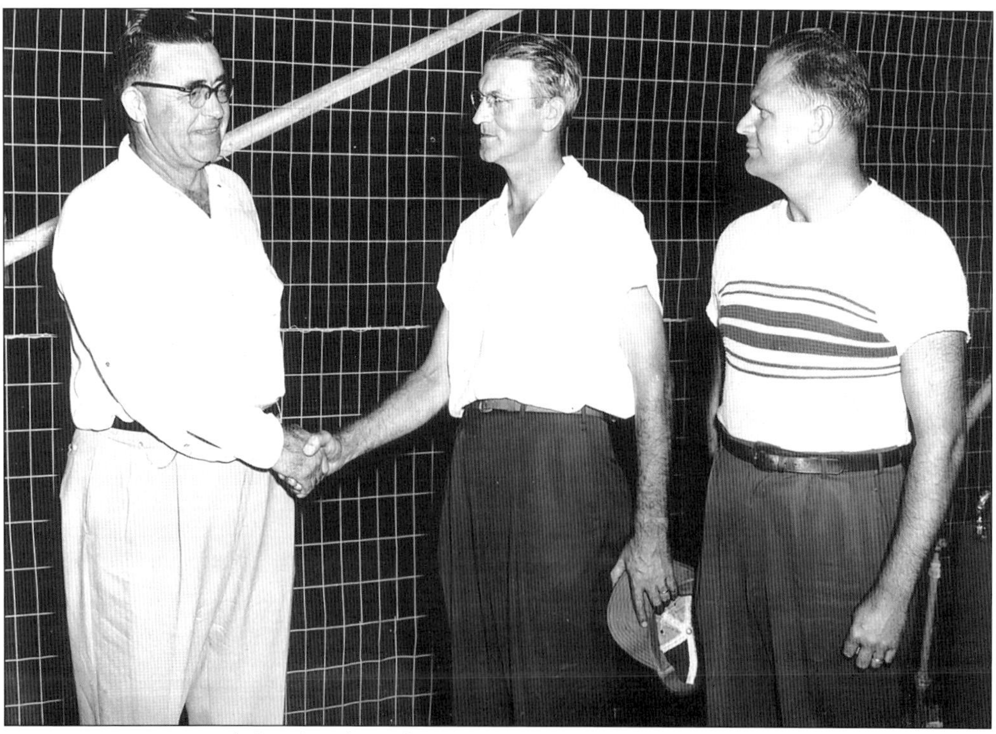

Mayor Lester Boggs shakes hands with J.D. McMichael of Jacksonville as J. Wilton Smith, Jacksonville's recreation director, observes. The photograph appears to have been taken at an athletic event. (General Collection.)

Mayor William G. Zinkil Sr. works at his desk on August 24, 1959. Zinkil was Hollywood's mayor from 1955 to 1957 and from 1959 to 1967. (General Collection.)

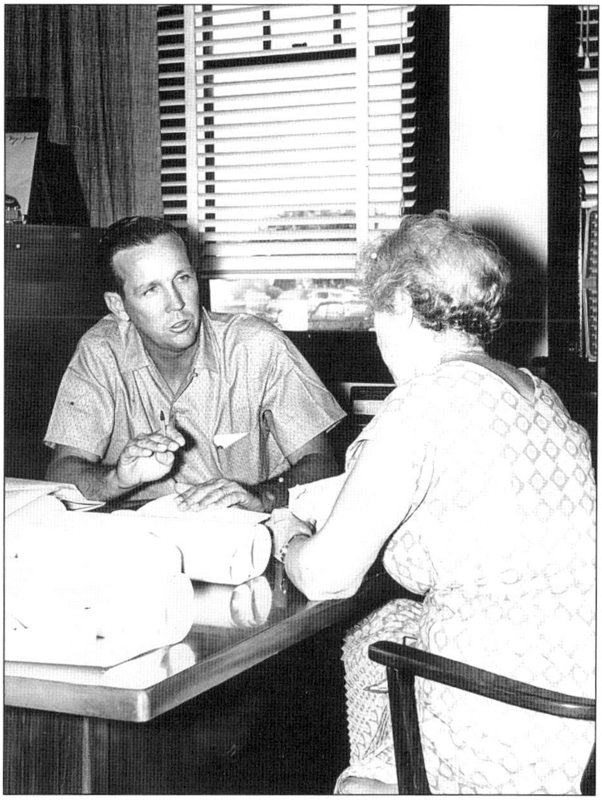

Hollywood's Administration Building, shown here as it appeared in the 1950s, was located in City Hall Circle. It was razed in the late 1960s after the new city hall was completed in 1968. (General Collection.)

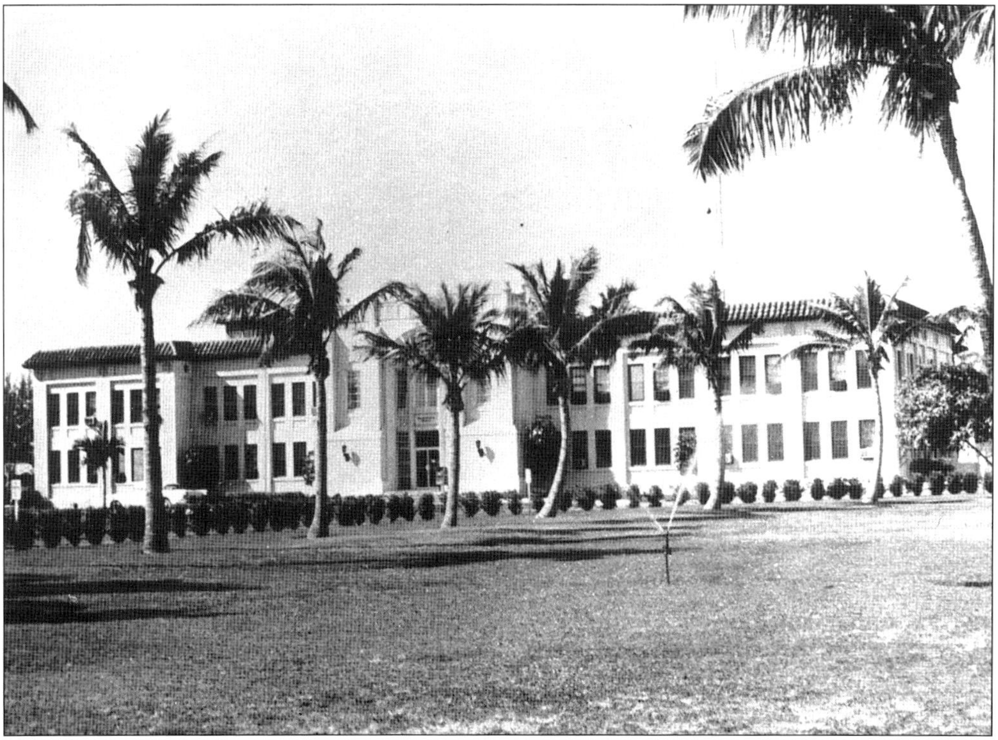

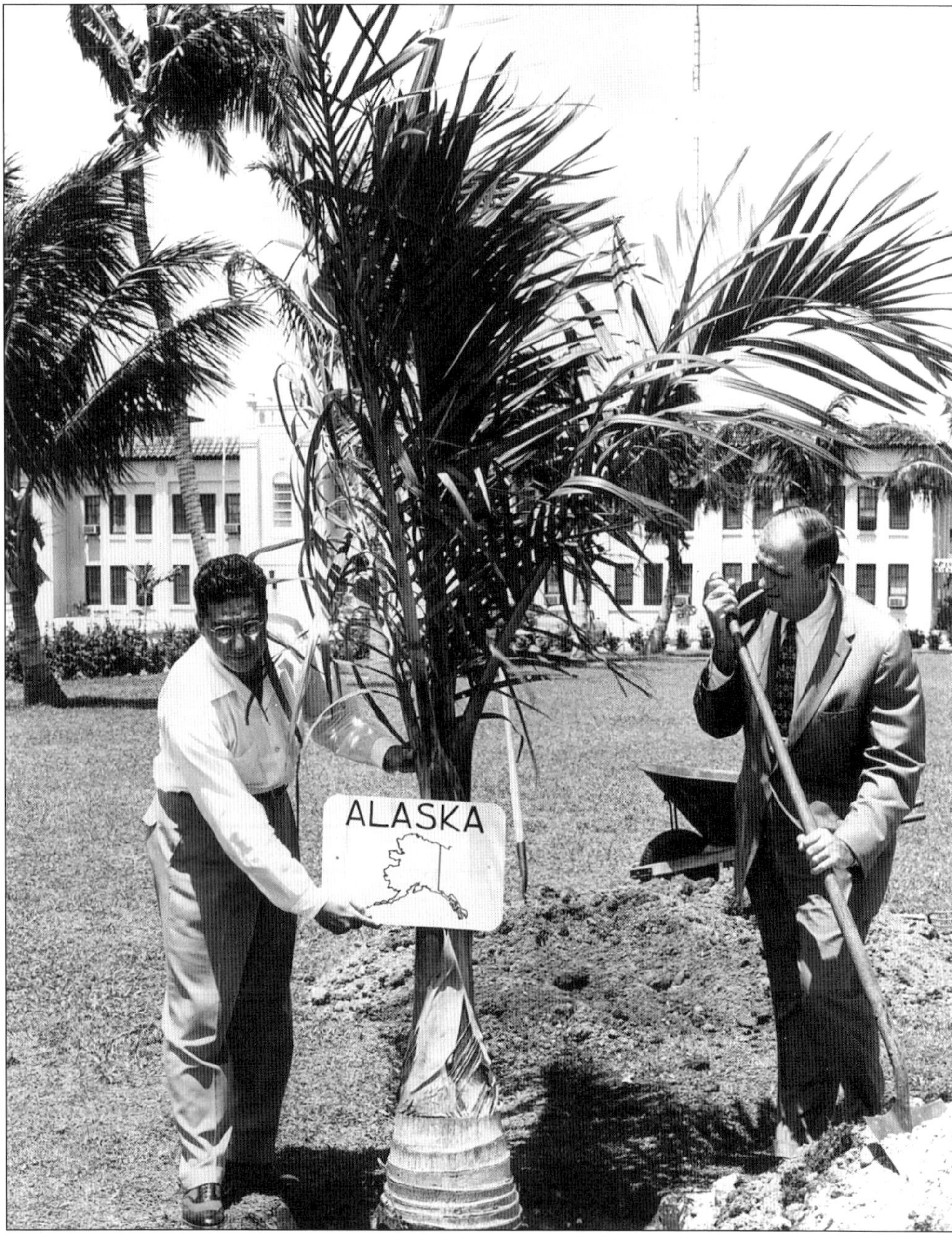

City Commissioner Jerry Tardiff holds a map of Alaska while Commissioner B.L. David ceremoniously plants a palm tree on city hall grounds in commemoration of Alaska's statehood on January 3, 1959. (General Collection.)

Five

THE 1960S

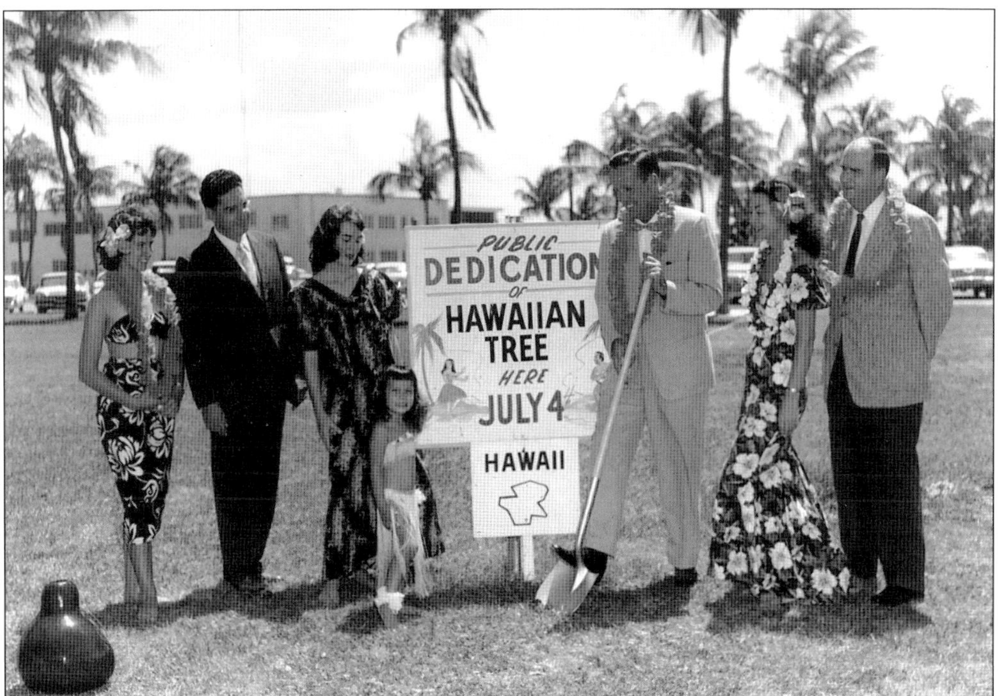

If you plant a tree for Alaska, you have to plant a tree for Hawaii. On July 4, 1960 the city did just that. Commissioner Jerry Tardiff and Commissioner B.L. David, along with three ladies in Hawaiian garb, assist Mayor William G. Zinkil Sr. in planting the "Hawaiian" tree in City Hall Circle. (General Collection.)

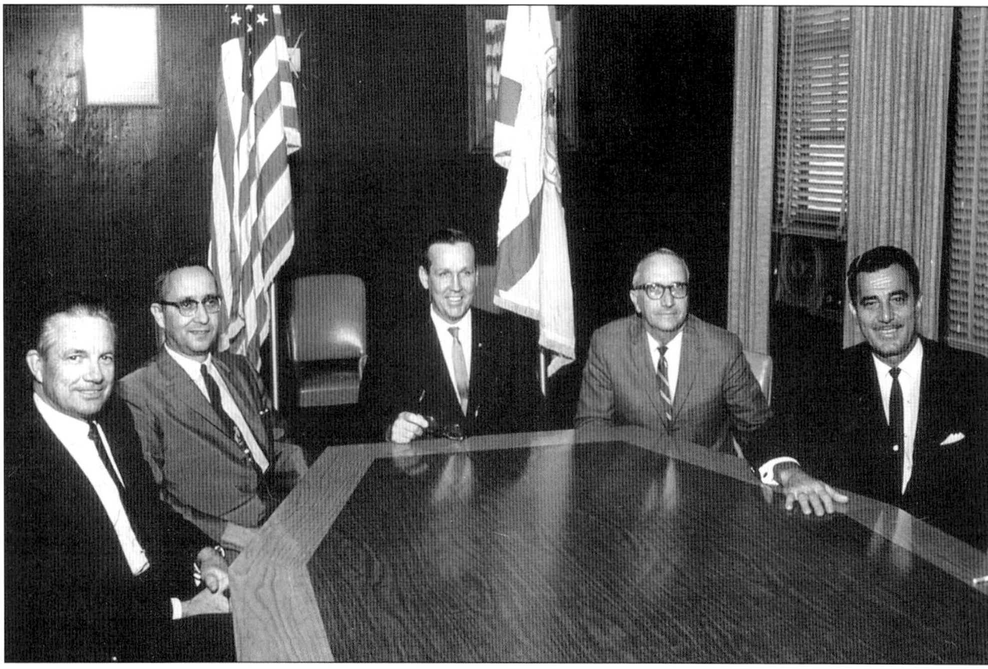

The Hollywood City Commission gathers for a formal portrait in 1963. From left to right are Commissioners Robert Anderson and Maynard Abrams, Mayor William G. Zinkil Sr., and Commissioners David Keating and Albert Montella. (General Collection.)

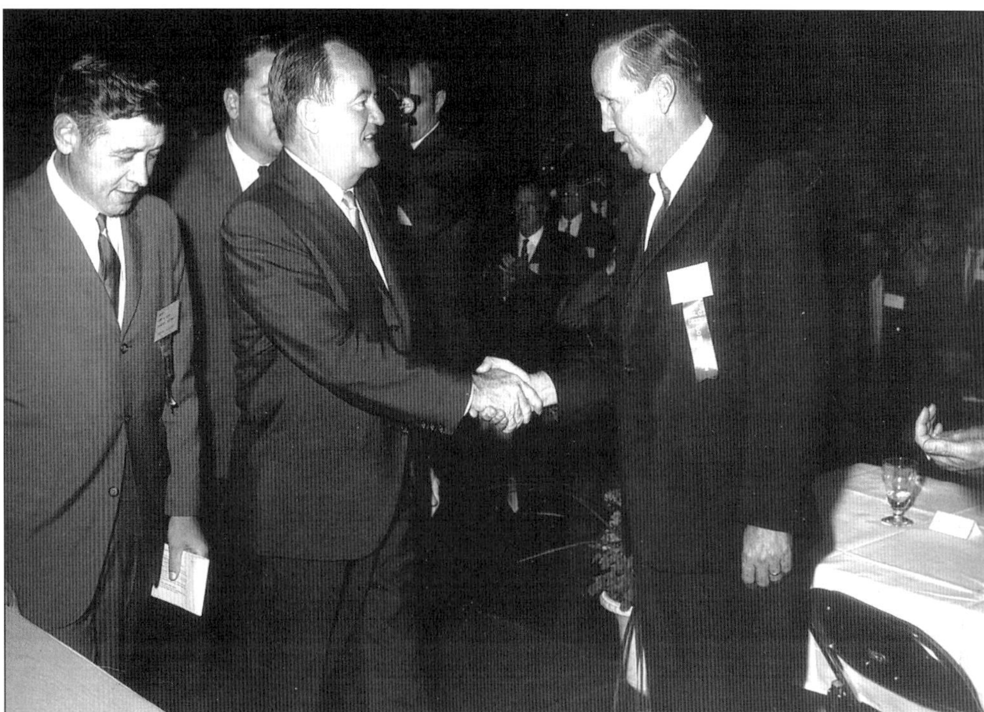

Mayor Zinkil greets Vice President Hubert H. Humphrey during a National League of Cities conference in 1965. (General Collection.)

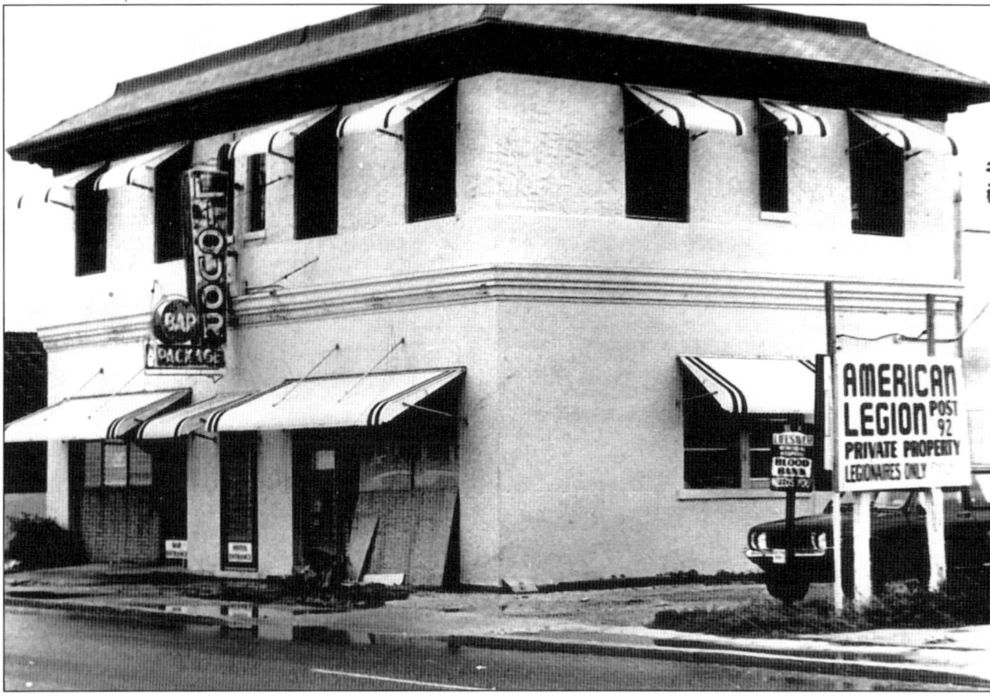

One of the many incarnations of the building that once served as the first Hollywood City Hall, the Continental Bar and Hotel was located at 219 North Twenty-first Avenue. It was originally built to house Joseph Young's publishing interests. (General Collection.)

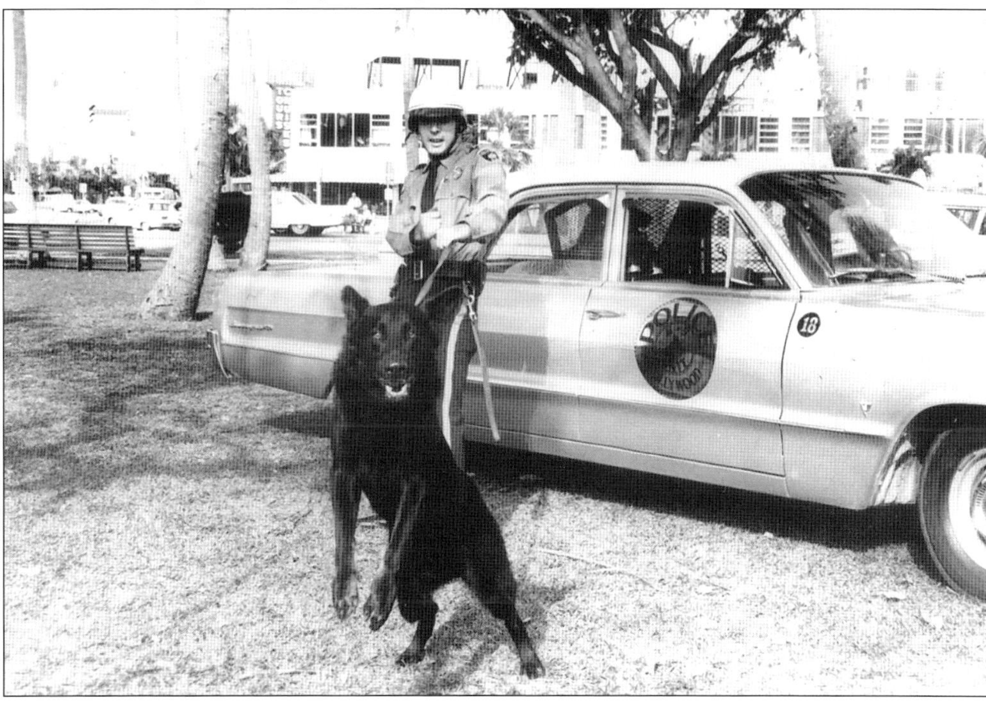

A Hollywood Police Department K-9 officer tries to hold on to his police dog during a public demonstration of police tactics in Young Circle Park. (General Collection.)

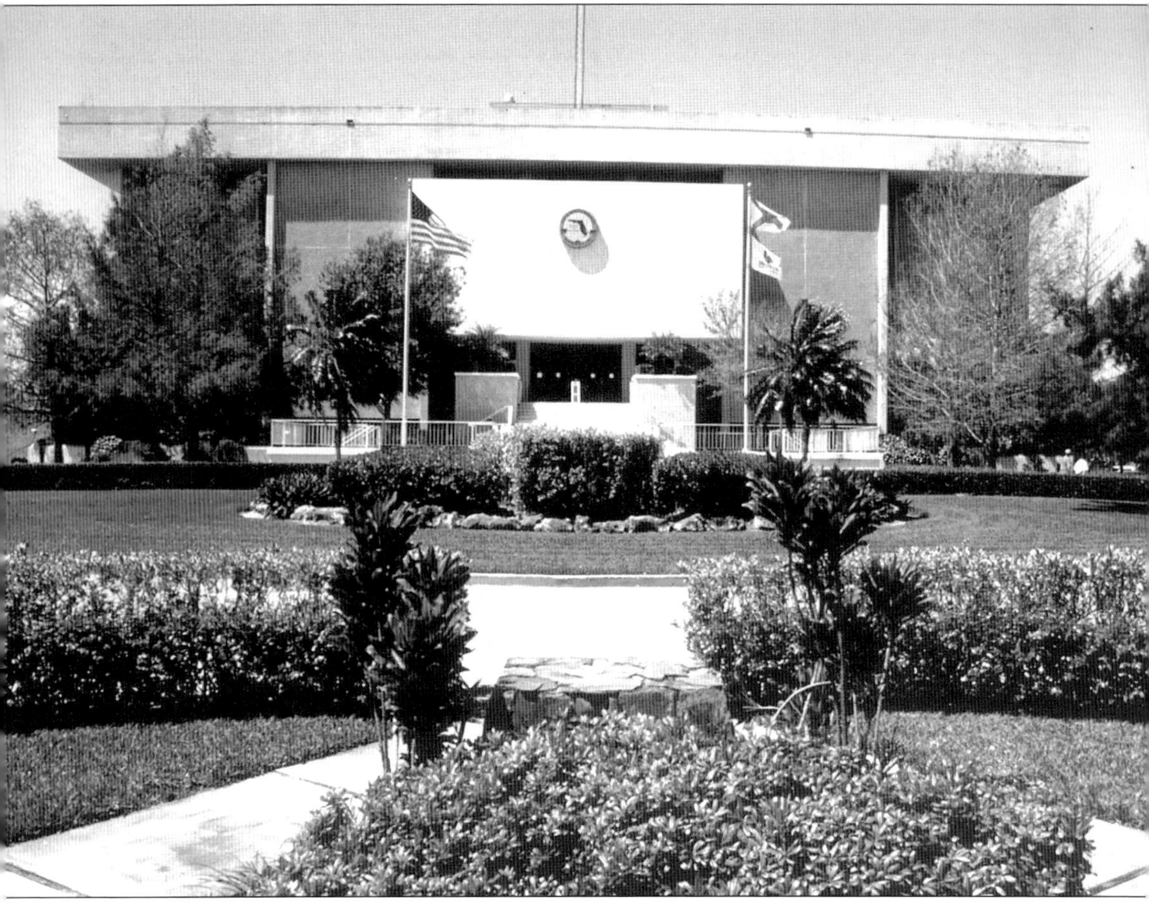

The "new" city hall was built in City Hall Circle on Hollywood Boulevard and was formally dedicated in 1968. This view is of the east entrance. (General Collection.)

Congressman J. Herbert Burke greets former child star Shirley Temple Black in his Washington office. Congressman Burke, a Hollywood resident, served in the U.S. House of Representatives from 1966 to 1978. (General Collection.)

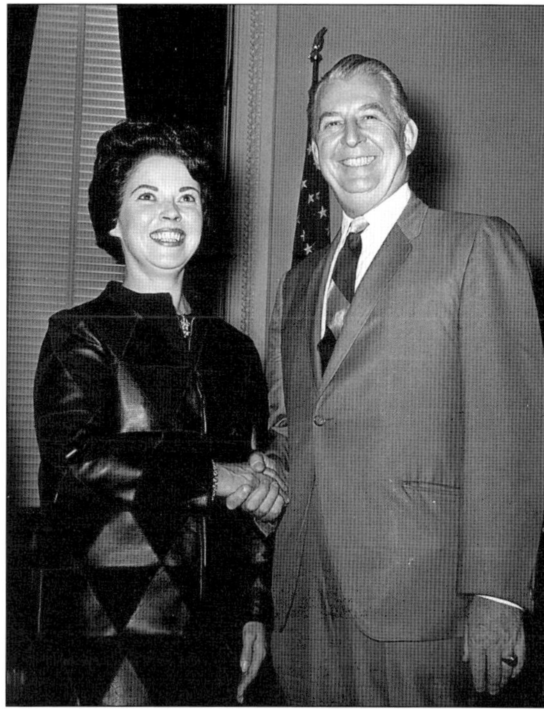

In 1965, Hollywood celebrated its 40th anniversary with a 10-day antique car cavalcade from Indianapolis to Louisville, Nashville, Chattanooga, Atlanta, Columbus, Tallahassee, Ocala, Cocoa Beach, and West Palm Beach, arriving for a community parade on November 24. The Tsarina of Russia (presumably the Dowager Empress Maria Feodorovna, who died in Denmark in 1928) reputedly owned this 1922 Rolls Royce. (General Collection.)

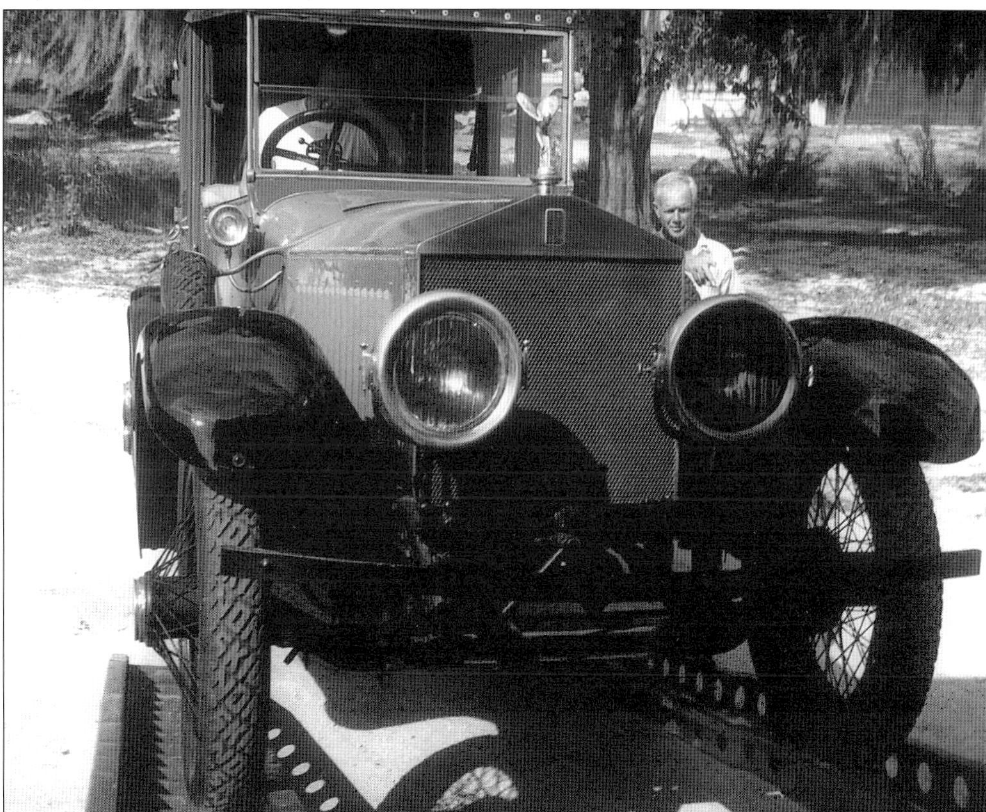

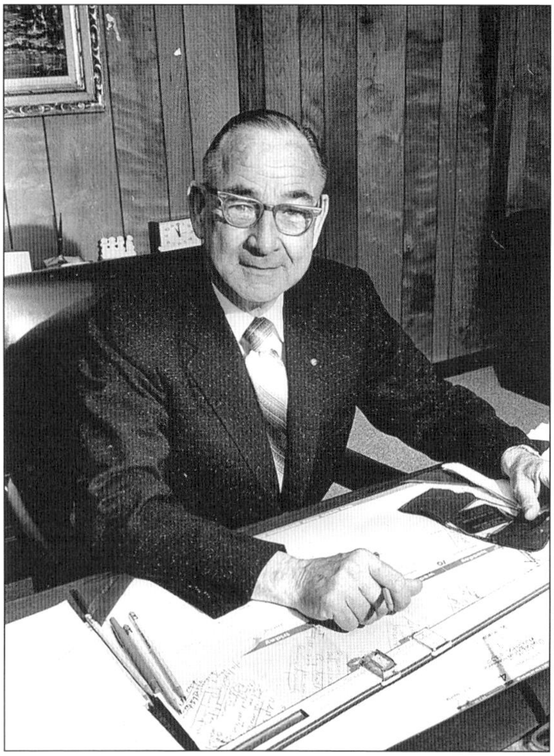

City Manager Joseph W. Watson works at his desk. Watson served as city manager from 1953 to 1970. (General Collection.)

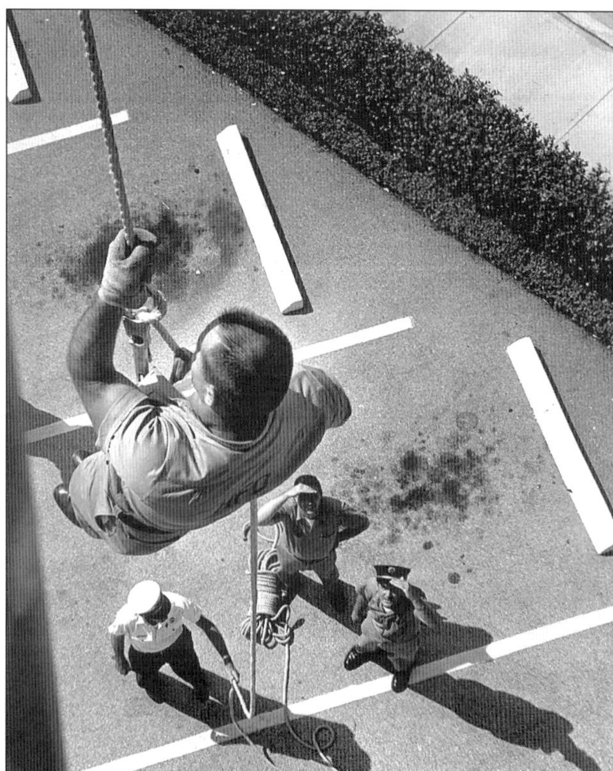

A Hollywood firefighter practices descending a rope while suspended above a parking lot. (General Collection.)

William D. Horvitz, left, president of Hollywood, Inc., confers with David F. Kelley and Jesse Martin, members of the Hollywood Industrial Board. The board was created to encourage industries to locate in the city. Hollywood, Inc. was the successor to Joseph Young's business. (General Collection.)

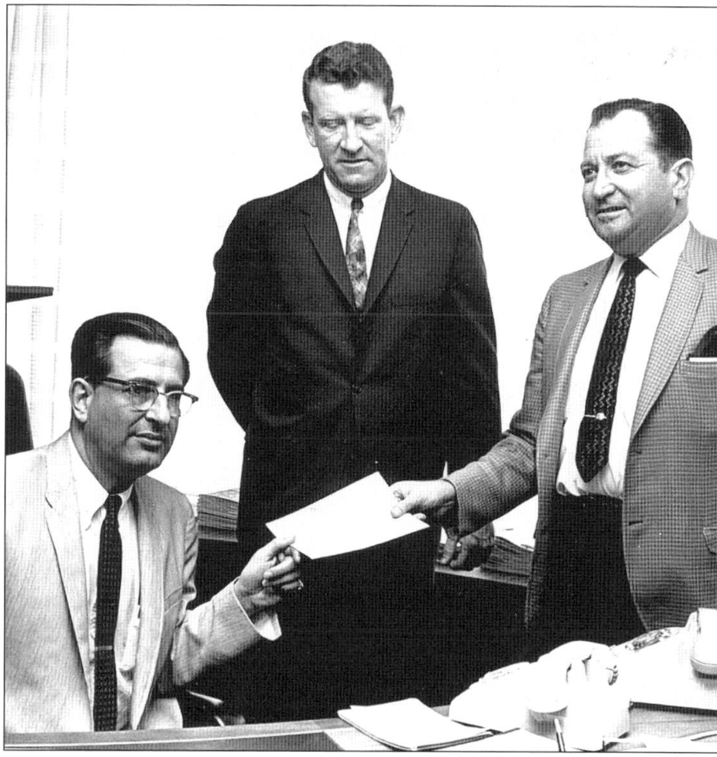

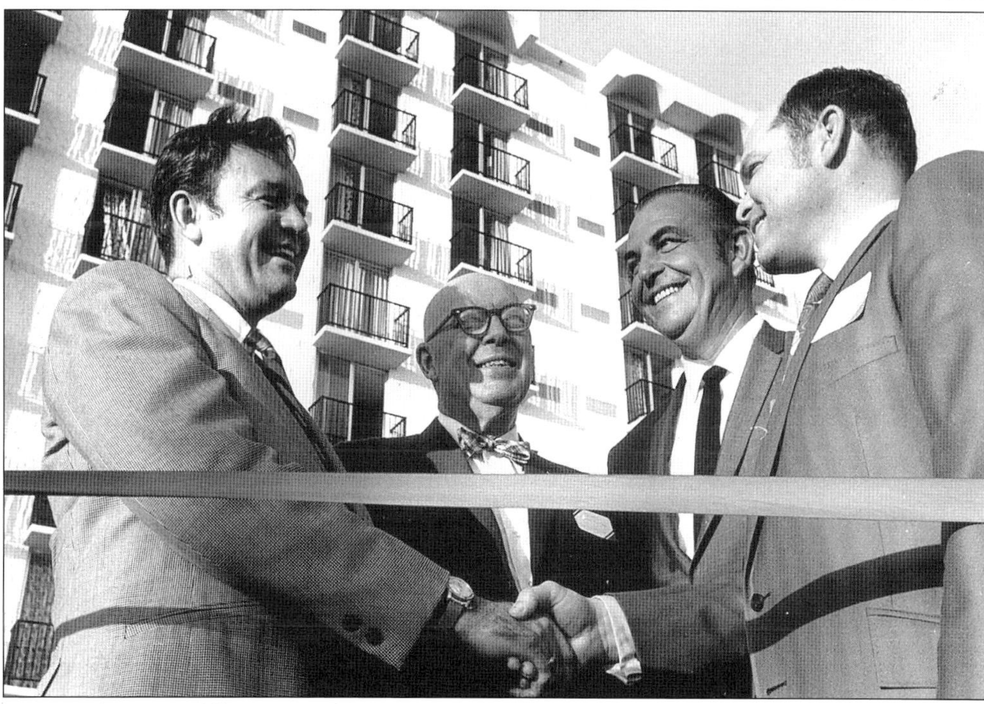

Mayor John T. Wulff, center in bow tie, stands behind the ribbon during the opening ceremony for the Town House Apartments at 1776 Polk Street. Wulff was elected mayor in 1969. (General Collection.)

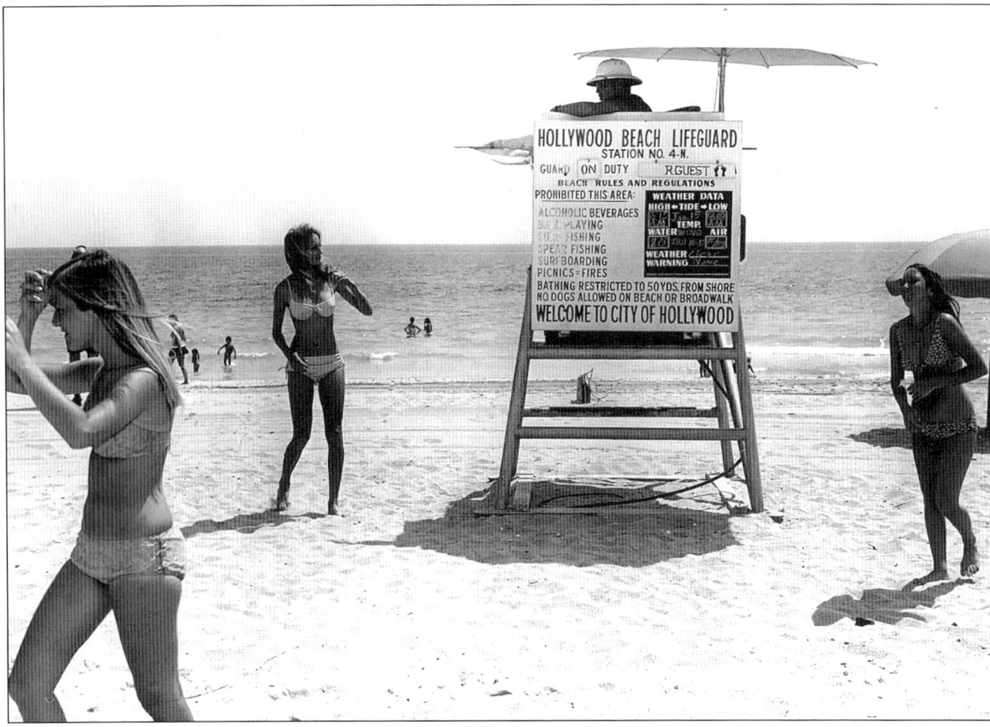

In this photo, a lifeguard keeps close watch on beachgoers.

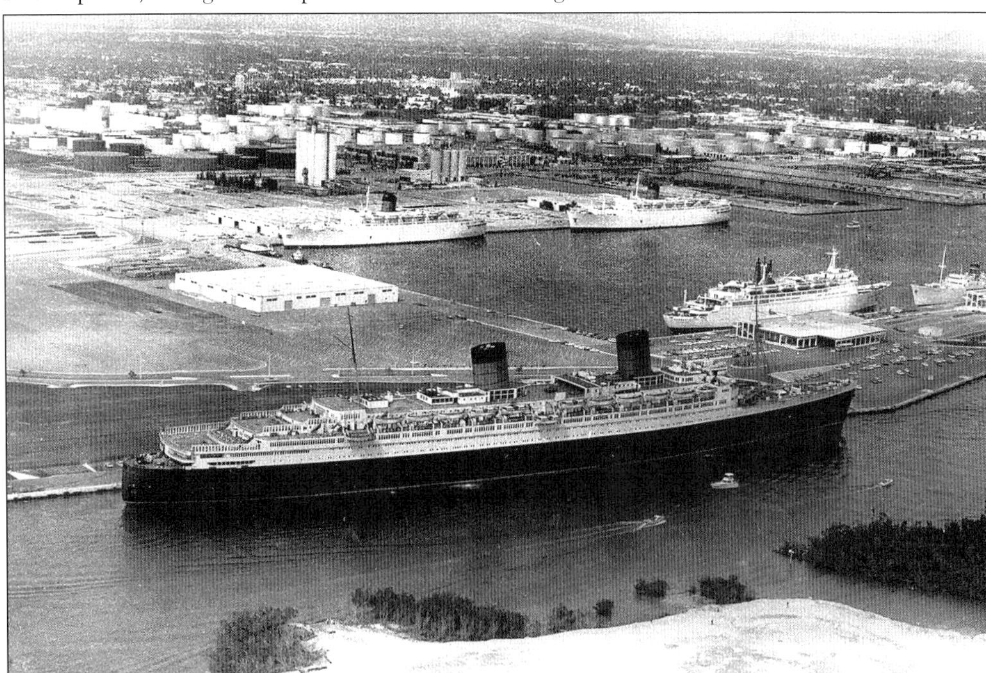

The *Queen Elizabeth* docks at Port Everglades in 1968 during one of her last voyages. The *Queen Elizabeth*, named for the British Queen Mother, was launched in 1938 and retired in 1968. (General Collection.)

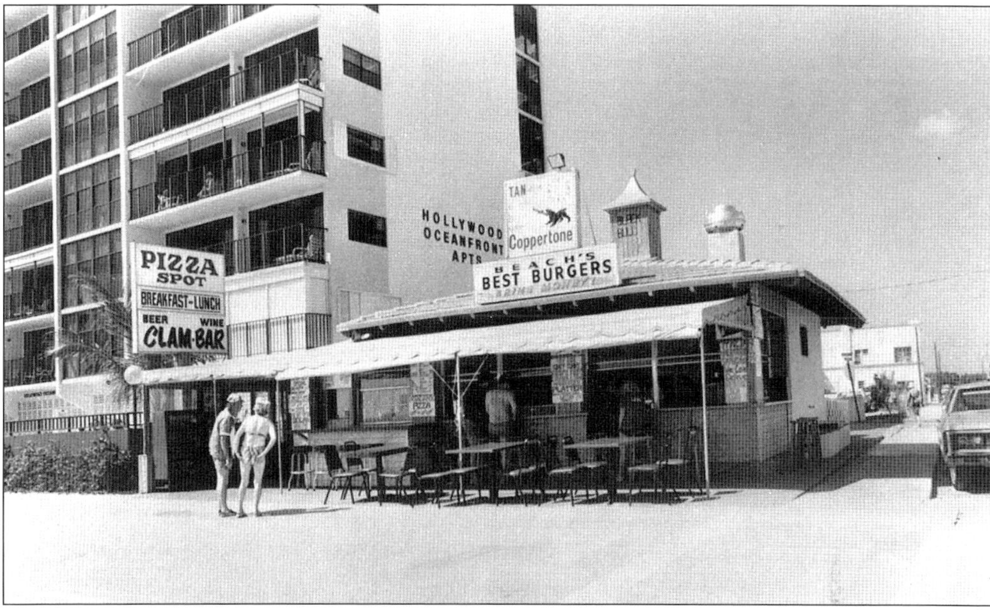

The Pizza Spot, located at 814 North Broadwalk, was a popular eatery for beachgoers and Broadwalk strollers. In addition to claiming to have the best burgers on the beach, the sign above the shop encourages customers to "Bring Money." (Manesiotis Collection.)

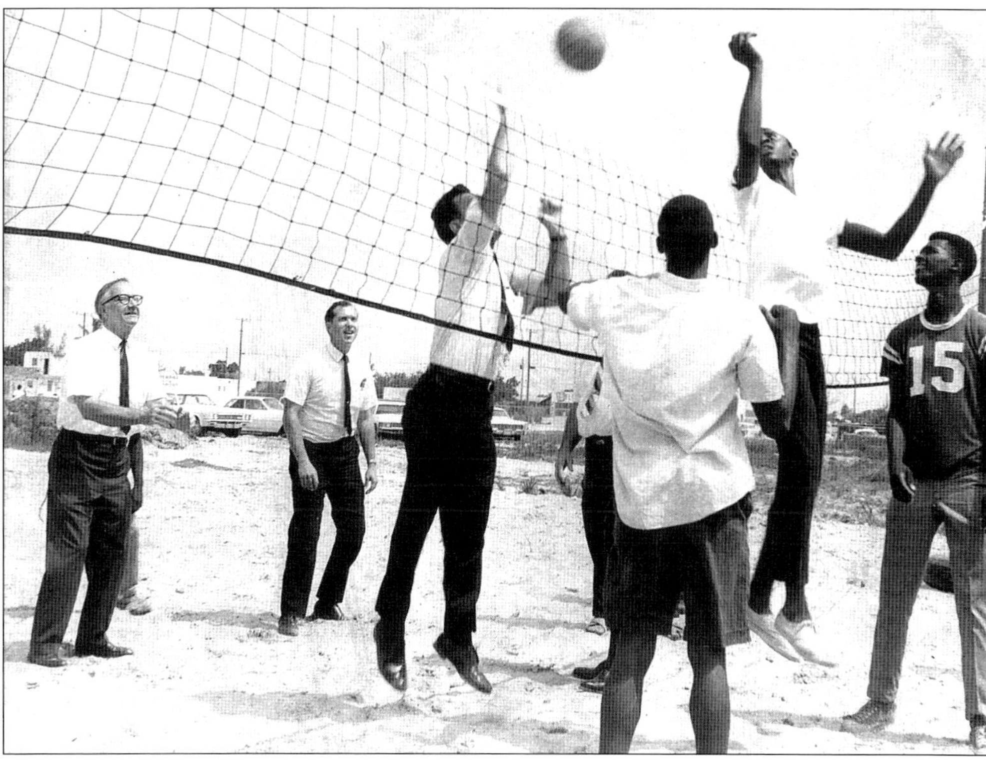

Commissioner Albert Montella goes for the spike during a June 23, 1967 volleyball game with young men from the Police Athletic League. Commissioner David Keating and Mayor William Zinkil Sr. also man the net. (General Collection.)

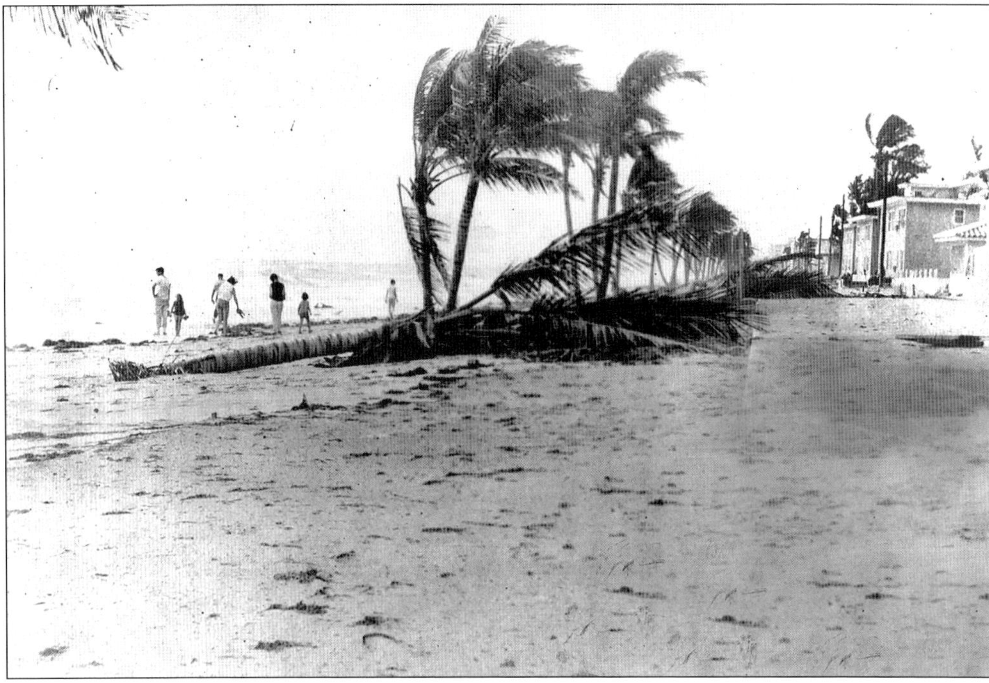

Hurricane Inez brushed the area on October 4, 1966. While the eye crossed well to the south at Marathon in the Keys, Hollywood endured some damage to its beach. (General Collection.)

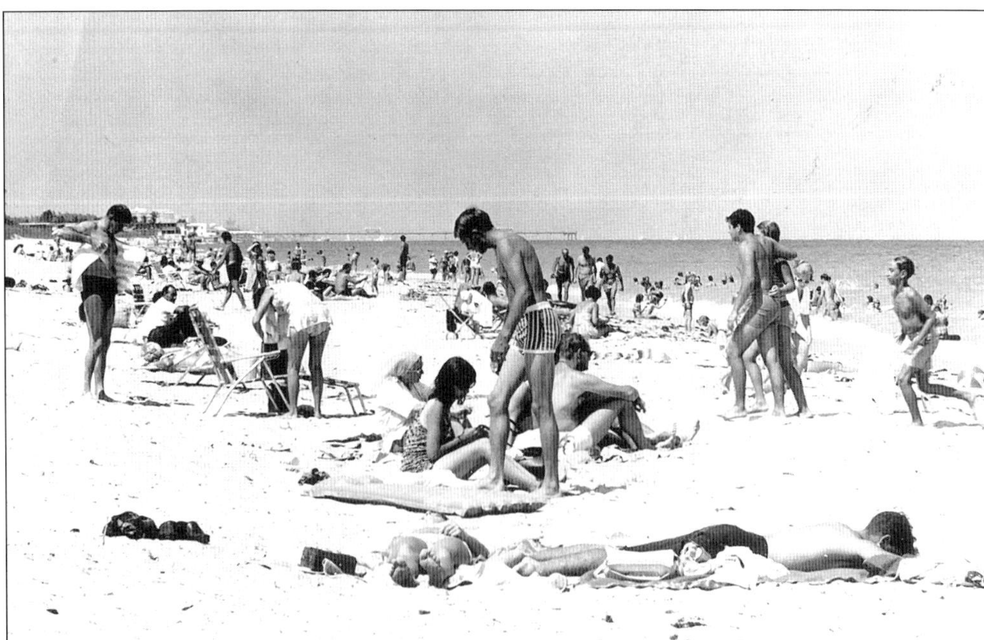

These sunbathers soak up the rays in September 1968. The Dania Pier is in the far background. (General Collection.)

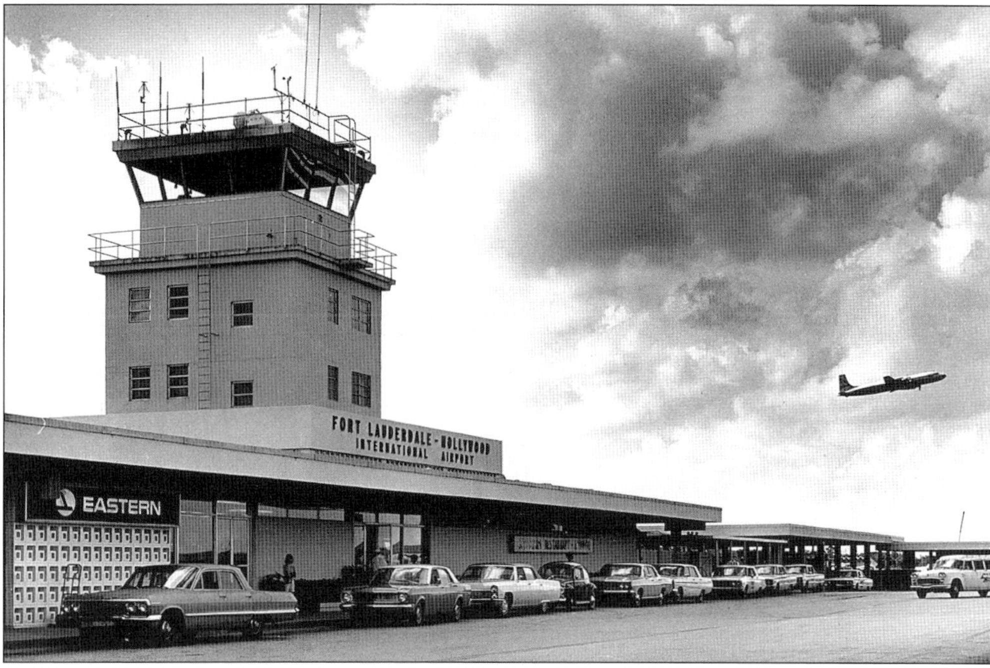

Eastern Airlines was one of the main carriers at the Fort Lauderdale–Hollywood International Airport. Originally known as Merle Fogg Field, the airport was purchased by the Navy for military use during World War II. After the war Broward County acquired the airport to operate as a general aviation facility. Passenger service began in 1953. (General Collection.)

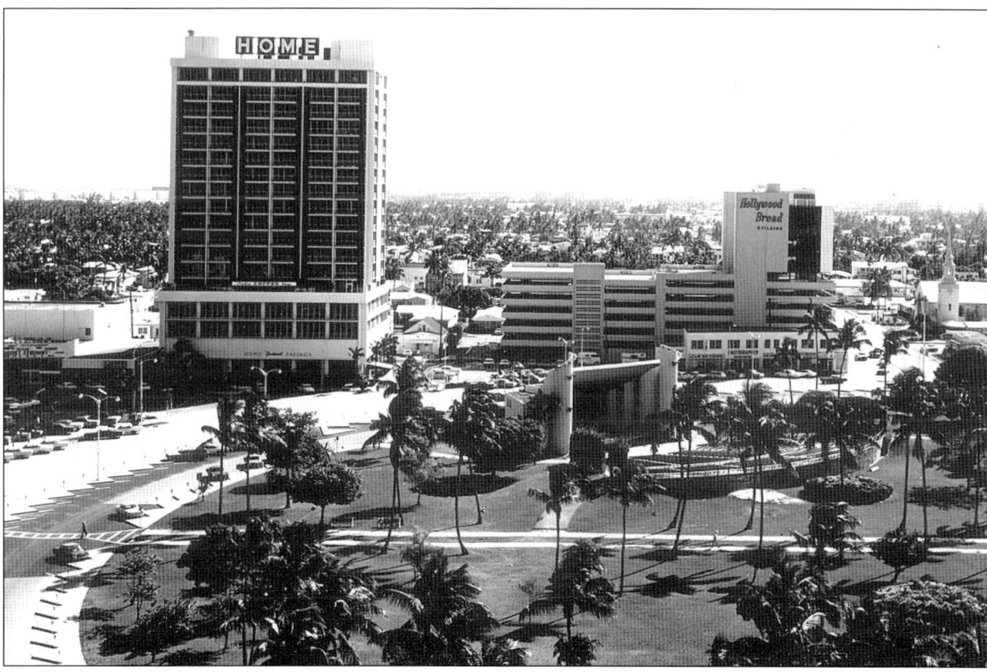

The 18-story Home Federal Tower was built across from Young Circle Park in 1964. At the time of its opening, it was the tallest cooperative office/apartment complex in Broward County. (General Collection.)

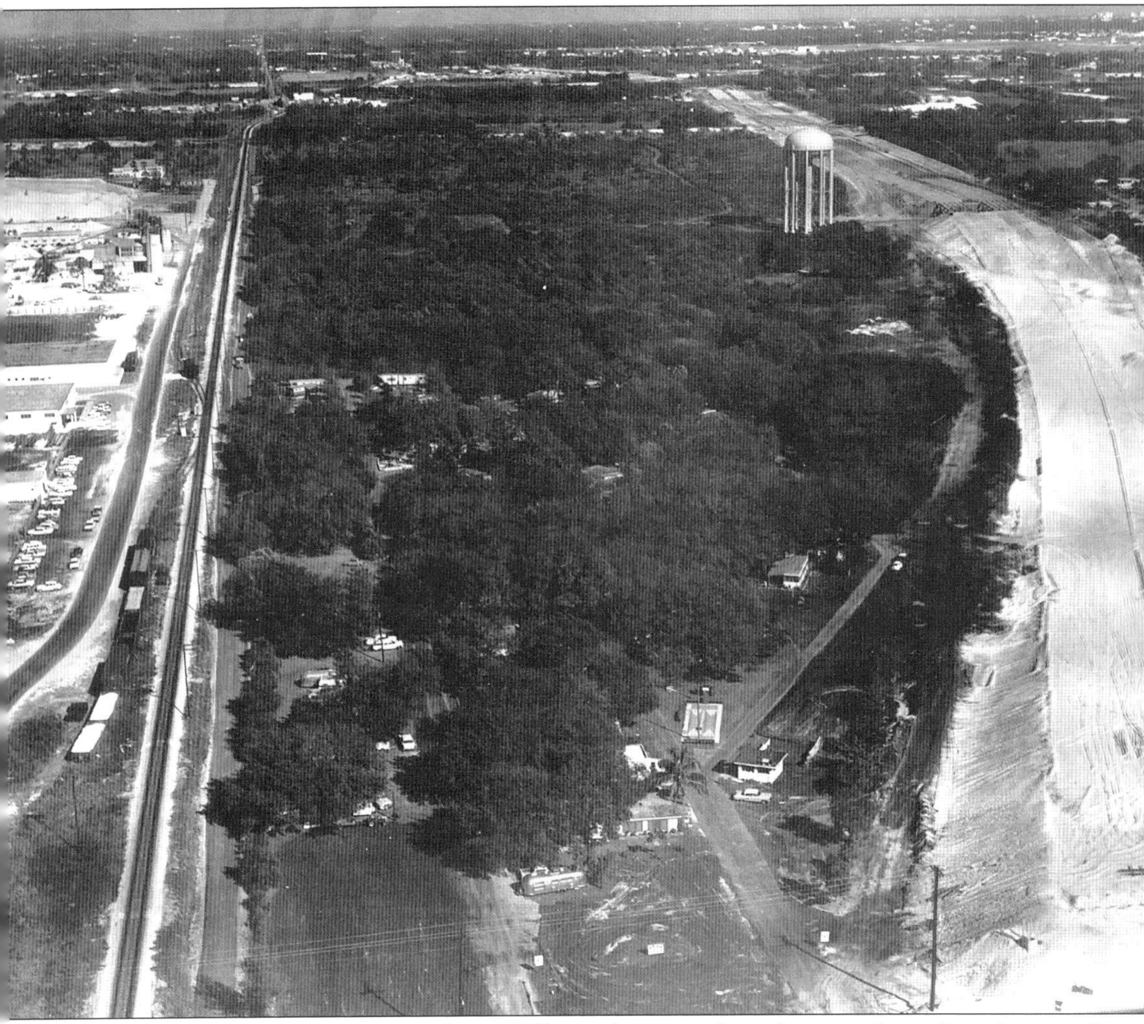

Construction on Interstate 95 in Hollywood was well underway when this photograph was taken on December 11, 1963. To give some perspective to the view, the water tower stands on Sheridan Street, which at the time did not extend across the Seaboard tracks. (General Collection.)

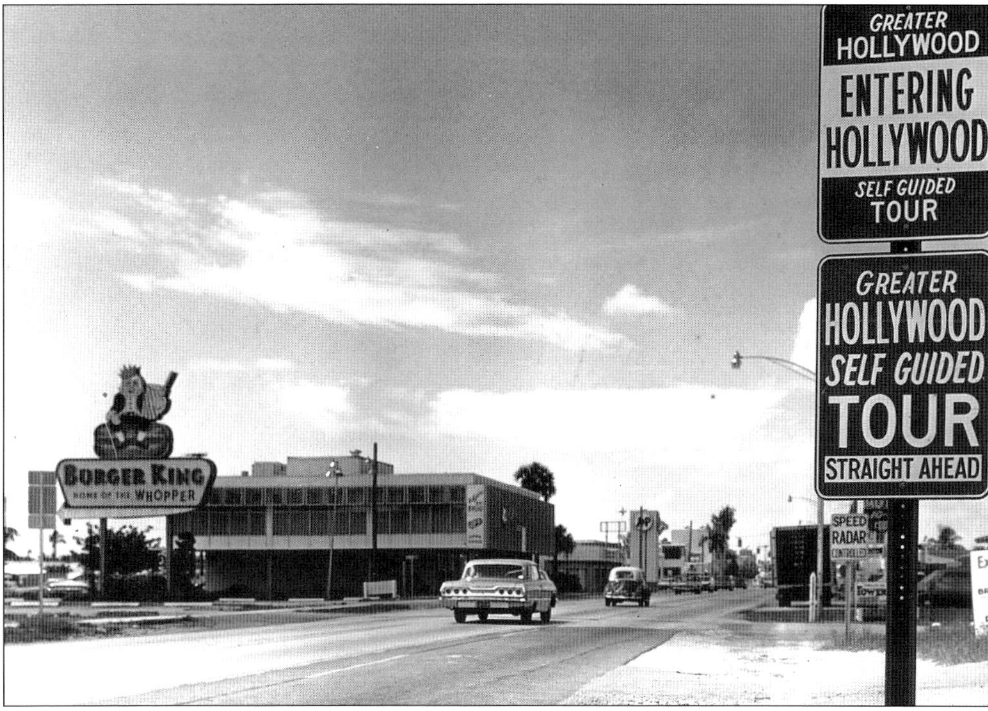

Motorists in 1966 could treat themselves to a self-guided driving tour of Hollywood. This image captures North Federal Highway looking south from Sheridan Street. Businesses in the area included a Burger King and an A&P grocery store. (General Collection.)

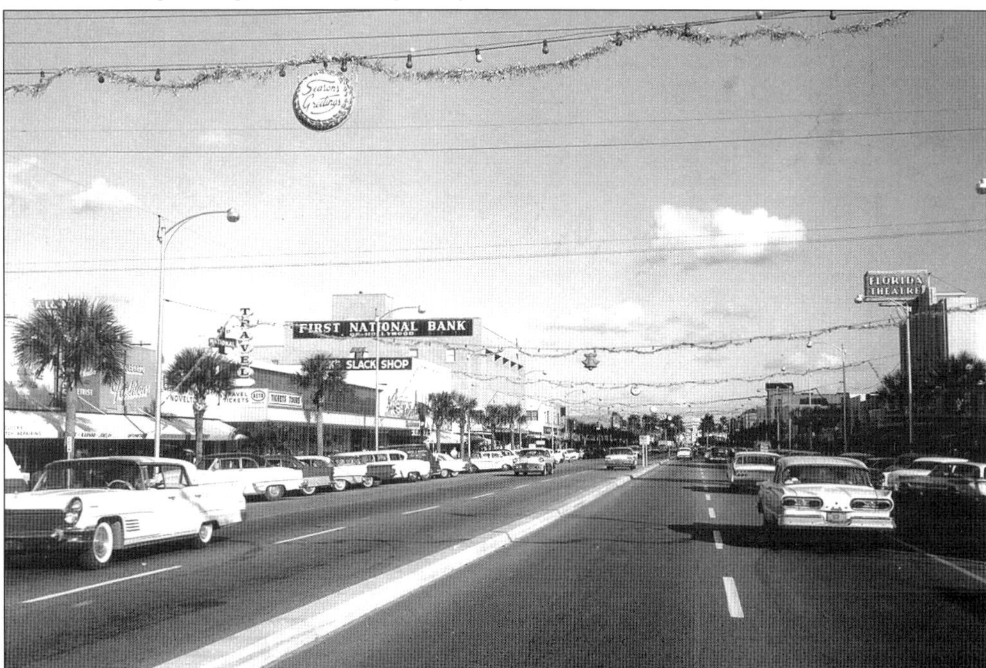

Looking east down Hollywood Boulevard between Twenty-first and Twentieth Avenues, the street is all decked out for holiday cheer. (General Collection.)

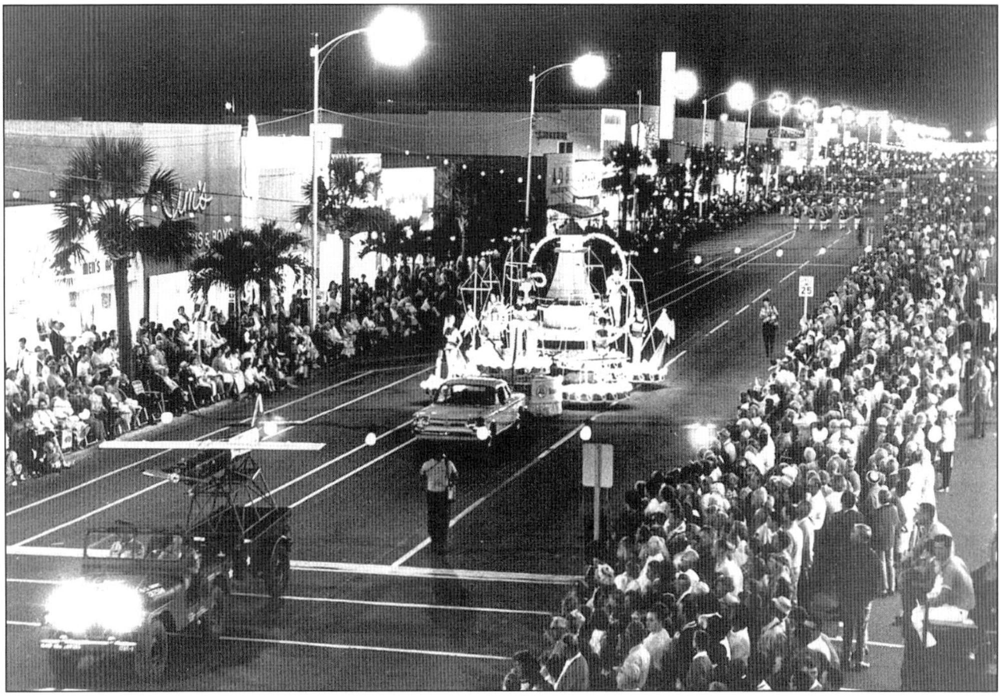

During a Fiesta Tropicale Parade, floats and bands make their way down the boulevard, passing Lee's Men's Wear at 2006 Hollywood Boulevard. (General Collection.)

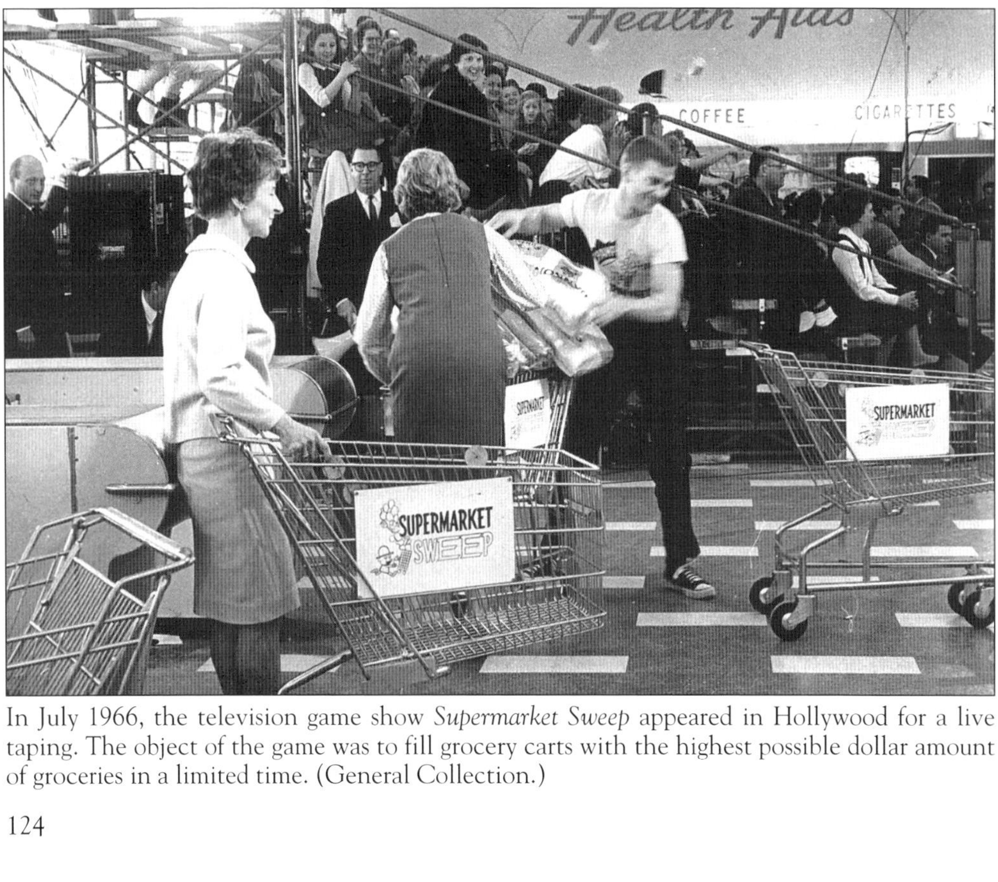

In July 1966, the television game show *Supermarket Sweep* appeared in Hollywood for a live taping. The object of the game was to fill grocery carts with the highest possible dollar amount of groceries in a limited time. (General Collection.)

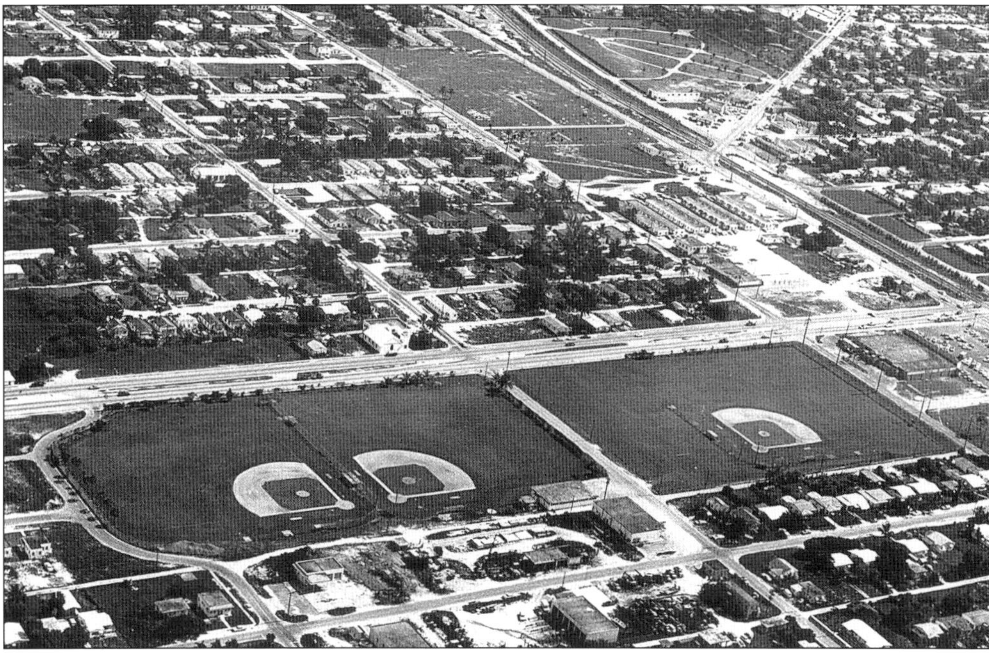

This aerial view encompasses Boggs Field, an athletic venue named for Lester C. Boggs, who was first elected to the Hollywood City Commission in 1935. He also served as mayor in the 1940s and 1950s. The area north of Boggs Field, across Sheridan Street, is Liberia, the African-American community planned by Joseph Young as a residential neighborhood for black workers in Hollywood. (General Collection.)

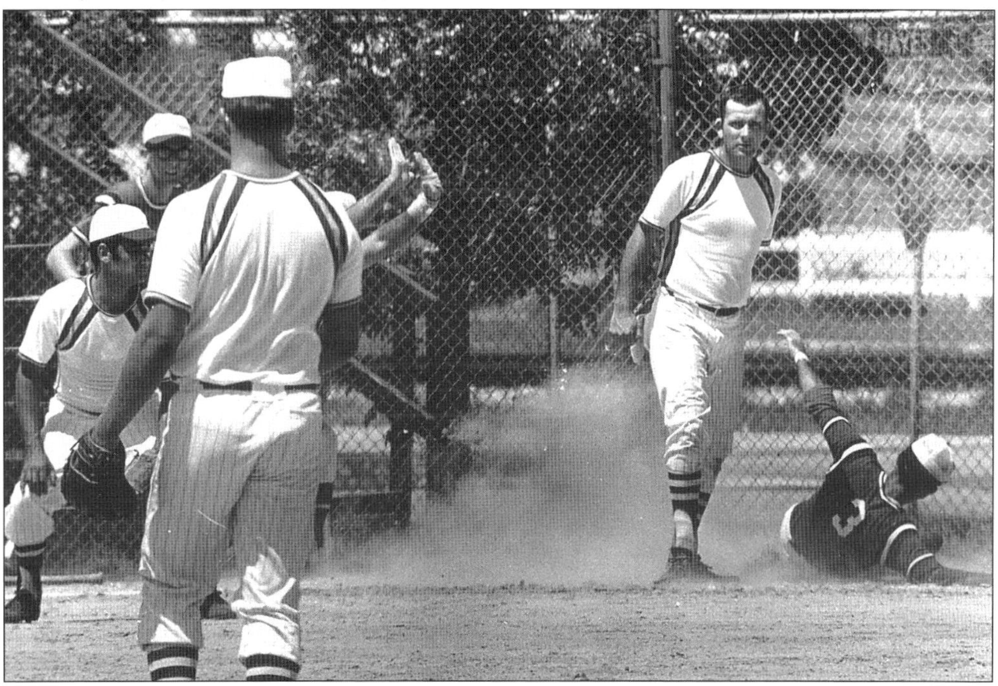

A softball player slides safely home during a game at Dowdy Field between Johnson and Hayes Streets. (General Collection.)

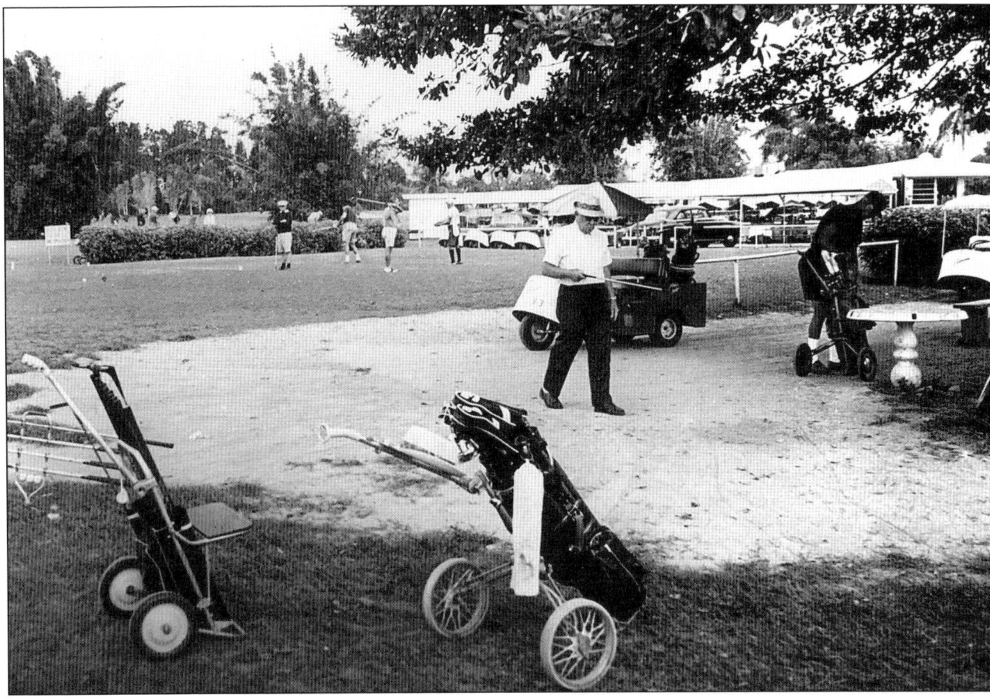

Golf aficionados at Orangebrook Golf and Country Club prepare for a trip around the course. (General Collection.)

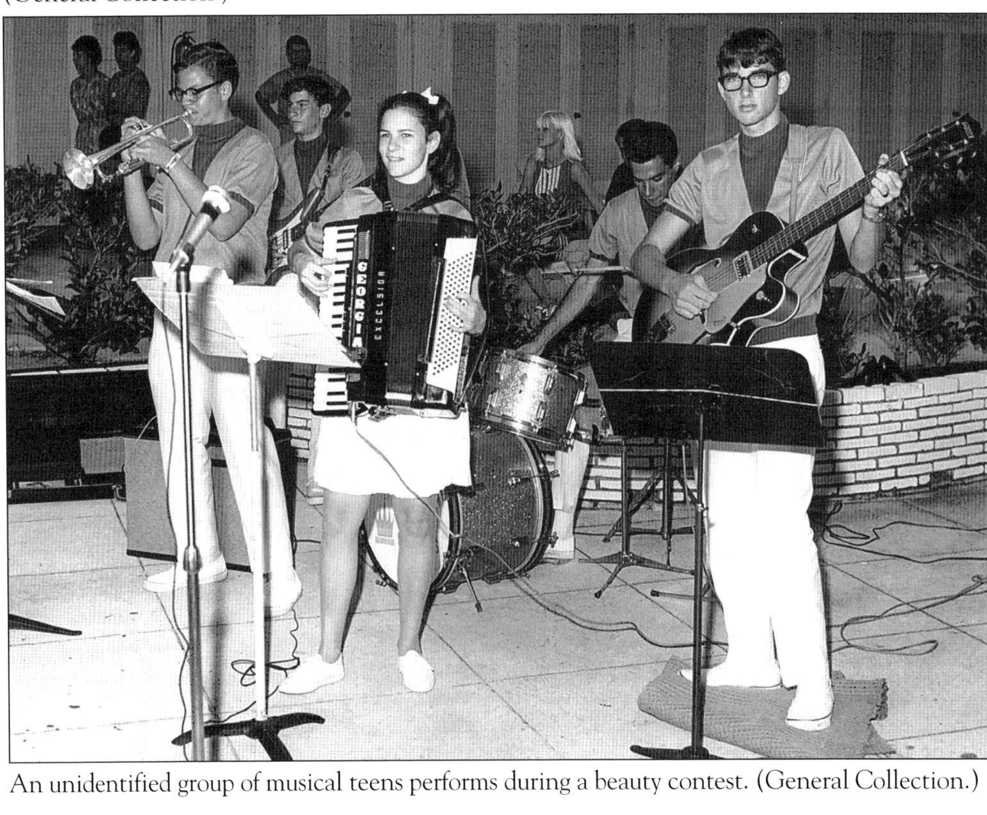

An unidentified group of musical teens performs during a beauty contest. (General Collection.)

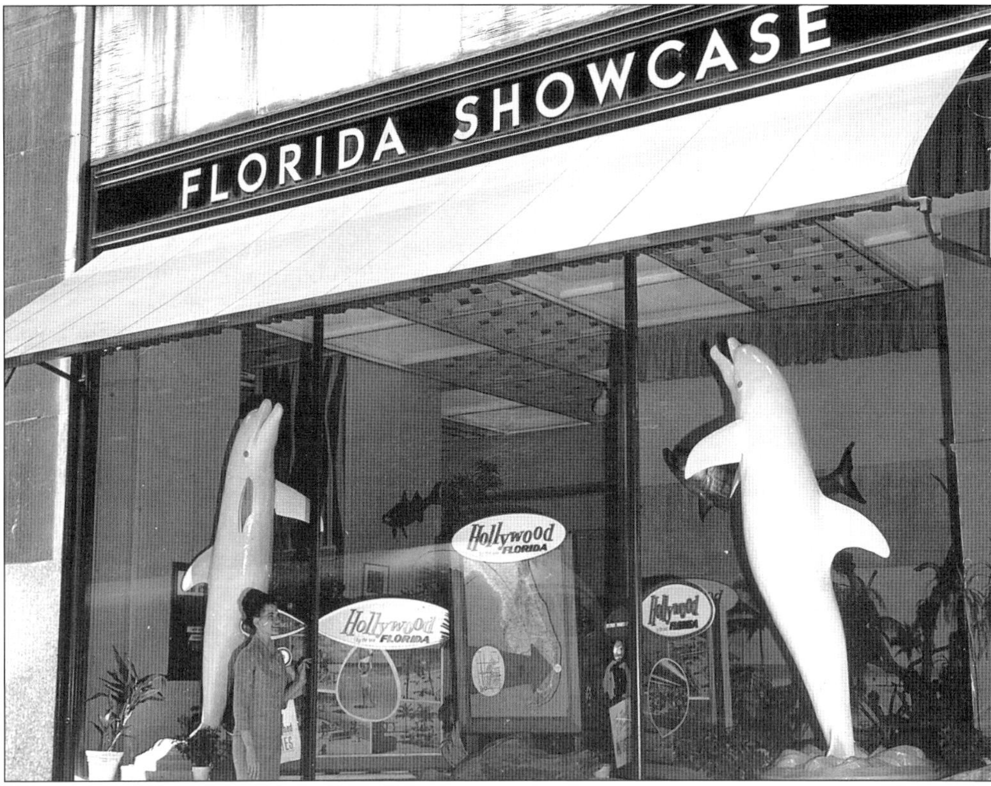

Hollywood was an active participant in the Florida Showcase in Rockefeller Center in New York City. The showcase, designed to promote tourism, opened on February 24, 1961 and was to run for two years. The dolphins were real attention-grabbers. (General Collection.)

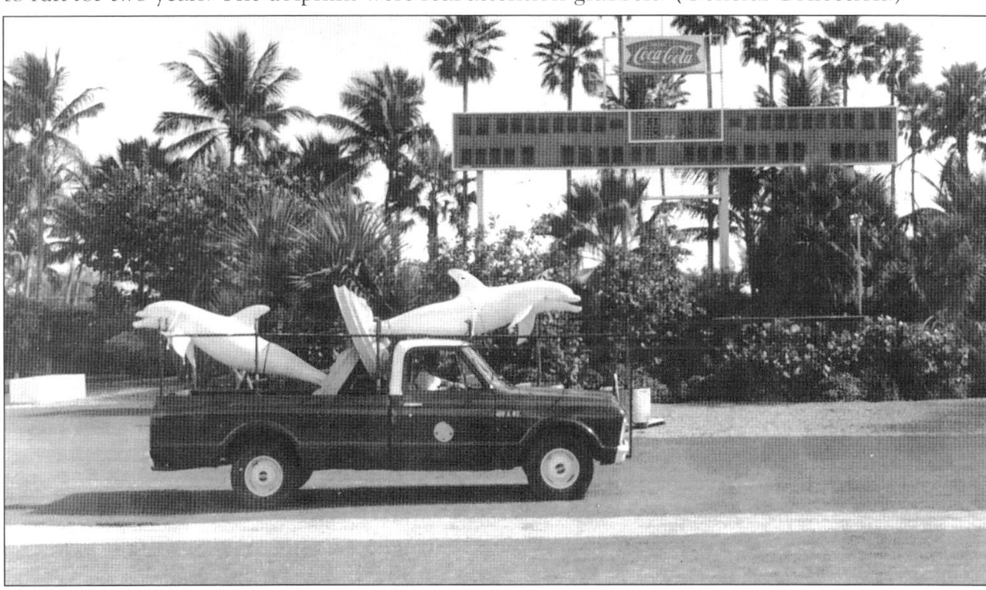

In December 1967, Hollywood's dolphins, home from New York City, were taken to Miami's Orange Bowl Stadium to celebrate Broward County Day during half-time of the Miami Dolphins–Boston Patriots football game. (General Collection.)

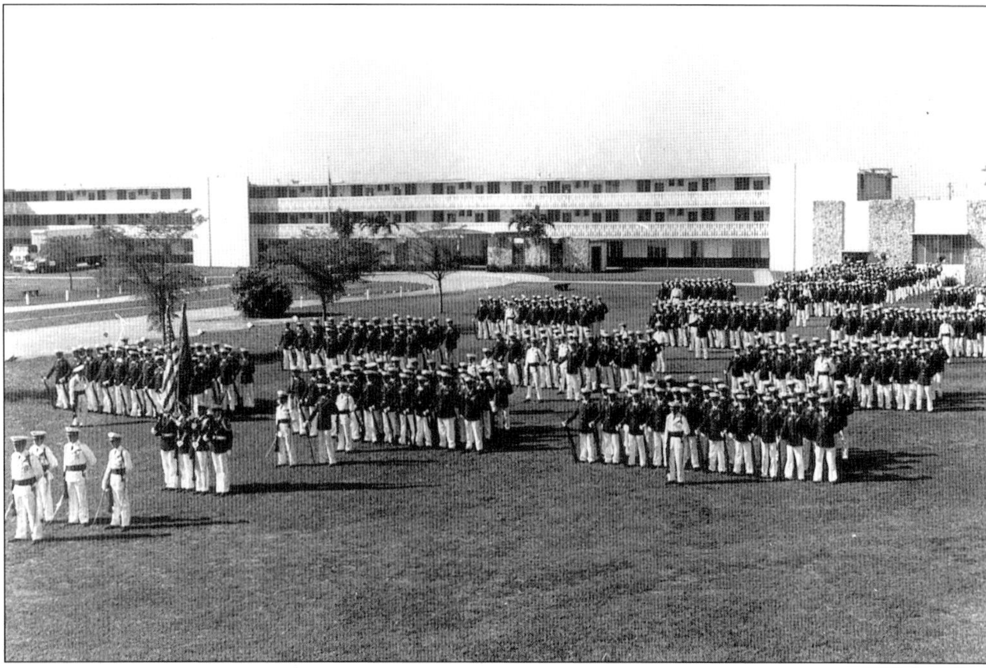

The cadets of Riverside Military Academy mass in formation outside their new building on the school grounds in Academy Circle. A fire in 1959 led to the construction of the new facility. Riverside held its final winter session in Hollywood in 1984. The Presidential Circle Building now occupies the site. (General Collection.)

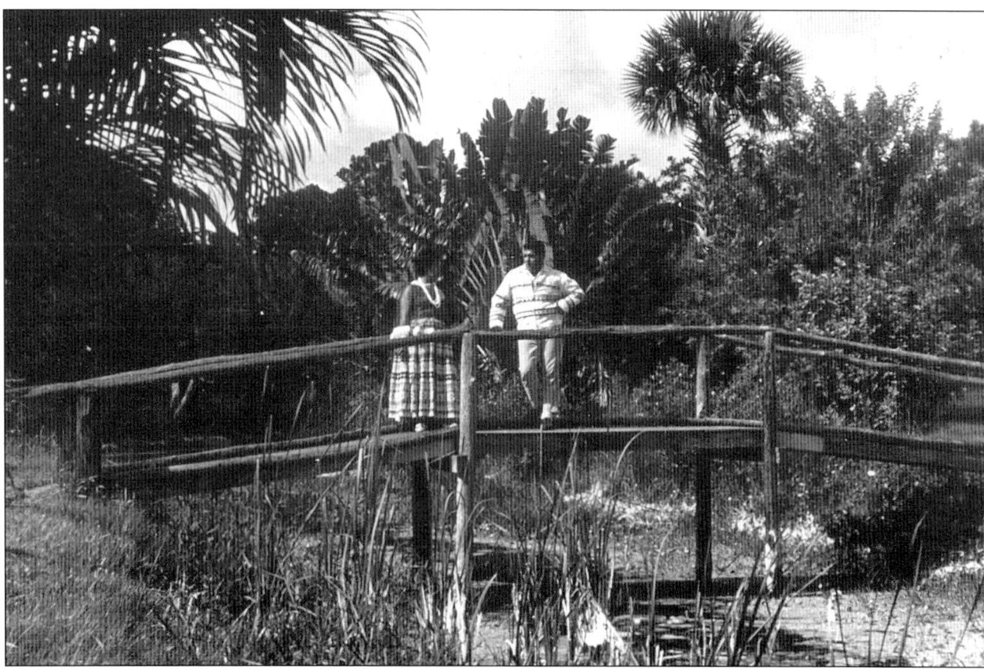

Hollywood is home to the Seminole Reservation of Florida and is the headquarters for the tribe's government and business interests. Two tribal members pause along a wooden bridge on the reservation. (General Collection.)